Photoshop Elements 2.0:
50 Ways to Create Cool Pictures

David Huss

New Riders
www.newriders.com

201 West 103rd Street, Indianapolis, Indiana 46290
An Imprint of Pearson Education
Boston • Indianapolis • London • Munich • New York • San Francisco

Photoshop Elements 2.0:
50 Ways to Create Cool Pictures

Copyright © 2003 by New Riders Publishing

International Standard Book Number: 0-7357-1323-5

Library of Congress Catalog Card Number: 2002107806

Printed in the United States of America

First edition: November 2002

06 05 04 03 02   7 6 5 4 3 2 1

Interpretation of the printing code: The rightmost double-digit number is the year of the book's printing; the rightmost single-digit number is the number of the book's printing. For example, the printing code 02-1 shows that the first printing of the book occurred in 2002.

Trademarks

Warning and Disclaimer

Publisher
David Dwyer

Associate Publisher
Stephanie Wall

Editor in Chief
Chris Nelson

Production Manager
Gina Kanouse

Managing Editor
Sarah Kearns

Senior Product Marketing Manager
Tammy Detrich

Publicity Manager
Susan Nixon

Acquisitions Editor
Jody Kennen

Development Editor
Chris Zahn

Project Editor
Michael Thurston

Copy Editor
Sheri Cain

Indexer/Proofreader
Lisa Stumpf

Composition
Jeff Bredensteiner

Manufacturing Coordinator
Jim Conway

Cover Designer
Aren Howell

Media Developer
Jay Payne

Photoshop Elements 2.0:
50 Ways to Create Cool Pictures

Introduction

Contents at a Glance

I	**Quick Start**	
1	Quick Tour	5
2	Getting Pictures into Your Computer	17
3	Adjusting and Enhancing Photos	31
4	Sizing and Saving Your Photos	51

II	**Making Photos Look Professional**	
5	Dealing with Composition Problems and Distortion	67
6	Fine-Tuning the Color	91
7	Correcting Lighting Problems	105
8	Putting on the Final Touches	119

III	**Getting Fancy**	
9	Cool Tricks with Text	133
10	Cool Photographic Techniques	163
11	Creating Stunning Panoramas	183
12	Rearranging and Replacing Objects in Photos	201

IV	**Photographic Repair Shop**	
13	Retouching Photographs	225
14	Restoring and Repairing Photographs	243

V	**Publishing Photos**	
15	Publishing on the Web	273
16	Making Great Photos on Your Printer	293

This book is dedicated to Megg Morin, my friend, critic, and acquisitions editor through more books than either one of us care to admit to.

Contents

Introduction   **1**

Part I   Quick Start

Chapter 1   Quick Tour   5

    Introducing Photoshop Elements 2.0   6

    What's New in Version 2.0   6

    A Cook's Tour of the Workspace   9

    Navigating Around the Workspace   12

    Undoing Mistakes   14

    Seeking Help   15

    Summary   16

Chapter 2   Getting Pictures into Your Computer   17

    Bringing Images into Your Computer   18

    Where Digital Pictures Come From   18

    Using Digital Cameras and Scanners   21

    Picture Management Suggestions   29

    Summary   30

Chapter 3   Adjusting and Enhancing Photos   31

    Understanding Adjusting and Enhancing Photos   32

    The Fast Track Method   32

    Summary   50

Chapter 4   Sizing and Saving Your Photos   51

    Resizing Photos for Email   52

    Changing the Size of a Photo—Basic Stuff   53

    Changing the Size of a Picture   57

    Resizing the Canvas   61

    Saving Your Work   62

    Types of Graphic Files   64

    File Management Suggestions   66

    Summary   66

Part II   Making Photos Look Professional

Chapter 5   Dealing with Composition Problems and
Distortion   67

Improving Composition   68

When Things Aren't on the Level   76

Straightening Out Scans   82

Correcting Distortion in Photos   84

Some Closing Thoughts About Composition   89

Summary   90

Chapter 6   Fine-Tuning the Color   91

Correct Color Versus Desired Color   92

Color Casts and Their Causes   93

Summary   104

Chapter 7   Correcting Lighting Problems   105

Understanding Lighting Problems   106

Basic Light Problem Solutions   106

Selective Highlights and Shadows   113

Real Fill Flash   115

The Darker Side of Washouts   115

Dealing with Red Eye   116

Summary   118

Chapter 8   Putting on the Final Touches   119

What's Wrong with This Photo?   120

Divide and Conquer   121

Introducing Tonal Adjustments   121

Framing Our Masterpiece   129

Summary   132

Part III   Getting Fancy

Chapter 9   Cool Tricks with Text   133

Adding and Editing Text   134

Introducing the Custom Shape Tool   145

Warping and Unwarping Text   148

Adding Styles for Great Effects   151

Making Semitransparent Text and
Transforming Text   154

Outlining Text   157

Summary   162

Chapter 10 Cool Photographic Techniques   163

    Creating Painterly Masterpieces   165
    Using Filters to Cover Up Poor Photos   172
    Other Painterly Options   178
    Selective Color Removal for Effect   180
    Summary   182

Chapter 11 Creating Stunning Panoramas   183

    Photomerge in Elements 2.0   184
    Taking Pictures for a Panorama   184
    Creating a Simple Panorama   186
    Creating a Panorama from Three Photos   189
    A Challenging Panorama   193
    Panorama Examples   198
    Summary   200

Chapter 12 Rearranging and Replacing
                Objects in Photos   201

    Harnessing the Power of Selections   202
    Introducing Marquee Tools   203
    Rounding Up the Lasso Tools   210
    Getting the Best Selections (In the Least
    Amount of Time)   211
    Let's Lasso Somebody   213
    Saving and Loading Selections   216
    Magic Wand Tool Magic   218
    Replacing an Overcast Sky   221
    Summary   224

Part IV   **Photographic Repair Shop**

Chapter 13 Retouching Photographs   225

    Photo Tips for Better Pictures   226
    Improving Appearances   230
    Further Editing Options   238
    Summary   242

Chapter 14 Restoring and Repairing Photographs   243

    Determining the Problem   244
    Making Copies Versus Using Adjustment Layers   249
    Multiple Corrections: Figure 14.1 Revisited   253
    How to Remove Dust and Debris   259
    Aligned Versus Non-Aligned Cloning   266
    Restoring Faded Color   268
    Summary   271

Part V   Publishing Photos

Chapter 15 Publishing on the Web   273

Sizing Up an Image for the Web   274
Making Images Web Friendly   276
Reducing Images for Internet Auctions   278
Making Images for Your Home Page   279
Saving for the Web   280
Attaching Your Images to Email   282
Automated Web Photo Gallery Creation   283
Generating a PDF Slideshow   287
Summary   292

Chapter 16 Making Great Photos on Your Printer   293

Fast Track Printing   294
Speeding Up Your Print Jobs   297
Getting the Best Quality Prints from Your Printer   297
Printing Multiple Copies of a Picture   299
Summary   302

Index   305

About the Author

Dave Huss has written over 14 books on digital photo editing. A photographer for over a quarter of a century, his photo-compositions and montages have won several international competitions. A popular conference speaker, he has taught classes and workshops on digital photography and photo editing in the U.S. and Europe. A third-generation Texan, he lives in Austin, Texas.

About the Contributing Authors

Mara Zebest Nathanson is a graphic artist who uses her knowledge and skills in both volunteer work and commercial endeavors. Mara donates much of her time to a local school corporation, providing technical support to teachers and administrators in designing brochures, letterhead, logos, and even T-shirts. In her commercial work, she designs newspaper and magazine ads, as well as a variety of other graphics. Mara has contributed chapters and has been a technical editor for several of the *Inside Photoshop* books published by New Riders.

Robert Stanley is a freelance artist living with his family in Southern California. His clients have included 20th Century Fox, MTV, Cigar Aficionado, and Grammercy Pictures. Robert can rip through a phone book with his bare hands and has created cold fusion in his bathtub. He was the real inventor behind Velveeta cheese and wrote several songs for Lennon-McCartney while in kindergarten. That same year, Robert told Thomas Knoll to call it the Toolbox instead of the Sandbox when he played with Thomas and the Photoshop interface at recess.

Al Ward, a certified Photoshop Addict and Webmaster of Action FX Photoshop Resources (www.actionfx.com) hails from Missoula, Montana. A former submariner in the U.S. Navy, Al now spends his time creating add-on software for Photoshop and writing on graphics-related topics. He co-authored *Photoshop Most Wanted: Design and Effects* and *Foundation Photoshop 6.0* for Friends of Ed Publishing. He has been a contributor to *Photoshop User* magazine, a contributing writer for *Photoshop 7 Effects Magic, Inside Photoshop 6,* and *Special Edition Inside Photoshop 6* from New Riders Publishing. He is a weekly columnist for *Planet Photoshop* (www.planetphotoshop.com) and the official NAPP web site, PhotoshopUser.com.

About the Technical Reviewers

These reviewers contributed their considerable hands-on expertise to the entire development process for *Photoshop Elements 2.0: 50 Ways to Create Cool Pictures*. As this book was being written, these dedicated professionals reviewed all the material for technical content, organization, and flow. Their feedback was critical to ensuring that *Photoshop Elements 2.0: 50 Ways to Create Cool Pictures* fits our reader's need for the highest-quality technical information.

Michelle Jones is a writer, editor, and technical consultant who makes her home in Louisville, Kentucky. Somehow, she has convinced people to let her write and play with computers and then they pay her for it. Even she is amazed at her luck. Her web site can be found at www.michellejones.net.

Seán Duggan is a photographer and digital artist who combines a traditional fine-arts photographic background with extensive experience in digital graphics. He has worked as a custom black-and-white darkroom technician, studio and location photographer, digital restoration artist, graphic designer, web developer, and educator. His visual toolkit runs the gamut from primitive pinhole cameras and wet darkroom alternative processes to advanced digital techniques. In addition to providing Photoshop training seminars and digital imaging color-management consultation services, he creates illustrations and image design solutions for the web- and print-based media. He is an instructor for the photography department of the University of California, Santa Cruz Extension, and the Academy of Art College in San Francisco where he teaches regular classes on Photoshop and digital imaging for photographers. His web site can be found at www.seanduggan.com.

Al Ward is a certified Photoshop addict and Webmaster of Action FX Photoshop Resources (www.actionfx.com). A former submariner in the U.S. Navy, Al now spends his time creating add-on software for Photoshop and writing on graphics-related topics.

Acknowledgments

This is my favorite page because it reminds me of movie credits that appear (endlessly) at the end of a flick. I am convinced no one ever reads acknowledgments unless they think that their name appears in them. I am one of those people who reads the credits in a movie, so the least I can do is acknowledge a few of the fine folks who make a book like this possible.

Top of the list is Jody Kennen, my acquisitions editor. Yep, she is the one who convinced someone at New Riders Publishing that this book was a good idea. In that, her job is not unlike that of a casting director.

Next is Chris Zahn, my development editor. It is his job to make sure that my Texan was translated into English and to sort out the hundreds of tiny details that make him more like a movie producer than many movie producers I know. This probably explains why he buys those really large bottles of extra-strength headache tablets at the superstore.

Although it is probably wrong for a Texan to admit this, I don't know how to do everything using Photoshop Elements. Therefore, I am grateful for the contributions of three talented individuals, Mara Zebest Nathanson, Robert Stanley, and Al Ward, who were able to give their time and expertise to several of the chapters in this book.

Another individual at New Riders who deserves a hearty thank you is Susan Nixon, whose tireless efforts ensure that the final result of all of our combined efforts actually get noticed by the press and their readers. Without Susan's work, this book would be lost in the tsunami of books that are released upon the shores of readers every day.

My thanks to Jim Patterson, who loves digital photography as much as I do, and who is always ready to share different ideas on how to improve our digital-camera experience. Of course, he has been taking photos a lot longer than I, being that his first job was working as an assistant for Matthew Brady during the U.S. Civil War.

Lastly, my thanks to Mark Dahm, product manager for Photoshop Elements 2.0, for patiently enduring, redirecting, or answering my questions about Elements during the beta testing.

Tell Us What You Think

As the reader of this book, you are the most important critic and commentator. We value your opinion and want to know what we're doing right, what we could do better, what areas you'd like to see us publish in, and any other words of wisdom you're willing to pass our way.

As the Associate Publisher for New Riders Publishing, I welcome your comments. You can fax, email, or write me directly to let me know what you did or didn't like about this book—as well as what we can do to make our books stronger.

Please note that I cannot help you with technical problems related to the topic of this book, and that due to the high volume of mail I receive, I might not be able to reply to every message.

When you write, please be sure to include this book's title and author as well as your name and phone or fax number. I will carefully review your comments and share them with the author and editors who worked on this book.

Fax: 317-581-4663

Email: stephanie.wall@newriders.com

Mail: Stephanie Wall
          Associate Publisher
          New Riders Publishing
          201 West 103rd Street
          Indianapolis, IN 46290 USA

Foreword

Dave Huss is a Texan with an insatiable curiosity about the things he experiences and sees. As a photographer for more than 25 years, Dave mixes his intellectual curiosity with an amazing eye—an eye for detail, light, texture, and often, even a feel for the weather conditions that prevail. Dave finds abstraction in almost any subject in front of his lens and transforms the commonplace into eye-pleasing compositions that defy identification.

Viewing Dave's work, one can almost taste the dryness of a dusty Hill Country trail or smell the fragrance of spring wildflowers. He is unusual in that, upon reviewing his take from a session, he will make a note to return to that location to improve upon his effort. Recently, he returned to the University of Tampa campus where I had photographed for many years. After one early morning, Dave returned with familiar scenes rendered in beautiful and unfamiliar ways. He blends the skills of a technician with the feeling of an artist to achieve uncanny photographic results.

He became interested in digital photography in 1992 and bought one of the first digital cameras offered by Agfa, the 1280. Like nearly every photographer, he progressed through the Nikon Coolpix 990 and now uses a Nikon CP 5700. One of his photo compositions was a Grand Prize winner in Corel's 1998 International Design Contest.

Combine these photographic skills and experience with the fact that Huss has worked in the computer industry for more than 30 years, and you have the ideal author to write about digital photography applications.

Dave is the author or co-author of 12 books and numerous magazine articles. His "Graphically Speaking" column is known throughout the Internet community. He is a teacher of digital photography and digital photo editing throughout the United States and Europe.

Adobe Photoshop has been a favorite of photographers for more than a decade. Since its early days as software used primarily for scanning, Photoshop has grown in features, size, and price to become a standard of the graphics industry.

Today, the term "Photoshop it" is part of the photographic and graphics vernacular. The application has become the standard for color separations and pre-press production and has spread to fields as diverse as textile design and sophisticated photo retouching.

Following in the path of Photoshop's growth has been the emergence of digital photography. As digital cameras have improved in features, especially resolution, the need for Photoshop has increased. But conventional photographers making the move to the digital medium have balked at the idea of "needing" a large, expensive application such as Photoshop. Recognizing this, Adobe introduced Photoshop Elements, an application seemingly tailored to the needs of digital photographers.

Although Photoshop Elements 2.0 has essential instructions available to the new user in its "Hints" and "How To" recipe palettes, the beginner may be awed and overwhelmed by its wealth of features.

In this book, Dave Huss attempts to bring understanding of these features to the reader with his friendly, often humorous style. This is not another rehash of the User's Manual, which the author and I staunchly advocate reading, but an interpretation of a wonderful, feature-packed program.

It's my hope that your creations with digital photography and Adobe Photoshop Elements 2.0 will be enhanced by reading and referring to this book.

Jim Patterson
Contributing Editor
Mac Design, Photoshop User magazines

Introduction

I want to introduce you to a cookbook for photographers (digital and otherwise). I call it a cookbook because, like a cookbook, it shows the steps necessary to cook up some great photos and other things using Photoshop Elements 2.0. For the record, you can also use it with the original Elements 1.0 because it didn't change all that much (don't let Adobe know I told you this). Back to the topic at hand, though. Let's face it: If you want to take a photo that's too dark and make it a little lighter, you don't want a five-page explanation about light theory. You just want to know what steps are necessary to do it. That's what this book is all about: how to do cool (and necessary) stuff using Elements.

Who Should Read This Book

If you are new to Photoshop Elements or you have dabbled with the program and want to do more with it, this is the book for you. To make this book, I used much the same material that I use to teach my digital photography classes—where time is a precious commodity. The content has been refined over the past few years and distilled into the topics that are most important to folks who want to make their photos look better, fix old or damaged photos, share them on the web, or just print them out.

Who This Book Is Not For

If you recently won a Nobel Prize, this book isn't for you. This book does not teach you the theory of color, light, or the secrets of alchemy. Also, if you need a book that explains how each tool in Photoshop Elements 2.0 works in minute detail, I can offer a recommendation…it's called the *User's Manual.* I have a copy myself and it comes with Photoshop Element 2.0. Although my book shows you how to do cool stuff with Elements, it is not a 1,000 plus page reference manual for the product that resembles the Manhattan-style phone directories that were so popular a few years ago.

Overview

As I said earlier, this is a visual cookbook that shows you how to cook up some great photos using Photoshop Elements 2.0. This book is divided into the five basic units that I use when I teach my classes.

Part I, "Quick Start," is just that; it contains the bare essentials that you need to know to begin using Photoshop Elements. Chapter 1, "Quick Tour," covers basic stuff, such as the layout of the program, tool names, and how to undo mistakes (very important). In Chapter 2, "Getting Pictures into Your Computer," we cover getting pictures into the computer by using either a scanner or digital camera. This naturally flows into the all-important topic of adjusting and enhancing photos (Chapter 3, "Adjusting and Enhancing Photos"). The last chapter in this part, "Sizing and Saving Your Photos," covers the many ways to save and organize your photos.

In Part II, "Making Photos Look Professional," we discover how to make photographs look just that—professional. The all-important topic of photo composition is explored in Chapter 5, "Dealing with Composition Problems and Distortion," after which you learn how to correct a myriad of common photo problems, such as incorrect color, bad or poor lighting, and different types of tonal corrections (Chapter 6, "Fine-Tuning the Color," Chapter 7, "Correcting Lighting Problems," and Chapter 8, "Putting on the Final Touches"). The point of all these chapters in this part is just to make your treasured photos look much better.

In Part III, "Getting Fancy," we move beyond the pedestrian and do the really cool stuff. We begin, in Chapter 9, "Cool Tricks with Text," by learning all the different text effects that are possible with Photoshop Elements. In Chapter 10, "Cool Photographic Techniques," we explore the different ways to make a photograph look like a painting before moving to my favorite topic: how to photograph and create panoramas that will impress all your friends (Chapter 11, "Creating Stunning Panoramas"). We round out this part by learning how to remove and replace parts of photos in Chapter 12, "Rearranging and Replacing Objects in Photos." Breaking up might be hard to do (as the song goes), but removing an old boyfriend from a photo is easy.

In Part IV, "Photographic Repair Shop," we cover two important topics: retouching and repairing photographs. In Chapter 13, "Retouching Photographs," we discover how easy it is to remove blemishes and other defects with the stroke of a brush tool. We also learn how to smooth skin to take years off of a face and to reshape body parts to compensate for bad camera angles during shooting. Chapter 14, "Restoring and Repairing Photographs," is an important chapter in which you discover how to salvage photographs that you might have thought were beyond repair.

Part V, "Publishing Photos," is all about publishing your work. Whether you just want to print photos to carry with you to show immediate friends or you want to go global and display your creations on the World Wide Web, this is the part of the book where you learn all about these important topics. Chapter 15 is titled "Publishing on the Web" and Chapter 16 is "Making Great Photos on Your Printer."

Conventions

This book follows a few conventions:

- Actions taken in the program interface are simply separated by a comma. For example, File, Save As, Save.

- When you are asked to type something in the program, the text to be typed appears in boldface. For example, **Ribbon**.

1 Quick Tour

Everyone always wants to skip this part of the book so that they can do the cool stuff as quickly as possible. With that in mind, this chapter introduces you to the bare essentials: Just what you need to be able to follow the directions in the remaining chapters.

If you have already worked with the original Photoshop Elements 1.0, you can skip this chapter because the operation of the program has changed very little from the previous version.

Introducing Photoshop Elements 2.0

If this is the first time you've used Photoshop Elements, let me tell you a little about what you can expect from this program. Not long ago, Adobe realized that a growing market of consumers were demanding professional-level photo-editing tools, but did not want or need many of the features in Photoshop—the industry standard for photo editing. As digital cameras have improved every year, so has the need for better tools to manipulate and output the resulting photographs. Photoshop Elements specifically addresses the needs of photographers, especially digital photographers.

Although it is easy to think of Elements as a stripped-down version of Photoshop because the two programs look and act in a similar fashion, it really isn't. Elements offers many of the professional-level tools found in the more expensive Photoshop. The major difference between Elements and its more famous cousin is that Elements focuses on the idea of making the process of digital photo editing easier, without resorting to the brainless automatic features of many bundled software programs that, many times, do more harm to the photo than good.

What's New in Version 2.0

This question is popular among owners of Elements 1.0. It's generally asked because the current owners are wondering if there are enough new goodies to justify the upgrade. To be honest, if you look at the list of new features, on the surface it doesn't appear that impressive. But, Adobe invested much effort into this release by improving the existing features so that they work even better than before. Now that we have covered that question, here are a few of my favorite things (raindrops on roses and whiskers on kittens...), which are either new or have been improved upon in Photoshop Elements 2.0.

Beefed-Up File Management Tools

The File Browser has been improved. It can now read and display information that the digital camera records with each photo (see Figure 1.1). Adobe has also added batch processing so that you can easily change existing digital camera filenames on a slew of images to names that have more meaning to you. Batch processing also enables you to automatically resize a group of images or change the file format of a collection of photos.

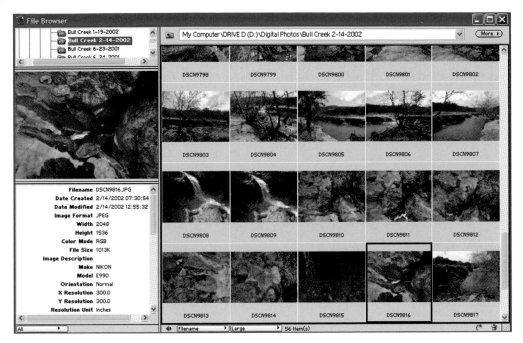

Figure 1.1
The File Browser gives you more information about your digital photos than you probably ever wanted to know.

Even Better Recipes and Other Online Documentation

Recipes, first introduced in version 1.0, continue to improve. Although Elements has a good help system, the recipes, just like recipes in a cookbook, are task-oriented, which means that they tell you how to complete photo-editing techniques. The good news is that, if you aren't big into reading, you can always click the Do This Step For Me command (see Figure 1.2), and Photoshop Elements automatically performs a recipe action.

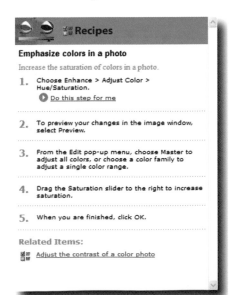

Figure 1.2
Recipes, similar to the one shown here, are helpful when you are learning new techniques or reviewing familiar ones.

Auto-Photo Correction

Although QuickFix is new to version 2.0, it just amounts to a handy placement of all the original tools in a centralized dialog box (see Figure 1.3).

Figure 1.3
QuickFix adds a "one-stop shopping" concept to Elements. From this dialog box, you can access the entire major photo-correction tool.

New Brush Selection Tool

Okay, I must admit: If there was one new feature in Elements 2.0 that would make me upgrade from 1.0, the new Brush Selection tool would be it. Until now, the only way to select an irregularly shape area or subject in Elements was to use the Lasso tool. Now, it's possible to refine that selection by using a brush. Thank you, Adobe.

Picture Package

The Picture Package feature is so cool, and it works even better in version 2.0. If you are not familiar with it, here's what it does: You can print out just about any combination of pictures on a single sheet of photo paper and Elements does all the work. All you need to do is select the photo you want multiple copies of, choose Picture Package (see Figure 1.4), and choose the combination that you like the best. (There are lots of them.) It doesn't get any easier than this.

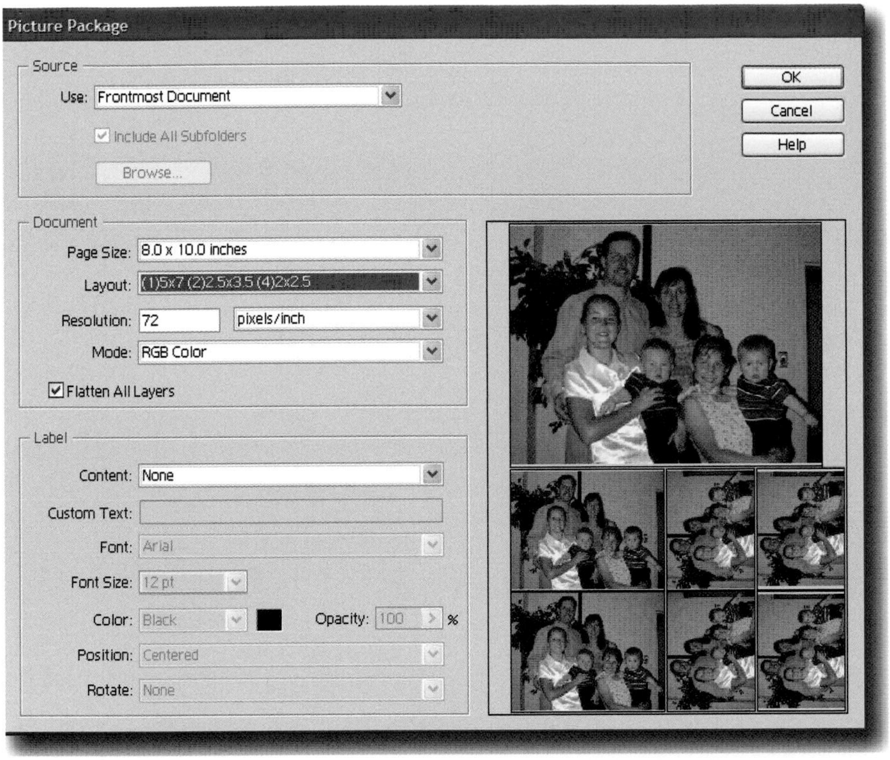

Figure 1.4
Picture Package enables you to automatically produce those crazy combinations of multiple copies offered by the professionals.

Photoshop Elements 2.0 has many more features, including a feature that enables you to make slide shows in portable document format (PDF), and another tool that automatically helps you publish your photos in a web gallery. For a more detailed description of the 2.0 release, go to www.adobe.com and locate the site for Photoshop Elements 2.0 (currently www.adobe.com/products/photoshopel/main.html).

A Cook's Tour of the Workspace

If this is your first time using Elements, let me give you a quick tour of the program's layout. Don't worry, it isn't complicated and I am not going into painful detail about how everything works and is configured. I cover these points throughout this book as, and when, necessary.

Free Copy of Photoshop Elements 2.0

If you haven't made the plunge and bought Photoshop Elements yet, Adobe lets you try it before you buy it by downloading the program from its web site at www.adobe.com. This download version is a complete copy of the program; it operates for 30 days after it is installed.

TIP

The Welcome Screen appears every time you start Photoshop Elements unless you uncheck the box that says, "Show this screen at startup" in the lower-left corner. Don't worry, you can always find this screen again. It is located in the Windows menu and is appropriately named Welcome.

Installing and Starting

Once upon a time, installing computer programs was a complicated process, but now it's pretty much automated. All you have to do is insert the CD and follow the directions. On a Mac, this is a bit more complicated (is that possible?) because the installer does not launch automatically.

After you launch Elements 2.0 for the first time, you see a screen that's similar to the one shown in Figure 1.5.

Toolbox   Menu Bar   Shortcuts Bar   Options Bar   Active Image Area   Palette Well   Palettes

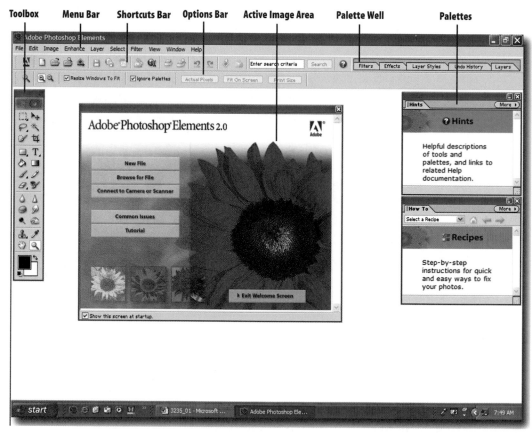

Figure 1.5
The layout of Photoshop Elements looks much like Photoshop, but the price tag doesn't.

Looking More Closely at the Parts

Figure 1.5 identifies the major parts of the Elements workspace. Each part could bear a lengthy exposition about how it works and how it's configured, and Adobe has provided a wealth of information about each part both in its online help and in its printed book (which you thought was only for those nights when you weren't able to fall asleep). In this chapter, I introduce these parts to you so you know what they do and why they exist.

The Toolbox and Options Bar

Of the three parts of the workspace that you will be using most often (the Toolbox, Shortcuts bar, and Options bar), two of them are related: the Toolbox and the Options bar. When you select a tool from the Toolbox, the Options bar displays the options for the currently selected tool. The Toolbox (see Figure 1.6) contains all the tools that you need to do the photo magic. If this is the first time that you have seen the Toolbox and its 25 icons, you might feel overwhelmed. I know I did the first time I saw it. At this point, you don't need to know the names of the tools; just be aware of two features of the Toolbox.

First, if you place your cursor over any icon in Elements for a moment, the name of the tool (or its function) appears. In Figure 1.7, the cursor shows that the small white square is used to set the background color. So, you really don't need to memorize a bunch of names because Elements always tells you what the names are.

Second, if you felt that the 25 icons in the Toolbox were a little frightening, I have some news for you: More icons are hiding in the Toolbox. If you look at the Toolbox again, you might notice that five of the icons have tiny black triangles in their lower-right corners. If you click and hold down the mouse button on one of these icons, an additional list appears. (Right-clicking the icon also makes the list appear.) The Text Tool icon, as shown in Figure 1.8, illustrates the four available options for this tool. When the drop-down list appears, selecting one of the tool options makes that tool the one that appears in the Toolbox.

Figure 1.6
The Toolbox can appear intimidating for first-time users. Don't worry; it will become familiar in no time.

Figure 1.7
Elements knows the names of all those icons in the workspace and displays their name or function when you position your cursor over the icon for a moment.

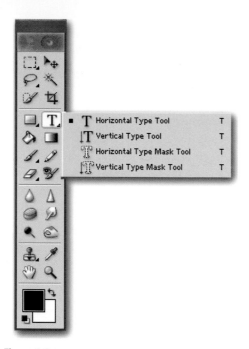

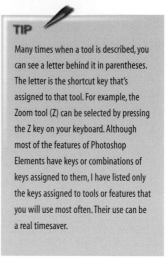

TIP

Many times when a tool is described, you can see a letter behind it in parentheses. The letter is the shortcut key that's assigned to that tool. For example, the Zoom tool (Z) can be selected by pressing the Z key on your keyboard. Although most of the features of Photoshop Elements have keys or combinations of keys assigned to them, I have listed only the keys assigned to tools or features that you will use most often. Their use can be a real timesaver.

Figure 1.8
Clicking the tiny triangle in a Toolbox icon reveals more related options for the tool.

The Shortcuts Bar

The Shortcuts bar (see Figure 1.9) displays buttons for common commands. You can quickly click commands as you need them while you're working in Photoshop Elements. Just like the other icons, to see the name of a button, hover the pointer over the button and its tool tip appears.

You can open or close the Toolbox and the Shortcuts/Options bars from the Windows menu. I recommend that the Toolbox, Options, and the Shortcuts bar always be left open in the work area so you can access all the tools and options without needing to open a series of menus.

Figure 1.9
The Shortcuts bar provides a fast way to accomplish many of the most commonly used tasks in Photoshop Elements.

Navigating Around the Workspace

One of the more important features of a photo-editing program is the tools needed to navigate around an image. If this is your first time working with a program like this, that first sentence might seem a little odd. It's like this: Performing touchup or color correction on a photographic image often requires getting very close to the area on which you are working. This presents some problems when your entire display screen is filled with your Aunt Hilde's lips. For this reason, Adobe built in some tools to make getting around the program much easier.

Zooming Around

Easily, the most important feature of the program is how the zooming is controlled. The Zoom tool (Z) is located in the Toolbox. Selecting it gives you control over how the currently selected image is displayed on your computer monitor.

Zooming and Its Pitfalls

Because zooming is such an important topic, I thought it deserved its own section. When an image is displayed on your computer, it is done so in one of two ways. It is either displayed at 100 percent (called Actual Pixels in Elements) or at some zoom level. In short, when viewing at any zoom setting other than the Actual Pixel setting, the image is not an accurate representation of the actual image. This is because Elements, like all other photo-editing programs, displays the actual pixels that make up the images. When displayed at the Actual Pixels setting, each pixel in the image is displayed on a screen pixel on your display—an accurate representation. When displayed at any other zoom setting, the computer can no longer display each pixel in the image on its own display pixel, but must mathematically approximate what color and brightness each display pixel must be to represent the image pixel at the assigned zoom level. Complicated? You bet, but with today's graphics hardware, it happens so fast that you don't notice it. As quickly as it happens, the display still only shows you its best guess of what the image will look like at the requested zoom level. I have personally, while teaching a photo-editing class mind you, tried to correct a color defect in a photo only to discover (when a bright student pointed it out to me) that the apparent defect wasn't a defect at all, but was introduced by the zoom level I was at.

So, how should you approach zoom levels? My suggestion: Don't worry about any distortion being produced and pick settings that are comfortable for you to work with. Just remember to always do the final check of your work using the Actual Pixels setting and/or printed output. So, let's see how this jewel works.

The Zoom Tool and the Options Bar

When you select the Zoom tool, the Options bar changes (see Figure 1.10) to show the options available with the tool. The two settings you will probably use the most are Actual Pixels (Alt-Ctrl-0) and Fit On Screen (Ctrl-0). If you do a lot of photo editing, you can save yourself time by

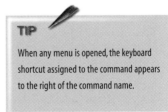

TIP

When any menu is opened, the keyboard shortcut assigned to the command appears to the right of the command name.

memorizing the keyboard shortcuts for these two settings. To be honest, I always forget them, so I constantly return to the Zoom tool to have access to the buttons in the Options bar. But if you like to memorize keyboard shortcuts, you will find that these two key combinations are useful to know.

The Print Size button attempts to display the photo at the physical size that it should be if it were printed. Sometimes, when I am working on what appears to be a huge image, I click that button and watch the image shrink to the size of a postage stamp.

If the Resize Windows To Fit check box is selected, every time you change your zoom level, the image window resizes in an attempt to fit the image. What happens if the image is larger than the display can accommodate? Scrollbars appear...what else?

Figure 1.10
The Options bar for the Zoom tool contains two of the most popular buttons in Photoshop Elements.

Undoing Mistakes

If there is one fact in photo editing, it is that you are going to take some action that you want to undo, undo again, and again, and again. One of the big problems in the early days of photo editing was the inability of the programs to enable you to undo something that you did. When Photoshop added the Undo command (Ctrl-Z), way back when, we cheered and then complained that we could only undo the last action. There was no pleasing us. Now, you can backtrack your actions in so many ways in this program that it's bewildering.

Classic Undo and Redo

With Photoshop Elements, every time you use Undo, you undo a previous action. To redo something, you use Ctrl-Y. I never understood this key choice. I realize the Y and Z are next to each other in the alphabet but, on the keyboard, they are separated by numerous keys. The most important use of Undo is not to undo a mistake, but it is used more often to get a "before and after" view of some action that you have just applied.

So how many steps can you go back? Unless you changed the default settings, you can backtrack (Texas term) 20 steps. If you have lots of memory, the answer is that you can go back as many History Steps as you want. You just need to change the History Steps setting shown in Preferences (Ctrl-K or Edit, Preferences). As you can see in Figure 1.11, many choices can be made in this single dialog box. You can even change the keyboard shortcuts for Undo and Redo. In Figure 1.11, the default number of History Steps shown is 20. If you change this to a larger number, you must restart Photoshop Elements before it takes effect. Remember that History Steps use memory, and more memory used by this feature means less memory space for you to work with large images.

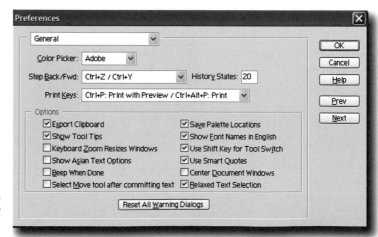

Figure 1.11
The Preferences dialog box is where the number of History Steps (Undo) is controlled.

Undo History Palette

When you need to remove many steps, Adobe has provided a way to let you view all the actions that you have applied to an image, or at least the last 20 (default setting) steps you applied. The Undo History palette, as shown in Figure 1.12, provides an easy way to go back many steps in a project with a single click. To go back to the point in the image where a command was applied, you only need to click the name of the command in the Undo History palette. All the steps you just undid now appear grayed out. You also can restore those same steps by clicking one of the steps, and the action's effect is immediately restored. This is a much better approach than some other photo-editing programs, which achieve this be reapplying all the actions one at a time.

Figure 1.12
The best way to go back many steps on a project is to use the Undo History palette.

Seeking Help

Adobe has made a great effort to provide plenty of online help to you. In the old days, user's manuals were a bad joke and the online help was a much abbreviated form of the user's manuals. When you need help in Photoshop Elements, just click the F1 key (or access the Help menu) and a large screen appears, as shown in Figure 1.13. Because it uses an HTML page for the front end, it looks like you are on the Internet (but you are not—the files are on your hard drive). From here, you can find the answer to just about any question that you might have.

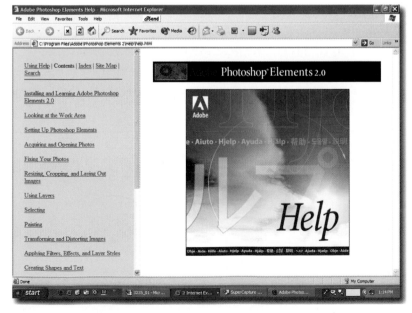

Figure 1.13
By simply clicking the F1 key, this enormous Help screen appears to answer your questions.

Recipes to Guide You

In addition to the main Help screen, other detailed procedures show you how to carry out commonly done tasks in Photoshop Elements. As previously mentioned, they are called recipes, and the beauty of this is that Adobe adds to its recipes all the time. Adobe puts up new recipes on its site that can be downloaded automatically. With the Recipes palette open, when you select Download New Adobe Recipes, the Online Services Wizard appears (see Figure 1.14) to help you download and install new recipes. Just a reminder, you must have an Internet connection to download recipes.

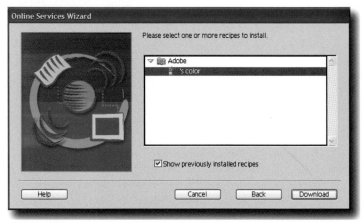

Figure 1.14
The Online Service Wizard helps you quickly download the latest Adobe Elements recipes from Adobe.

Summary

In this chapter, we covered the bare essentials that you need to know to use the techniques described in the remainder of this book. Although there seems to be way too many palettes, tools, and other items to recall, remember that you can get great results from this program by using just a small part of it (the parts described in this chapter).

In the next chapter, you learn about all the ways to get images into Photoshop Elements.

2 Getting Pictures into Your Computer

Before we can use Photoshop Elements to work on pictures, we first must get the images into the computer. With the advent of inexpensive scanners, relatively inexpensive digital cameras, and the Internet, we now have the ability to digitize our existing treasured photographs and have access to hundreds, if not thousands, of digital pictures. In this chapter, you learn how to get pictures into the computer from various sources (scanners, digital cameras, and so on) so that they can be opened in Elements. Also, we look at ways to capture better images with your scanner to obtain improved output and ultimately better pictures from Photoshop Elements.

Bringing Images into Your Computer

Regardless of what you plan to do with or to an image, the first step requires that you get the picture into your computer. Although it would be nice to just stick your favorite photograph into a slot on your computer and have it appear on the computer screen, things aren't that simple. A photograph must be converted to a digital file before it can be opened in Photoshop Elements. But it cannot be just any digital file; it must be in a graphic file format. Some images, such as photographs taken by digital cameras, are already in a file format that can be opened by Photoshop Elements, while photographs taken with traditional film cameras must be converted into graphic files using a scanner. In this section, we learn about available sources of digital images and what equipment is necessary to convert non-digital images (such as photographs) into graphic files (see Figure 2.1).

Figure 2.1
Existing photos must first be made into a digital file using a scanner before they can be opened in Photoshop Elements.

Where Digital Pictures Come From

Digital pictures that can be used in Photoshop Elements are available from various sources. It's impossible to list them all, so this section summarizes the more popular sources for digital images.

Digital Cameras

In a few short years, *digital cameras* (also called digicams) have, and will continue to, change the way we approach photography. Early digital cameras were expensive and they produced poor quality photographs. Today's entry-level digital cameras produce excellent results, cost much less, and give you the ability to take thousands of photos at little to no cost (see Figure 2.2).

Figure 2.2
DigItal cameras come in different sizes and prices, but they all produce pictures
that can be read by Photoshop Elements.

Scanners

A *scanner* can turn almost any photograph, printed image, or even a 3-D object into a
graphic file that can be brought into Photoshop Elements for enhancement, correction,
or restoration. Even if you own a digital camera, you might still need a scanner because,
most certainly, you have old photo albums with photographs or negatives tucked away
that need to be scanned and converted into digital images (if only to preserve them).

It might surprise you to know that five different types of scanners are used in the graphics industry, but only two types of these scanners are of interest to Photoshop Elements
users (see Figure 2.3): Flatbed scanners and Film scanners.

Figure 2.3
A flatbed scanner (left) and a film scanner (right) convert photographs, slides,
and negatives into digital images.

Flatbed Scanners

Scanners can convert just about anything into a digital image. Most people are unaware that scanning is not limited to flat objects, such as photographs. Resembling a flattened version of its cousin the copier, this scanner captures an image of whatever is placed on the scanner glass. Then, the captured image is sent to the computer in the form of a digital graphics file. In Figure 2.4, I scanned in four different objects individually and, using Photoshop Elements, made them into a montage. (Don't try and interpret any meaning in this, I was just scanning stuff around my office.) These objects could have been photographed with a digital camera, but using the scanner allows the image to be captured without the distortion introduced when the camera is at something other than a perfect perpendicular angle to the subject being photographed.

> **NOTE**
>
> Almost every personal flatbed scanner sold today connects to a computer using either a USB or a FireWire (IEEE-1394) interface. Newer scanners use the new, faster USB 2.0 specification. (Your computer must support USB 2.0 to get the maximum benefit of the improved scanning speed.) If your computer supports only the original USB, your scanner can still scan using it, it just won't be as fast.

Figure 2.4
You can use a flatbed scanner to capture a wide variety of objects.

Film Scanners

Film negatives and slides require a film scanner that's specifically designed to scan the very small 35mm originals. Some of the more expensive flatbed scanners offer transparency adapters for scanning color slides and negatives. Dedicated film scanners have traditionally provided noticeably superior results when compared to a scan obtained by using a flatbed scanner, but now that's beginning to change. Today's combination flatbed scanner with transparency adapter produces adequate to good results. Similar to the scanner market in general, the price of film scanners has dropped over the past few years, but they still cost more than the equivalent quality flatbed scanner. The Pacific Image Electronics PrimeFilm 1800 film scanner, shown in Figure 2.5, was the first film scanner to sell for under $300.

Figure 2.5
The availability of low-cost film scanners provides a way for consumers to scan in their existing film and slide collections. (Photograph courtesy of Pacific Image Electronics.)

Other Picture Sources

The Internet is a great source of images ranging from crummy home web page collections to royalty-free professional photographs that are available by subscription. My personal favorite is Hemera (www.hemera.com), a vendor of great collections of photo objects and clip art. Many of the figures in this book (such as Figure 2.1) were made using Hemera's photo objects.

Using Digital Cameras and Scanners

Now that we have some basic concepts under our belt, let's look at how to use these digital technologies, including how to use them with Photoshop Elements.

Connecting Camera and Computer

Whichever type of camera you use, you need a way to get your pictures from the camera into the computer. To do this, you need a physical connection between the camera and the computer. This is done by using one of the following connection types:

- Serial connection
- Dedicated card reader
- USB connections to the camera

The type of connection determines how long it will take to move pictures from your camera to your computer. Outside of buying a different camera, you cannot control the type of connection that your camera has.

How your digital camera is hooked up to the computer and which operating system is used determines what methods can be used to copy pictures from your camera to your computer. Generally, to copy pictures directly from the camera into your computer, you use either the software that came with your digital camera, use the Import feature of Photoshop Elements, or use the File Browser.

NOTE

Not all digital cameras are recognized as cameras by PC computers. Most often, I see this in older computers that have early versions of USB hardware. For this reason, your digital camera software might not automatically launch when you connect a camera. The software still works—it just doesn't start automatically.

Using Digital Camera Software

Most software that comes bundled with digital cameras provides a full range of features, such as image management, camera control, and the ability to rotate, flip, name, and move pictures to and from the camera. An example of such software is the Nikon View software, shown in Figure 2.6. The camera's software is launched automatically when a digital camera (with a USB interface) is plugged into the computer.

Figure 2.6
Nikon View 5 is a good example of full-featured camera software that makes the process of getting pictures into the computer a breeze.

Using Photoshop Elements's Import Command

The Import command, located in the File menu, brings in pictures from a digital camera and scans pictures (if a scanner is attached). When the Import command is selected, a list of devices that can import images appears (see Figure 2.7). Select either the camera software or the WIA support from the list and load the picture(s) you want.

Figure 2.7
This list appears when Import is selected. The content of the list is determined by how many imaging devices are installed.

NOTE

If your digital camera is attached to a computer using either Windows XP or Windows ME, each time you attach your camera to the computer, you are asked what you want the computer to use to talk with your camera. One of those choices is to move pictures from the camera into the computer using the Windows Imaging Acquisition (WIA) interface. Although it provides a simple way to move pictures directly from your digital camera (or scanner) to the computer, there's a disadvantage to using the WIA interface: It's a generic "no frills" control interface and, therefore, not as full-featured as the controls found on the software that comes with your camera (or scanner).

NOTE

Although a digital camera is properly attached to the system shown in Figure 2.7, the digital camera does not appear on the list. This is because Windows (ME and XP) didn't recognize the camera as an imaging device, but only saw it as a USB mass storage device. Using the WIA Wizard will not locate the camera either. When this happens, you cannot use the Photoshop Elements Import command to load pictures from your digital camera. You can still copy the pictures from the camera to the computer by using the software that came with the camera or the File Browser.

TIP

Click the Import button in the Shortcuts bar to quickly import an image (see Figure 2.8).

Figure 2.8
The Import button in the Shortcuts bar.

When Photoshop Elements launches, a welcome screen appears (assuming that you haven't disabled it, as discussed in Chapter 1, "Quick Tour") (see Figure 2.9). One of this screen's choices is Connect to Camera or Scanner. Selecting this button is equivalent to using the Import command in the File menu.

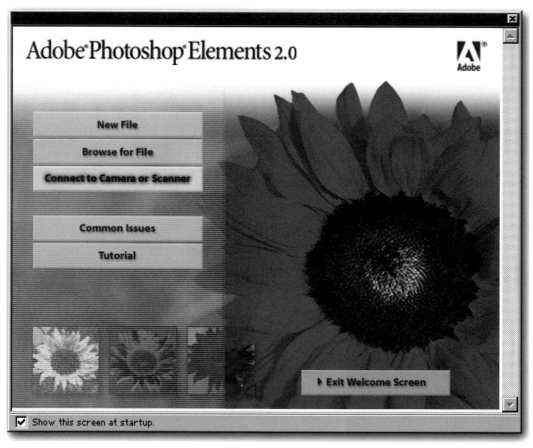

Figure 2.9
The Welcome Screen can be used to immediately begin getting pictures from an imaging device.

Using the File Browser

The *File Browser* is a great visual picture manager that provides an easy way to move, view, and manage images on your computer. The File Browser's operation couldn't be simpler:

1. With Photoshop Elements open, launch the File Browser (Shift-Ctrl-O or Window, File Browser). The File Browser window (see Figure 2.10) opens and displays the currently selected folder on the left and thumbnails of its contents on the right.

Figure 2.10
The File Browser lets you see thumbnails of all the pictures in the selected folder.

2. With the Explorer-like interface on the left, select the folder containing the pictures with which you want to work. The first time you open a folder, you see question marks in the right pane (see Figure 2.11); Photoshop Elements will take a few moments to generate the preview thumbnails in the area on the right side of the window. After the File Browser creates the thumbnails, it saves them in a special file in the same folder so that the next time you open it, the thumbnails appear instantly.

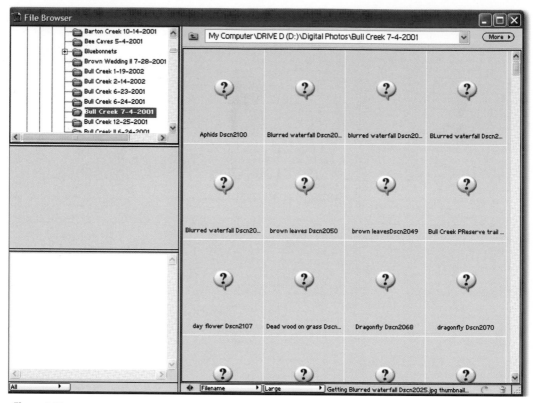

Figure 2.11
The File Browser takes a few moments to create thumbnails the first time a folder is opened.

3. Select individual pictures by clicking them one time. Select multiple individual pictures by holding down Ctrl while clicking the thumbnails or select all the pictures in the folder by using Ctrl-A.

4. After your pictures are selected, drag them to another location by clicking one of the selected thumbnails and dragging it to one of the folders on the left side of the File Browser window. You can also load the picture into Photoshop Elements by dragging it to the Photoshop Elements Image window or just by double-clicking the thumbnail.

TIP

Picture Information—Place the cursor over a thumbnail in the File Browser and, after a moment, a drop-down list opens and displays information about the picture.

Rotating Pictures

One of the File Browser's features is the capability to rotate pictures. By right-clicking the thumbnail image in the browser, you can select the direction and amount of rotation (see Figure 2.12). Be aware that although the thumbnail is rotated, the actual image is not. When the picture is actually opened, it is rotated, but the rotation will not be permanent unless you save the image.

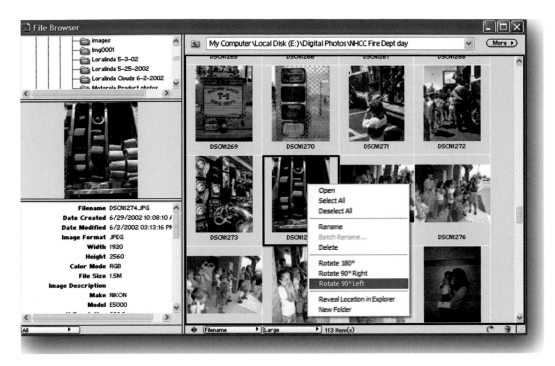

Figure 2.12
The File Browser provides a fast way to rotate images so they are oriented correctly for viewing.

Scanning with Elements

When you start scanning using the Import command, the software that came with your scanner is launched inside of Photoshop Elements (see Figure 2.13). Depending on the scanning software, this might be confusing. If you are using the Precision Scan software that comes with HP ScanJet scanners, it doesn't say anything about scanning (only Return to Photoshop Elements). Other applications are more direct and say something like Scan Now, or there might simply be a Scan button (how original). After the scan is complete, the scanning user interface (UI) closes and the scanned image appears in the Photoshop Elements workspace.

NOTE

You can customize several features in the File Browser by clicking the More button on the thumbnail side of the File Browser and choosing Preferences. The Photoshop Elements Preferences dialog box opens on the Browser page with several features that you can customize. From this page, you can change the size of the thumbnails so that they are large enough to recognize the image, but small enough to fit the maximum number of thumbnails per screen. I recommend using a size of 100 pixels (the default is 80).

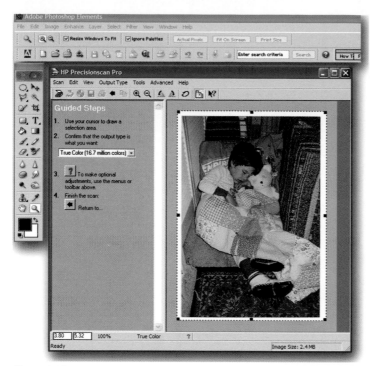

Figure 2.13
The scanner software launches within Photoshop Elements when Import is selected.

Scanning Printed Material

When you scan a printed image, such as a picture in a magazine article, the image usually develops a checkered or plaid pattern. Regardless of what it looks like, this pattern has a name—*moiré pattern*. When the patterns of the tiny dots that are used to print the picture (called screens) are scanned, it develops its own pattern for technical reasons beyond the scope of this book. Your scanning software might have the capability to minimize the moiré effect. (It might be called descreen.) What has become increasingly popular is to have a preset for the subject that you are scanning. For example, my scanning software has a setting for newspapers and magazines where descreening is accomplished automatically.

Be aware that regardless of how an image is descreened, the result is a softer picture, which means that it loses some of its sharpness. This is a small price to pay for the reduction of those annoying moiré patterns.

So much for importing pictures from a digital camera and scanning non-digital pictures to make them digital; now we'll consider some ways in which you can organize this tidal wave of images that is about to engulf your computer.

Picture Management Suggestions

One of the big advantages of digital cameras is its capability to take an almost unlimited number of pictures at little to no cost. As a result, most of us end up with many photos on our computer. (I have over 25,000 photos stored on my computer!) Keeping track of all those pictures can be challenging, so this section lists some ideas to help you keep track of them.

Use Folders to Categorize Photos

Keep photos organized in folders named for an event (for example, Amanda's Wedding, Baby's First Birthday). If the photos are not of specific events, use subject matter with dates (for example, Bluebonnets 03-04-2001 or Clouds 12-15-2001). The best time to do this is when transferring the photos from your camera to your computer. I recommend maintaining a master folder on a hard drive in which you keep all the digital photo folders.

Naming Pictures—A Real Timesaver

All digital cameras automatically assign numbers to photos when the pictures are taken. Some cameras reset the numbers each time the media is removed from the camera. This can be a problem because the result is many photos files with a label similar to AGF0001.JPG. If your camera works this way, having them categorized in individual folders keeps the duplicate names from becoming problematic.

Other cameras make life easier in this regard by not resetting the picture-number counter each time, so each photo has a unique number. Regardless of how your camera works, you will want to give your pictures unique names that describe the picture. This brings up another potential headache. Say you have six pictures of Uncle Bob sitting in front of a fireplace. Two possible solutions can prevent duplicate filenames. You can use sequential numbers following the description (for example, Uncle Bob fireplace 01, Uncle Bob fireplace 02...). Because I usually like to keep the original photo files under the original number assigned by the camera, I give the picture file a name by adding a descriptive name in front of the number. For example, Uncle Bob's photos would be Uncle Bob fireplace DCN0001, Uncle Bob fireplace DCN0002.... I do this because I apply all changes, enhancement, or corrections to the named copy of the photo. Having the original photo number as part of the name allows me to locate the original picture file when necessary—and believe me, it is often necessary. Without the number, I'd have to wade through dozens of images trying to see which original image is Uncle Bob fireplace 01.

Using File Info to Add More Information

In addition to the filename, you can use the File Info feature of Photoshop Elements to input additional information to the photograph. With an image open, selecting File, File Info opens a dialog box that provides two selectable pages for information (see Figure 2.14): General and EXIF. The General page displays a wealth of information (that you must add) including copyright, title, comments, and so on. If you make the image copyrighted, a copyright symbol appears in the title bar whenever the image is opened.

Figure 2.14
Use the File Info feature to store important information with the image.

The EXIF page displays all the technical information that was provided by the camera when the image was made (see Figure 2.15). Many times, this page is blank because the information is lost in most copies of the image.

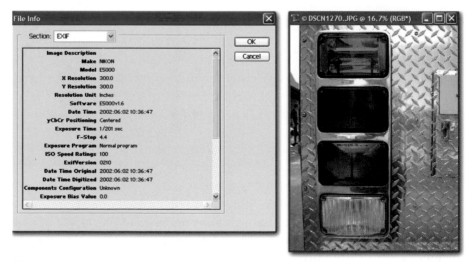

Figure 2.15
The EXIF page displays a wealth of technical information about the actual photograph—if the camera recorded it.

Summary

We covered plenty of material in this chapter. We learned about how to import pictures from imaging devices using the Import command, whether they come from a digital camera or a scanner. Now it's time to move to the next chapter and discover how easy it is to quickly tweak those digital pictures and make them look great.

3 Adjusting and Enhancing Photos

Some photo printers on the market today enable you to print pictures without using a computer. You need only to insert the camera's memory card into the printer and—Presto!—you have a photograph. Although I can understand the appeal of popping in the media and having a photograph appear, I always want to fiddle with the photo a little (sometimes a lot) before I print it. In this chapter, we discover how easy it is to improve the appearances of your photos when you print them.

Understanding Adjusting and Enhancing Photos

I wish that you could just click a button in Elements that automatically makes all the adjustments you want to your picture. The reason this button doesn't exist is because the computer doesn't have any way of knowing what's right and what's wrong with your photo. But, if you learn to identify parts of the photo that need improvement, Elements provides various tools to fix them. Before going any further, we need to first understand the difference between adjusting and enhancing a photograph.

Adjusting Versus Enhancing Photos

This isn't about the actual names—adjustment and enhancement—it's about the concepts. There is a difference in what is done with these two actions. When we talk about *adjustments,* we talk about corrections applied to photos to make them as they are supposed to be. If the orange in the photo is green, the color needs to be adjusted (corrected). If a digital image is too large to post on the web or too small to print, it needs to be adjusted. On the other hand, if you want to make a photo look better by making the colors look richer, remove a blemish from a face or blur a background to emphasize a subject, you're *enhancing* the photo. That being understood, take a look at how to perform some of the most common basic photographic adjustments and enhancements.

The Fast Track Method

Here's the quickest way to get pictures from your camera ready for printing. It involves only four steps:

1. Rotate the picture (if necessary).

2. Crop the photo (if necessary—and it probably is).

3. Apply the QuickFix.

4. Sharpen the photo.

Rotating the Photo

This is the first and most common correction we make with Elements. Anytime you take a photograph with the camera in portrait orientation, it needs to be rotated. For the record, when we talk about the orientation of the camera, we mean what part of the image is on top—the wide part or the narrow part. Figure 3.1 shows the same subject taken using two orientations: landscape and portrait.

Figure 3.1
The left photo is taken in landscape; the right photo is taken in portrait orientation.

With Photoshop Elements, you can rotate a picture in two ways: by using the File Browser or the Rotate command.

Rotating with the File Browser

Rotating a photo by using the File Browser is the simplest and quickest way to rotate a photograph. You simply right-click a thumbnail and choose the rotation direction from the menu that appears (see Figure 3.2).

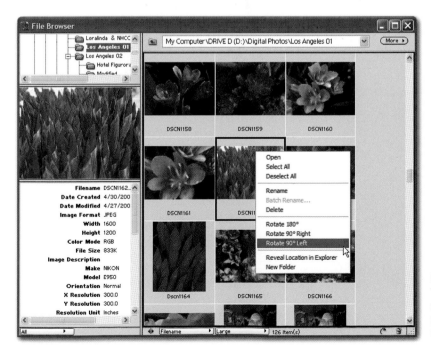

Figure 3.2
The File Browser provides a quick way to rotate photographs to their correct orientation.

The first time you attempt to rotate a photo using the File Browser, a dialog box appears that's similar to the one shown in Figure 3.3. It tells you that you are not actually rotating the image, but rotating the thumbnail. The next time that Elements opens the image, it will rotate it to match the thumbnail. There is a trick to this, however; you must save the file when you close it. If you don't save it, the rotation will be lost. You also need to take note of the Don't Show Again check box in the lower-left corner of the dialog box. Unless you really want this warning appearing every time you rotate a photo, I recommend that you check this box.

Figure 3.3
This dialog box lets you know that you are only rotating the thumbnail and not the photo.

It isn't necessary to use the File Browser to rotate a photo. You can also choose Rotate from the Image menu and select the rotation that turns your photo right side up.

Yet a Third Way to Rotate a Photo

I mentioned that there were two ways to rotate a photograph using Photoshop Elements—that's true. Here's a third way that might be better than those offered in Photoshop Elements. If your digital camera came with its own software, you might discover that it provides a neat and tidy way to rotate its images. I use the NikonView 5 software provided by Nikon (see Figure 3.4), and I think it is the best way to transfer and rotate all the images that need to be rotated.

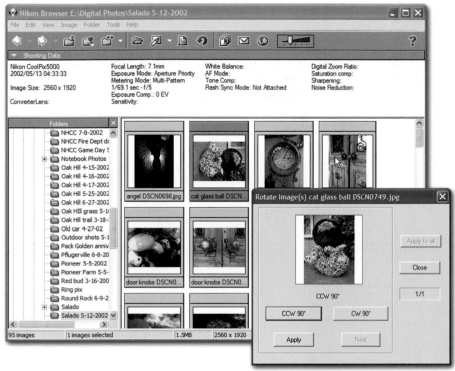

Figure 3.4
The software that ships with your digital camera might provide the fastest and quickest way to rotate your photos.

Figure 3.5
The Crop tool provides a quick and simple way to Improve the composition of most photographs.

Cropping

Now that your photos are all pointed the right way, the next step is to crop them. Generally, people don't think about cropping their photos because of the feeling that they want to keep every part of the photo. The truth is that most photographs are greatly improved by removing the part of the scene that distracts the viewer's eye. You can crop photos using the Crop tool (C), which is shown in Figure 3.5. Its operation is pretty obvious. The part that requires judgment on your part is what to crop and what to leave in the photo.

Using the Crop tool is simple. After you select the Crop tool (C), drag it over the part of the image that you want to keep. When you release the mouse button, the crop marquee appears as a bounding box with handles at the corners and sides. You can use these to adjust the crop marquee. When the photo is cropped the way you want it, double-click the image. It crops according to your specifications.

35

Why Crop Before Doing Anything Further?

There's a very good reason why you need to crop your image before making any tonal or color corrections. The automatic correction features of Photoshop Elements read the information contained in the entire image to determine what and how much correction to apply.

For example, in the squirt gun mêlée shown in Figure 3.6, the girl on the far right is in deep shadows. Although it's possible to recover her from the darkness, so to speak, the focus of the photo is the action in the center. If you apply any of the automatic features of QuickFix, it tries to balance out the dark (shadow) and bright (highlight) portions of the photo using a part of the photo that we will ultimately remove.

Figure 3.6
The girl in the shadow affects the automatic tonal correction if she's not cropped before it's applied.

What to Crop

Consider these general rules and examples when you decide what to crop in your photos. First, decide the subject of the photo and remove anything that distracts from the subject. The two girls in Figure 3.7 are lost in a large room. By cropping the photo to what's shown in Figure 3.8, the girls become the focus of the photo. Don't be afraid to remove part of your subject to get up close. People are not going to look at the photo and ask what happened to the rest of the girls' bodies.

Did you notice the other trick I used to center the focus on the subjects? I used the Clone tool to remove the display that was on the bulletin board behind them. (You learn about the Clone tool in Chapter 13, "Retouching Photographs.") In this case, the part that I removed had no bearing on the subject matter. When cropping, be careful not to remove items that reinforce the photo's subject.

Figure 3.7
The girls should be the subjects of the photo, yet they appear to be part of the room.

Figure 3.8
With the expanse of the room removed, you can now see the girls' faces.

Here's another example of improving a photo by using the Crop tool. From a composition perspective, the original has just about everything wrong with it (see Figure 3.9). It was taken at a slight angle because I was leaning back in a chair. Other people clutter the bride and her dad, who are the subjects, so they are lost in the crowd. By cropping out the non-important stuff, we end up with a lovely shot of Amanda, the bride, and her dad (see Figure 3.10). (For the record, this is the second daughter to get married within a month. I think Jim is holding up quite well.)

Figure 3.9
The father and the bride are somewhere in this photo.

Figure 3.10
With the expanse of the room removed, we can now see the faces of the bride and her dad.

Cropping Versus Picture Size

If you watch TV or go to the movies, you have probably seen a critical scene where someone asks a technician to zoom in on some part of a video or satellite photo, at which point, my favorite line is said— "Now enhance it." Amazingly, the blurred license plate or face or whatever suddenly comes into crystal-clear focus. Don't believe it—it only happens in the movies. The point is, when you zoom in on a small part of the photo to emphasize it, be careful that you haven't reduced your photo to the size of a postage stamp. For digital camera users, it is when you are cropping a photo that all those extra megapixels come in handy. If you want only to show the picture on the web, you can really make it small. If, on the other hand, you want to print a photo, you need to have enough size to print it at a resolution of 150dpi for most inkjet printers. We touch more on this subject in Chapter 4, "Sizing and Saving Your Photos."

Other Cropping Suggestions

Never feel that you must crop a photo. Sometimes, all the extra space around a subject can draw attention to it, or the space is necessary for the composition. In Figure 3.11, a young man is sitting on the edge of an empty parking lot eating a snow cone on a hot Texas afternoon. In my opinion, the emptiness around him is part of the composition, so I left it.

Figure 3.11
The emptiness around the subject helps viewers see how that snow cone holds this young man's attention.

My last cropping suggestion (in this chapter, at least) applies to both cropping a photo and taking one. Whenever possible, avoid placing your subject in the center of the photo. Having a photo with the subject in the dead center is used for passports and drivers licenses—and we all know how good those photos look. In Figure 3.12, we have a girl in her Easter outfit (with a matching doll, of course) in a playground. I love this shot because, on most days, this girl would not have been posing for me, but would have been all over that swing set. So, how can we improve the composition of this photo? We could crop most of the background, except for her, which results in an oddly shaped narrow photo. Although it isn't necessary to have every image in standard photo sizes, cropping the photo that way would look weird.

Figure 3.12
Great photo of the girl, but once again, she's not the focus of the composition.

Another possible solution is to remove everything to the left of her, leaving her alone on the playground. The problem with that solution is that, without the playground equipment, she's standing alone on sand in front of a chain-link fence. The viewer has no real visual clues that she is standing in a playground. The cropping decision that I made was to leave the playground equipment in the background, but blur it slightly with the Blur tool (R) to make it slightly out of focus (see Figure 3.13). Can you figure out what else I did to this photo? Remember the pole that was behind her? Once again, the Clone tool helped remove a fixture that distracted from the overall composition. In Chapter 12, "Rearranging and Replacing Objects in Photos," we learn many tricks for removing objects from photos.

Figure 3.13
Cropping, and using a few other tricks, results in a more interesting composition than the original.

QuickFix: One-Stop Image Correction

QuickFix is a new feature of Photoshop Elements 2.0. It opens a dialog box from which you select and adjust the brightness, color, sharpness, and even the rotation of your image in a single dialog box. It's sort of a Swiss Army knife approach to image correction and, like that famous knife, it has more features on it than you will probably ever use.

Located in the Enhance menu, selecting QuickFix opens the dialog box that's shown in Figure 3.14.

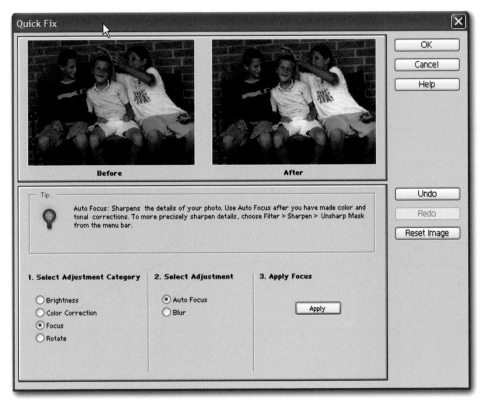

Figure 3.14
QuickFix provides selection and control over many of the automatic correction tools in Elements.

Adobe has done a good job of making this feature easy to use. Simply select the Adjustment Category, pick the specific adjustment, and click the Apply button (if available) or make the actual adjustment if the slider controls appear. You have a before-and-after preview window so that you can see the cumulative effects of your changes. If your screen is large enough, you can also preview the effect on the actual image, which is better because previewing changes on a small screen is difficult.

As I said, I don't think that you need to be concerned with all the features in QuickFix. But, here are my recommendations for using this helpful tool.

Using QuickFix Quickly

Three commands in QuickFix are used most often for quickly fixing photographs:

- Auto Contrast
- Auto Levels
- Auto Color

Here's my recipe for using QuickFix:

1. In the Brightness category, choose Auto Contrast and click Apply. What happens to the image? Do the colors change? Depending on the photo, they might not change with Auto Contrast. Does the image change at all? If not, look on the right side of the dialog box and click Undo. Although undoing a step that appears to have no effect isn't critical, it is just good housekeeping because some of the effects actually do alter the image slightly, even if they are not apparent on the screen.

2. Apply Auto Levels. With this command, the colors might change slightly. The main question is, "Does the change look better or worse?" For example, did a photo of some children with lots of warm colors suddenly develop a bluish cast? If it does, click the Undo button. That removes only the last applied effect. Because Elements doesn't tell you what effect you are undoing, it's possible to get a bit lost. If you do, just click Reset Image, and you go back to the original photo.

3. Select the Color Correction button, choose Auto Color, and click Apply. The same rule applies to Color Correction that applies to Auto Levels. Did the colors change? If they did change, was the change something that you wanted?

4. After doing these three steps, click the OK button, and you're done. Yeah, there are several more categories to pick from, including Focus (sharpening)—don't use this one.

There is no way to tell in advance what type of images will be improved by QuickFix and which ones won't. Because it just takes a moment to run the three auto features, I always check how each one affects the image.

Trying Out QuickFix

To demonstrate QuickFix in action, download the sample file `pink_flowers.jpg` from this book's web page on the New Riders Publishing web site and open it in Elements:

1. Select QuickFix and, in the Brightness category, select Auto Contrast and click Apply. The colors appear brighter but they didn't change (we can also say the colors didn't shift). So far, so good.

2. Choose Auto Levels and click Apply. Wow! Who turned on the green light? (See Figure 3.15.) This effect is not uncommon for a photograph taken on an overcast day, as this one was. Click the Undo button.

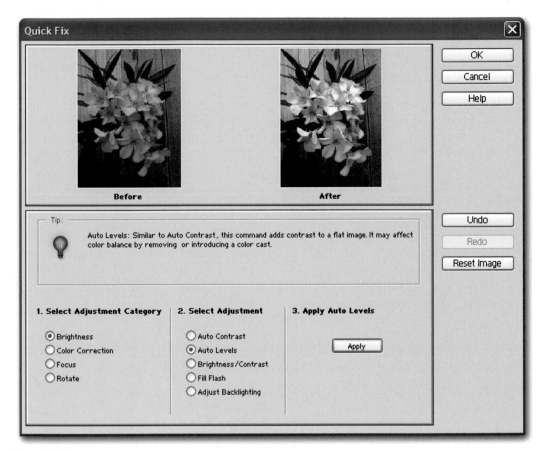

Figure 3.15
Auto Levels makes the flowers appear brighter, but changes their color.

3. Choose Color Correction, select Auto Color, and click Apply. That same greenish color appears in the upper-left corner. So, click Undo. We are left with only one of the three recommended automatic corrections having been applied to the photo. Click the OK button, and you are done. Remember that it is all right to only use one correction (or even none of the corrections), which is why I picked this photo for the first QuickFix tutorial. I want you to get familiar with the fact that it isn't necessary to use every correction.

Trying Out QuickFix: Part II

It might seem like I'm being too harsh on the other features of QuickFix and, in retrospect, I thought it would only be fair to include a sample image to try that does use something other than the "Auto trinity." The photograph called Friends.jpg (which you need to download from this book's web page on the New Riders Publishing web site) is one that I took at the wedding of my daughter's close friend, Ashleigh. It's a great shot except that the flash didn't fire. Let's see if we can salvage it by using some QuickFix magic:

1. With `Friends.jpg` open, click the QuickFix icon on the Shortcuts bar (see Figure 3.16) and select Auto Contrast. Surprised? Well, we're not done yet.

Figure 3.16
The QuickFix icon provides a fast way to open the QuickFix dialog box.

2. Don't apply Auto Levels or Auto Color because they won't improve the photo. Next, in the Brightness category, choose Fill Flash and change the Lighter value to +9, as shown in Figure 3.17. Be patient; depending on the size of the image and the speed of your computer, it sometimes takes a few moments for the preview to catch up to the setting. Click OK. You have a good recovery of an underexposed photo, as shown in Figure 3.18.

Figure 3.17
Using QuickFix's Fill Flash adjustment, we are able to improve a photo that was too dark.

A

B

Figure 3.18
The original photo is underexposed (a), but after QuickFix (b), it's ready to use.

Sharpening—The Last Step

After you are happy with the color and other adjustments that you made to the photo, you can sharpen it. Here are a few things to know about sharpening photos. First, if the photo is out of focus, after you apply sharpening, it will still be out of focus. Second, Photoshop Elements (and Photoshop) offers several different types of sharpening. Ignore all of them except Unsharp Mask. They provide a fixed amount of sharpening that's either too little or too much, but rarely the right amount. For the record, any Photoshop instructor will tell you the same thing. Even the Adobe Photoshop

Evangelists (yes, Adobe has them) will tell you to ignore the other sharpen settings (which is called Focus in QuickFix), and that's why I told you to ignore them. Last point before we proceed: If you are going to change the size of the image (which is described in the next chapter), don't apply sharpening until you have the image at its final size. So much for general knowledge about sharpening; let's see how it is done.

Unsharp Mask: Great Tool with a Weird Name

In the Filter menu under Sharpen, you will discover Unsharp Mask at the bottom of the drop-down list, as shown in Figure 3.19. The three dots (ellipsis) that follow the name indicate that a dialog box is associated with the filter. (Notice that only the Unsharp Mask filter has a dialog box.)

Figure 3.19
Although it's buried deep in the menu tree, the Unsharp Mask filter is the sharpen filter of choice.

When the Unsharp Mask dialog box appears, you are presented with three adjustment sliders: Amount, Radius, and Threshold, as shown in Figure 3.20. Three controls that interact with each other can seem complicated, so for most sharpening, I recommend that you keep the Threshold at 0 levels, the Radius at a value between 1 and 2, and adjust the Amount slider until the image looks right.

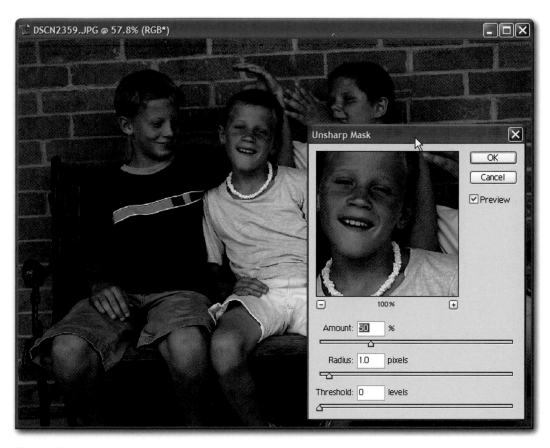

Figure 3.20
The Unsharp Mask filter dialog box is simple to use despite all its adjustment sliders.

How Sharp Is Sharp Enough?

How much sharpening should you apply? It depends on what you are sharpening. Don't you just love that answer? I should run for a political office. It's true, though. If you are sharpening a portrait of a middle-aged person, sharpening will bring out all the details (wrinkles) in his or her face, so you wouldn't necessarily want too much, if any, sharpening. If you are applying sharpening to man-made objects, such as buildings or cars, you can get away with almost any amount. You know you have applied too much sharpening when lighter parts of the image begin to loose their details and become solid white. This phenomenon is called a *blowout* and should be avoided.

The Best Zoom for Previewing Effects

When you are viewing the photo on your computer screen at anything other than 100 percent, the image that you see is not an accurate representation of the actual photo. Although it might not fit on your screen, always view any sharpening changes using the Actual Pixels setting in the View menu.

Another potential problem when sharpening a photograph that was scanned is that sharpening emphasizes all the dust, hair, and other debris on the photo or scanner glass. This is especially noticeable if a photo has many dark areas, such as someone wearing a dark suit or dress. Apply too much sharpening to a photo like that and it appears that the photograph has developed a case of dandruff. Sometimes, even a moderate amount of sharpening can light up all the debris that you should have cleaned off the photograph and/or scanner before scanning it. Also be aware that problems caused by over-sharpening are more apparent in black-and-white (grayscale) photographs than color.

Next, let's look at some examples of Unsharp Masking. Figure 3.21 shows the original photograph with which we'll be working.

Figure 3.21
Here is the original photograph, taken with a digital camera.

In Figure 3.22, I applied a strong amount of Unsharp Mask filter. Notice the difference around the necklace the middle boy is wearing, how it now appears whiter. The fact is, the overall contrast of the photo was increased, but now the white portions are beginning to blowout.

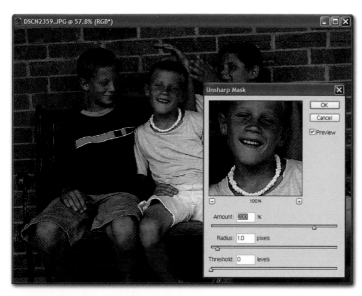

Figure 3.22
Here is the same photograph with a hefty, but not excessive, amount of
Unsharp Masking applied.

Figure 3.23 represents an example of oversharpening. Don't be seduced into adding
either too much contrast or sharpening. A quick glance at an oversharpened picture
gives the impression that it is more vivid. In fact, a lot of detail in the photo is lost in
oversharpened pictures.

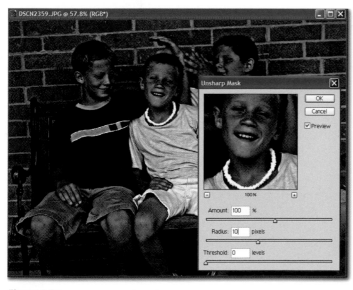

Figure 3.23
In this case, the amount of Unsharp Masking applied is excessive and causes
much of the detail to be lost.

When the same amount of sharpening that was applied to the boys in Figure 3.23 was applied to the close up of the Texas doorknobs on the old door in Figure 3.24, it made the photo more vivid by bringing out the detail and the great contrast of the wood and peeling paint.

Figure 3.24
Applying large amounts of sharpening to vivid objects that have great texture brings out its details.

Summary

Now that you know how to do the quick and slick photo fixups, the next chapter teaches you how to change the size of a photo so it fits on the web or in an email. It also discusses how many different ways you can save an image.

Sizing and Saving Your Photos

When you take a picture with a film camera, just about the only choice you must make concerning size involves what print size you want. When it comes to digital photos, you have more choices, so it can be more confusing. In this chapter, we learn how to make digital photos so that they are the size you want. I also cover the many different formats in which they can be saved—hallelujah.

Resizing Photos for Email

Let's start by taking a quick look at what is probably the most popular thing digital-camera owners do—share photos through email. The problem with sharing photos through email is that, as digital-camera sensors get larger (mine gets up to five megapixels), so does the file size of the photos that they produce. Because most email recipients have size limits on email attachments, if the attached photo is too large, the receiving mail server might refuse it. Some might just delete the email. Even if the mail server accepts the attached photo, if the poor soul downloading your photographic masterpiece has a slow dial-up connection, it could tie them up for a while. To prevent all this, you need to reduce the photo's file size.

One of Photoshop Elements' great features is the capability to automatically downsize a photo and attach it to an email. Because the operation is totally automatic, there are no choices about how small to make the photo. That's OK; it's still a great feature. Here's how to use it:

1. Open the photo that you want to send. From the File menu, select Attach to Email. If the file is wider or taller than 1,200 pixels (we learn about pixels in the next section) or isn't in JPEG format, the warning message shown in Figure 4.1 appears. The presented choices are self-explanatory.

Figure 4.1
This message appears when you attempt to attach an overly large photo to an email.

2. If you click the Auto Convert button, a copy of the image is reduced and attached to a blank email, as shown in Figure 4.2. The original remains unchanged.

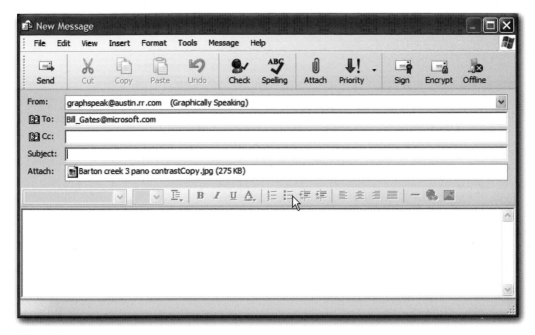

Figure 4.2
The Attach to Email feature provides the quickest and easiest way to resize photos being attached to emails.

Although the Attach to Email feature provides a quick-and-dirty sizing of your photos for email, it lacks some sophistication. We look at this feature and preparing photos for email more in Chapter 15, "Publishing on the Web."

Changing the Size of a Photo—Basic Stuff

Changing the size of a digital photo using Photoshop Elements is relatively easy. The only problem most users experience is that it involves some technical jargon that can be bewildering. So, our first course of action is to come to grips with a few of these terms.

The Anatomy of a Digital Picture

Working with digital pictures is easier if you understand a few things about them. If you read and understand the concepts in this section, working with digital images and all of their techno jargon will make more sense. It isn't brain surgery—it isn't even hard, and it involves very little math.

Pixels: Picture Building Blocks

All digital pictures are made of building blocks called *pixels*. No, these are not characters from *The Lord of Rings*, but a term that describes the smallest part of a digital picture. Pixels have two characteristics: They are square, and they can be only one color. So, a digital picture is much like the mosaic shown in Figure 4.3. It's made from a bunch of colored squares put together.

Figure 4.3
This mosaic is composed of hundreds of small and different-colored tiles that results in a picture.

The dimensions of a digital picture are measured in pixels. For example, my Nikon Coolpix 5000 digital camera produces a picture that is 2,560 pixels wide by 1,920 pixels high. When the File Browser is open, as shown in Figure 4.4, you can see the dimensions listed below the selected preview image.

Where Do Pixels Come From?

All digital pictures are made up of pixels. The two most common sources of digital pictures are scanners and digital cameras, which operate in a remarkably similar fashion. Digital cameras contain millions of tiny light detectors that are all jammed together to form a sensor that produces the digital picture when the shutter is opened. If you look at a digital camera, you can see a number emblazoned on the body that advertises how many millions of pixels (megapixels) are produced by the camera's sensor. Looking at my Nikon Coolpix 990, I can see it has 3.36 megapixels. This means that when I push the camera's button, the shutter opens and light strikes each of the millions of little light detectors that make up the camera's sensor. Each light detector in the sensor produces a digital value that represents the color of the light that struck it. My Coolpix camera combines all these values to produce a digital picture containing over three million pixels. As a side note, the term megapixel describes only the size of the sensor in a digital camera; it never describes the size of a digital image.

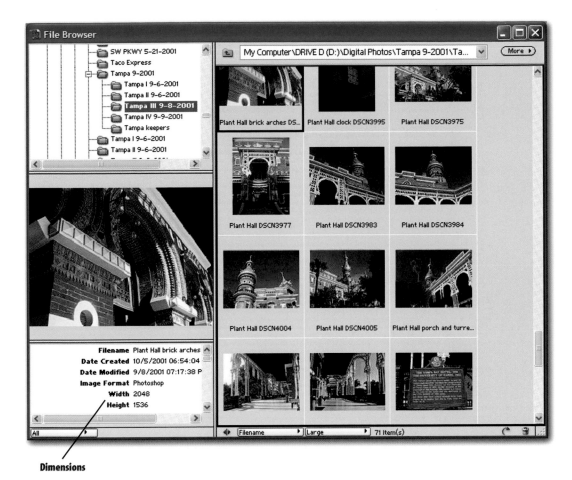

Dimensions

Figure 4.4
The File Browser provides plenty of information about a photograph, including its dimensions, given in pixels.

How Big Is Your Pixel?

At this point, the question you're probably asking is: How big is a pixel? The answer is both simple and complex. (Don't I sound like one of the judges on *Iron Chef?*) The fact is that a pixel can be as large or as small as it needs to.

To help you better understand pixels, pretend we have an image that's 600 pixels wide by 300 pixels tall (referred to as 600×300). If you print this image so it is 6 inches wide and 3 inches tall, every square inch of the image will be 100 pixels wide and 100 pixels tall. Here comes the math (but don't be afraid).

Example 1

600 pixels divided by 6 inches = 100 pixels per inch

300 pixels divided by 3 inches = 100 pixels per inch

In this example, each pixel is 1/100 of an inch square.

What if the same picture is printed on a billboard that's 50 feet (600 inches) wide?

Example 2

600 pixels divided by 600 inches = 1 pixel per inch

300 pixels divided by 300 inches = 1 pixel per inch

Each pixel is now 1 inch square (or 100 times larger).

Resolution: Defining Pixel Density

The number of pixels in both of the previous examples remains the same; only the resolution (number of pixels per inch) changed. A digital image has no absolute resolution. All it has are a fixed number of pixels in each dimension. As the resolution changes, the physical size of the output changes because the number of pixels that make up the image are being spread over a greater or lesser area. Figure 4.5 shows three copies of the same photo. The only difference between them is their resolution setting. Because each photo has the same number of pixels, they appear as the same size in a photo-editing program, such as Elements. In Figure 4.6, the three photos were imported into Microsoft PowerPoint, which displays each photo at the size determined by their resolution setting. The result is three different-sized photos.

One question remains unanswered. Look carefully at the photos in Figure 4.6. What's "Real Food?" I shot this photo in a small Texas town and would have loved to ask the owners, but the Old House Cafe had gone out of business. I guess real food wasn't that popular.

Figure 4.5
Although these identical photos have different resolutions, they appear to be the same size in Photoshop Elements.

Figure 4.6
The effect of the resolution becomes evident when the three identical photographs are imported into PowerPoint.

Resolution is commonly (and erroneously) stated in dots per inch (dpi), even when what's being measured has nothing to do with dots. Table 4.1 shows the relationship between the resolution of an image and the size of the printed output when the file size remains unchanged.

Table 4.1 Relationship Between Image Resolution and Size of Printed Output

Resolution	File Size	Output Pixel Size	Output Size of Image
Increases	Unchanged	Smaller	Decreases
Decreases	Unchanged	Larger	Increases

Changing the Size of a Picture

Changing the output size of an image by changing its resolution is called *scaling*, or *resizing*. Because it does not add or remove pixels from an image, scaling doesn't degrade the picture. So, what determines the resolution of a picture? The answer might surprise you. The photo-editing program you use to open a picture usually determines its resolution setting. For example, many images that are opened in Photoshop Elements display a resolution of 72dpi.

NOTE

Pixels per inch (ppi) and dots per inch (dpi) are frequently used interchangeably by both professionals and amateurs. Although this is wrong, it's not a problem because we usually understand what we're talking about. To be absolutely accurate, be aware that scanners, digital cameras, and computer monitors are all measured in ppi, while printers are measured in dpi. I just want you to know that there is a difference.

The Resize Image Dialog Box

This is as good a time as any to open up the Resize dialog box because it reinforces what we have learned about resolution. With an image open in Elements, from the Image menu, choose Resize and Image Size. This opens the Image Size dialog box, as shown in Figure 4.7.

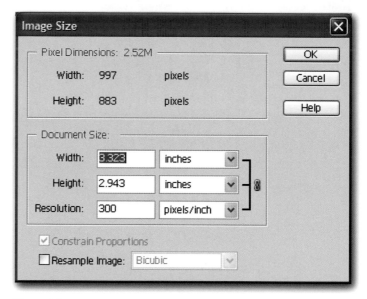

Figure 4.7
Everything that has to do with resizing an image can be done from the Image Size dialog box.

Now, if this is your first time seeing the Image Size dialog box, it might appear somewhat complicated. Let's concern ourselves with the parts that interest us at the moment. First, you might notice that it is neatly divided into sections. The top section tells you the width and height of the selected photograph (in pixels). It also shows the uncompressed size of the file—we talk more about compression later in this chapter. The next section shows what the dimensions of the photo are if it's printed at a resolution of 300dpi. The bottom section of the dialog box controls how the resizing is done.

Most of the time, the only parts of this dialog box that are of any concern to most users are Resolution, Width, Height, and Resample Image. At this point, let's learn how to use this dialog box and learn a little about resolution while we're at it.

Figure 4.8 is a photo that I took of our children (Grace and Jon) at a friend's wedding. (I must point out that one of the perks of being an author is the ability to insert photos of family and friends as examples.) The Image Size dialog box (Image, Resize, Image Size) that's shown in Figure 4.9 tells us that the image is moderate in size—596KB. The size information displayed is how large the image file is after it's opened. The actual size of the file on the disk drive is usually smaller, especially if the file is compressed.

Figure 4.8
Meet Jonathan and Grace. This photograph demonstrates that we have some good-looking kids.

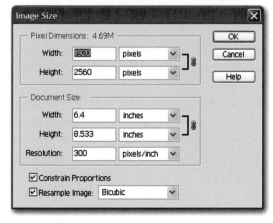

Figure 4.9
The size information for the photograph shown in Figure 4.8 is displayed in the Image Size dialog box.

The Best Way to Resize

When resizing an image, the best way to do it is to change the resolution. This method doesn't add or remove any pixels and, therefore, it prevents any degradation of an image. This is accomplished by unchecking the Resample Image check box. With this box unchecked, changing the resolution causes the Document Size values to change, but the Pixel Dimensions remain fixed. In Figure 4.10, the resolution was halved from 300dpi to 150dpi and, because Resample Image was unchecked, the dimensions doubled. This verifies what we discovered earlier: If the resolution decreases, the size increases. The size of the image displayed in Elements doesn't change. Why? Because the physical dimensions of the photograph (in pixels) haven't changed. Only the resulting image size when it's printed or placed in another program has changed.

59

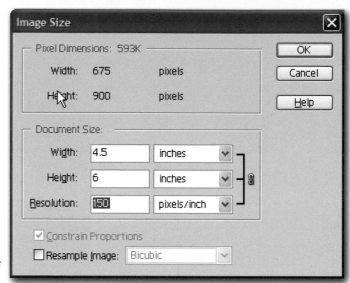

Figure 4.10
The Image Size dialog box shows that, if the resolution is halved, the dimensions of the image double.

Resampling—Another Way to Resize

The second way to resize an image is to resample it. *Resampling* involves having the computer add or remove pixels from an image to make the requested size change. By its very nature, resampling degrades an image. This doesn't mean you shouldn't do it—most of us who do photo editing resample all the time—it just isn't our first choice. Another factor that influences resampling is whether you are making the image larger or smaller. Technically, it is called upsampling and downsampling, but I don't hear folks using those terms much any more. When you make an image smaller, there is a perceived increase in sharpness. To demonstrate this principle, the next time you go to your local appliance superstore, check out the TVs. Compare the same picture on a 32" and a 24" monitor and the smaller image appears sharper or more vivid. OK...back to resampling.

To change the size of an image using resampling, check the Resample Image box. Several choices for types of resampling algorithms can be used. Use the default Bicubic setting and ignore the other choices (see Figure 4.11)—they were really handy back when we had 386 computers running at 25MHz. I really don't know why Adobe hasn't removed these choices.

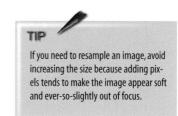

TIP

If you need to resample an image, avoid increasing the size because adding pixels tends to make the image appear soft and ever-so-slightly out of focus.

With Resample Image checked, you can change any of the dimensions to fit your needs. Elements will calculate and display the resulting dimensions or file size that will result. When you click the OK button, the size of the image displayed in Elements changes, but pixels were either added or removed.

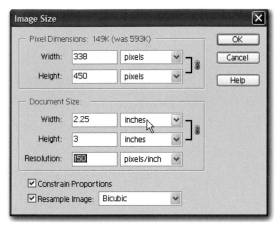

Figure 4.11
The Image Size dialog box shows that if resolution is halved with the Resample Image checked, the dimensions of the image remain the same, but the physical dimensions (in pixels) are also halved.

Resizing the Canvas

Another command changes the size of an image by either adding or subtracting pixels from the edge. It's called *Canvas Size*; it's located in the Image menu under Resize. When you select it, the dialog box that's shown in Figure 4.12 appears. The layout of the dialog box is easy to figure out. By entering a new value, the picture either has pixels added to or removed from (cropped) the existing image. When pixels are added, they are the color of the current background color. One little check box might not be obvious, however: Relative. When checked, you enter in the amount that you want added to an image. I use this feature all the time when I want to add a half-inch white border around a photo. By changing the background color, you can also make a colored border around an image.

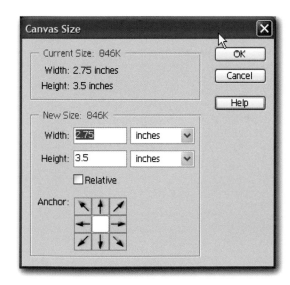

Figure 4.12
The Canvas Size dialog box provides an easy way to create a border around an existing image.

After you have an image at its desired size, it's time to save it. This opens up a whole new bunch of choices.

Saving Your Work

Saving images in Photoshop Elements is not much different than saving images in any other computer application, there are just a few more choices to make.

When you save an image (Ctrl-S), Elements assumes that you want to save it using the graphic format that it was in when you opened it. If you want to save the image in a different format, select Save As from the File menu (or hit Ctrl-Shift-S); the Save As dialog box appears. In the example shown in Figure 4.13, the original file was a JPEG, so to change it to a TIFF format, you just need to open the Format drop-down list to see all the available formats.

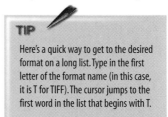

TIP

Here's a quick way to get to the desired format on a long list. Type in the first letter of the format name (in this case, it is T for TIFF). The cursor jumps to the first word in the list that begins with T.

Figure 4.13
The Save As dialog box gives you more choices for file formats than you ever thought existed.

After you name the file, you need to be aware of a few save options in this dialog box.

Saving Options

If the As a Copy check box is checked, the file is saved but the currently open image maintains its original filename. This is handy for preserving the image without changing the name of the copy on which you are working. When it is used, a copy of the file is saved to the desired location, but the open image remains unaffected.

You can also select the box that saves the color profile that's associated with an image. This is helpful when the photo will be reproduced by a system that can use the color profiles. But profiles are not magic—assigning a profile does not make the colors accurate, it just provides specific parameters to help a color-management system produce accurate colors. If you have layers on your image and the file format you selected supports them, you have the option of saving the layer information with the image. If the format you pick doesn't support layers or other Elements-specific features, it attempts to warn you and have you save a copy of the file, as shown if Figure 4.14. You can still override this feature, just be aware that the image will be flattened, and any information unique to Photoshop Elements, such as saved selections, will be lost.

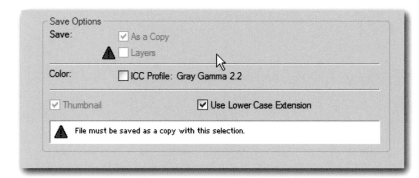

Figure 4.14
The Save As dialog box tries to warn you if you attempt to save in a format that doesn't support layers or other Elements-specific file information.

You're not done yet if the file format you picked has additional options. Most of the options involve picking a level of compression for JPEG or a type of compression for TIFF. One odd little check box exists in the TIFF options that refers to an Image Pyramid (see Figure 4.15). This has to do with a feature that supports multiple resolutions that cannot be created in Photoshop Elements, but the file you open might have the information in it. Therefore, Adobe felt you need the option to preserve that information.

We're almost done.

Let's look at a few of the most common file formats and then wrap things up with some recommendations about file management.

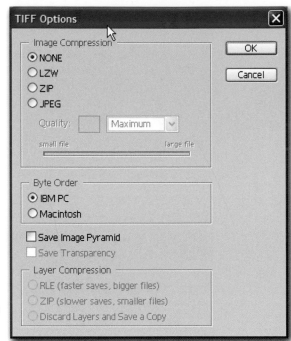

Figure 4.15
The available options for TIFF files are numerous and now include some JPEG compression.

Types of Graphic Files

Saving a photo in Elements is just like saving a letter in your word processor or any other Windows program. What makes it appear complicated is when you notice that you can save the files in many different formats. If you are new to computer graphics, looking at the list of graphic formats that Photoshop Elements supports almost takes your breath away; however, you will actually use only a few formats.

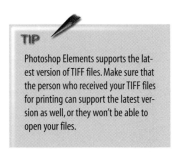

TIP

Photoshop Elements supports the latest version of TIFF files. Make sure that the person who received your TIFF files for printing can support the latest version as well, or they won't be able to open your files.

Don't let all the names of these formats confuse you. Essentially, all the formats can be categorized into the following groups:

- **Internet formats**—Used with emails and to post photos on web pages. They are used because most Internet browsers recognize and display them.

- **Graphic standard formats**—When you need to save the file in a format that some one else can open, use one of the formats that are considered industry standards for graphic exchange.

- **Native formats**—When saving files for later use with Photoshop Elements or Photoshop, you can save it in a file that maintains all the information that's unique to Elements, such as layers, selections, and so on. Any file format that's unique to the program that saved it is called its *native format*.

Internet Formats

The size of graphic files sent over the Internet must be as small as possible to ensure a quick download. To make files smaller, *compression* is applied to the files. The two most popular formats that have built-in file compression are GIF and JPEG (including JPEG 2000). Two types of compression are used in file formats: the type of compression that reduces file size by roughly 50 percent and preserves the image (lossless), and a compression that achieves a great amount of compression (up to 90 percent) with some image degradation (lossy). Table 4.2 summarizes the difference between these two formats.

Table 4.2   GIF Versus JPEG

Characteristic	GIF	JPEG
Compression	Lossless—Fixed amount of compression applied. There is no loss of image quality.	Lossy—User selects the amount of compression. Some loss of image quality occurs, depending on the amount of compression applied.
Compression results	Moderate file size reduction.	Greatly reduced file size.
Color depth	Can be used only on 256-color images.	Can be used on 24-bit color or grayscale images.
Best used with	Low-color cartoon-like images, line drawings, and logos.	All photographs.
Allows for transparency, giving the appearance of seeing through an image or of an image floating on a background	Yes.	No.

Graphic Standard Formats

When you need to send an image to a printer, it will most likely ask for it in a format that has become the de facto standard. Its official name is *Tagged Image Format File* (*TIFF* or *TIF*, they're both pronounced the same). TIFF files also offer several lossless compression options but, similar to GIF files, you can only expect a 40 to 50 percent reduction in file size. Photoshop Elements also offers the option of using a lossy compression format (JPEG), but use it cautiously because some older graphic programs cannot decode JPEG in a TIFF file format. Another format that is often used in the Windows environment is bitmap (BMP). When you want to save an image for use as wallpaper on your Windows platform, save it as a BMP file. Many of the other formats are used only if you have someone who specifically requests them. So, unless that happens, there's no need to use them.

Photoshop Elements Native Format

The native format for Photoshop Elements and Photoshop are one and the same. This means that you can save a file in Photoshop's native format (PSD) and open it in Elements without any information loss. This is the format of choice for important images that you might want to revisit at a later date. Why not save all the images in native format? Well, first of all, the files can get somewhat large, especially if the image contains many layers. Secondly, few people have the software necessary to open the file.

File Management Suggestions

If you are working on images that must be maintained and possibly revisited at a later date, always save the file in native format. For sending files to a printer or for placement in a page-layout program, save a copy as a TIFF file. If you want to share photos with a friend, save a copy as a JPEG file. Although JPEG uses a lossy compression scheme, the effects of the compression are typically visible only when you apply a ridiculously high level of compression. One of the new features in Photoshop Elements 2.0 is JPEG 2000. This offers greater compression than JPEG with less image degradation. Before you get all excited and begin to save images in this format, I recommend that you wait until most of the major Internet browsers support this new JPEG standard. If you don't, I promise that you will discover that many of your friends and associates cannot open or view your files. It's a great new standard, but it is still new.

Summary

If you read this entire chapter, you covered some of the most important fundamentals in computer digital graphics. To that end, I recommend that you reread this chapter every now and again to make sure that you have a firm grip on the fundamentals. Resolution is a tough concept to grasp, and when I first began to work with digital photo editing, I spent much time trying to understand why the printed image got smaller when the resolution increased. If you understand resolution and its relationship to digital images, you're way ahead of the game.

In the next chapter, we explore how to improve the composition of your photographs by removing distortion that's introduced by the angle at which we take our pictures. Also, we learn how to improve existing photos by straightening them and removing backgrounds.

5 Dealing with Composition Problems and Distortion

In Chapter 3, "Adjusting and Enhancing Photos," we explored some basic techniques to improve the overall appearance of a photo. In this chapter, we learn some more advanced ways to improve the overall composition of an image, including how to straighten out crooked scans and remove the distortion produced by camera lenses.

Improving Composition

When you bring up the subject of image composition, most people think about cropping. Although cropping is one way to change an image's composition, we will discover that more ways exist to focus a viewer's attention on a photo's subject. With that being said, let's look at a few examples of how easy it is to correct a photo that was taken with a camera in less than optimum (just plain wrong) orientation.

Let's begin by looking at Figure 5.1, which is a poorly composed photo that I took of Alison during an outdoor wedding. I had to take the shot quickly to capture her expression before she posed, turned away, or did something else that would have taken away from the photo's candidness. Isn't that a great excuse to use for poor composition? Feel free to use it yourself.

Figure 5.1
Here is an example of a poorly composed photo. The young lady should be the subject, but the stranger is distracting.

Download this photo (named `Alison.jpg`) from the New Riders Publishing web site and follow along in the next section.

Initial Cropping

Because the subject is vertical in orientation, we need to use the Crop tool (C) to remove the part of the image that distracts from Alison. You can crop this photo in several different ways. Figure 5.2 shows the crop I chose. My reasoning was that her elbow sticking out like a wing wasn't going to add to the photo and, this way, I could place her in the right-third of the photo. After the cropped area is selected with the Crop tool, you can sort of see what the cropped photo will look like; you can adjust any of the crop lines until you have it just the way you want. When you're satisfied, double-click anywhere in the image and the crop is complete, as shown in Figure 5.3.

Figure 5.2
Using the Crop tool, some of the distracting parts of this photo are removed.

Figure 5.3
This photo looks better, but we can still do more to improve it.

Removing Items from a Background

We can use the Clone tool to remove the part of the suit on the left side of the photo, but it takes some time to cover an area that large, so let's try another trick.

Choose the Rectangular Marquee tool (M) and select the area shown in Figure 5.4 that's just to the right of the suit sleeve and pant leg.

Figure 5.4
By using the Rectangular Marquee tool, we created a selection of grass.

Now comes the fun part. Select the Move tool (V) and, while holding the Alt key, click inside the selection and drag it to the left. Let go of the mouse button and, while still holding the Alt key, move it over again until most of the suit is gone, as shown in Figure 5.5. After you finish, release the mouse button and Alt key, and complete the job by deselecting the grass selection (Ctrl-D).

Figure 5.5
Holding the Alt key, we use the Move tool to place duplicate selections of grass over the suit.

Removing the chair is done in the same fashion, except we use a chunk of grass from the left side and move it to the right side, as shown in Figure 5.6.

Figure 5.6
Using the same technique that we used on the suit, we can quickly remove the chair from this photo.

The only two items remaining are the upper part of the suit and a piece of a branch that was hanging in the upper-left corner. Both are dispatched using the selection-move technique. Figure 5.7 shows the result.

Figure 5.7
We successfully recropped this photo and removed the distracting elements.

Blurring the Background

This last step is optional, but it gives a professional touch to the finished photo. Select the Magnetic Lasso tool from the Tools bar, and make a rough selection around Alison. Don't forget to remove the selection inside her arm on the right side of the photo. You can do that by holding the Alt key and selecting the grass inside of the existing selection. The Magnetic Lasso tool works great, and it took me only about a minute to make the selection that's shown in Figure 5.8.

Figure 5.8
By selecting the subject and then inverting the selection, we slightly blur the background.

From the Select menu, choose Invert. At this point, only the background should be selected. Choose Filter, Blur, Gaussian Blur, and use a setting of 2.0, as shown in Figure 5.9. Any more than that makes it look like Alison is standing in a fog.

Figure 5.9
The selective application of a Gaussian blur subtly adds emphasis to the subject.

You could include several more optional items. With the background still selected, you could also use the Levels (Ctrl-L) to darken the background ever so slightly, or selectively apply effects such as Hue/Saturation or Unsharp Mask to the subject. Figure 5.10 shows the final image.

Figure 5.10
In a few minutes, we converted a poorly composed photograph into a much better one.

When Things Aren't on the Level

When action is happening quickly, the camera doesn't always end up being level with the horizon. There are times when having the photo at an angle produces a desired effect, but as a general rule of composition, you want the horizon to be level. Another guideline for action shots is that they need to be in a landscape orientation. With this in mind, let's look at the photo that's shown in Figure 5.11. In this case, I tried to capture the action of the team roping at a small Texas town in the late afternoon.

Team roping original color DSCN0722.tif @ 46.3% (RGB)

Figure 5.11
In this photo, the horizon is off level, the scene is cluttered, and it's slightly out of focus. It doesn't happen very often where so many things can go wrong in the same photo.

Action Events and Digital Cameras

Digital cameras can present problems to the photographers in low-light action events because most digital cameras have a small delay from the time the shutter button is pushed until an image is captured. To compensate for this, it's necessary to click the shutter about a half second before you want to take the shot. As I said, it was late afternoon (less light) so to keep a slow shutter speed from blurring the photo, it was necessary to pan the camera as the riders came out of the gate. *Panning* means to move the camera in the direction of the action so as to follow the subject and reduce the amount of speed relative to the camera. It also helps to take lots of pictures—lots and lots of pictures.

Leveling the Playing Field

The first step to fixing this photo is to make the horizon level. To accomplish this, we need a point of reference. Photoshop Elements provides a grid for such purposes. Located in the View menu, clicking Grid makes the grid visible. In the Image menu, select Transform, Free Transform, and rotate until the image is level with the grid. Figure 5.12 shows the result. Notice that, when the image was rotated, the dimensions of the image were increased so that none of the photo was cropped.

Figure 5.12
When the image is rotated, the image dimensions are automatically increased to prevent cropping.

Replacing the Cluttered Background

Using the same technique that we learned at the beginning of this chapter, I selected the Rectangular Marquee tool and made a large selection of the dirt in the mid-right side of the photograph. Next, I chose the Move tool (V) and, while holding the Alt key, moved a copy of it up to cover the fence. Then, with the Alt key still held, I moved it around the photo; each time I released the mouse button, a copy of the selected dirt was applied over the existing background pixels, as shown in Figure 5.13. At this stage, the photo looks somewhat ugly.

Figure 5.13
By making copies of the area using a selection, we can begin the process of replacing the background.

The next stage takes the most time—but having said that, it only took me about 15 minutes to do the entire photo. After the big chunks of selections are placed, the next step is to make smaller selections and fill in the gaps. Each subsequent selection gets smaller. At some point, it became necessary to use the Zoom tool and get in at about the 200 percent level, and then use the Clone tool (S) to cover the remaining old background and to smooth out the blocks in the replaced background. In Figure 5.14, I already smoothed out the rider on the right, but you can see that work still needs to be done on the young man on the left.

Figure 5.14
The blockiness of the selection is apparent on the left rider. By using the Clone tool, the background on the right rider has already been cleaned up.

Using the Clone Tool Effectively

In this type of work, we are actually doing two completely different tasks: removing the blockiness caused by the selection copies, and covering the old background in the remaining areas of the photo.

To remove the blockiness, I recommend initially using a large brush and unchecking the Aligned box in the Options bar. By clicking the parts of the new background that show the difference in colors or shades, it will break up the patterns. After you think you removed all the signs of your new background, zoom out and look for patterns. Expect to see stuff you missed when you were zoomed in. The human eye is marvelous at detecting repeating patterns. At this point, just get the major stuff and try not to get too close to the subjects.

To remove the old background close to a subject, I suggest that you protect the area that you don't want to be covered with the replacement background. You can do this by selecting the area that is to receive the replacement background with a selection. In Figure 5.14, the rider on the left was easy to select using the Magic Wand tool. Then, I used the Selection brush to fine-tune the selection. After I selected the rider, I inverted the selection and used the Clone tool to apply the replacement background. The result is a complete background replacement. Figure 5.15 shows the riders with the old background replaced and the evidence of the replacement removed.

Figure 5.15
The hard part is finished. Now we just need to crop this photo to create the final composition.

Creative Cropping

All that remains is to crop the photograph. It might seem that the decision is simply a matter of removing the white parts of this photo. Although that's true, let's see if some creative alternatives are possible. Figure 5.16 represents standard cropping. The white parts from the rotation are removed and the riders and the bull fill most of the frame. It's OK.

Figure 5.16
By cropping the extra material, the photo composition is complete— or is it?

Consider this alternative: Use the Canvas Size feature to add two inches to the right side of the photo. (Make sure that your background color is set to white.) Add additional background by dragging a selection over the new space and cleaning it up with the Clone tool. Crop the riders close on the left side. By doing this, we give the impression that the bull has still got someplace to run, which enhances the action of the scene. It also produces a stronger horizontal image, which produces a stronger action scene (see Figure 5.17).

Figure 5.17
Adding more background on the right of the photo emphasizes the action of the riders and the bull.

Straightening Out Scans

Photoshop Elements has a feature that automatically straightens and crops photos. (I am actually reluctant to tell you about this feature because I see it, and other features like it, used to degrade images when the user could have spent an extra minute to realign the photo in the scanner. OK, I'll get off of my soapbox now.) Just remember that anytime you rotate an image (in something other than 90-degree increments), it causes the image to be slightly degraded. The answer to your next question is, "Yes, the photo of the ropers earlier in this chapter was slightly degraded when it was rotated to make the horizon level." Of course, if someone else scanned the photo and sent you the electronic file, you wouldn't have the opportunity to rescan it, so this feature can be useful.

Figure 5.18 shows a photo of three boys in a very small pool. It pretty much puts the phrase "everything is bigger in Texas" to rest. After the photo was placed in the scanner, I flopped down the scanner lid, which caused this photo to do exactly as predicted— move. I realized this when I did the scan preview; under normal circumstances, I would have lifted the lid and repositioned the photo.

Figure 5.18
Here is a classic example of a photo not being aligned correctly on the scanner.

In the Image menu under Rotate, there are several choices at the bottom, one being Straighten and Crop. When this option is selected, the active image is automatically straightened and cropped to fit the new edges, as shown in Figure 5.19.

Figure 5.19
The Straighten and Crop feature automatically corrects a crooked scan.

Correcting Distortion in Photos

When you take a photo of a building, or anything large for that matter, a certain amount of distortion is introduced. When I stand in front of a large building looking up, the distortion is apparent, as shown in Figure 5.20. The top of the building appears to be smaller than the bottom. This effect is called *keystoning*. We are about to learn how to correct this kind of distortion.

Figure 5.20
The distortion created by taking this photograph at an angle is obvious.

Most digital cameras on the market today come with a zoom lens that can get really wide. The good news is this feature's capability to capture more of the landscape. The downside is that these wide lenses introduce distortion (called *barrel distortion*). Figure 5.21 shows a photograph of a mural on the side of the Hard Rock Café in Austin. This photo provides an example of this combination distortion. Two types of distortion exist in this photo: keystoning, which is caused by shooting from the far end of the mural (instead of shooting in the middle), and barrel distortion, which is produced by the wide-angle lens that was used. The keystone distortion is where one end of the image is either smaller or larger based on its position in relation to the camera lens. A classic example of this is railroad tracks. When you look down the tracks, they appear to come together at the horizon. The point where they appear to come together is called a *vanishing point.*

The lens actually fitting more of the scene into the picture than would normally occur produces barrel distortion. A classic example of this is a picture taken with a fisheye lens.

Figure 5.21
Two types of distortion exist in this photo: keystoning and barrel distortion.

The first step to fixing this photo is to correct the keystoning. Here is the procedure (if you want to follow along, download Hardrock.jpg from the book's web page on the New Riders web site):

1. Make a layer of the background (Layer, New, Layer from Background).

2. With the top layer selected, choose Image, Transform, Distort. Now, to be able to see the handles necessary to make the correction, make the image window larger than the photo. You can do this by grabbing one of the corners and dragging it to the larger shape, as shown in Figure 5.22.

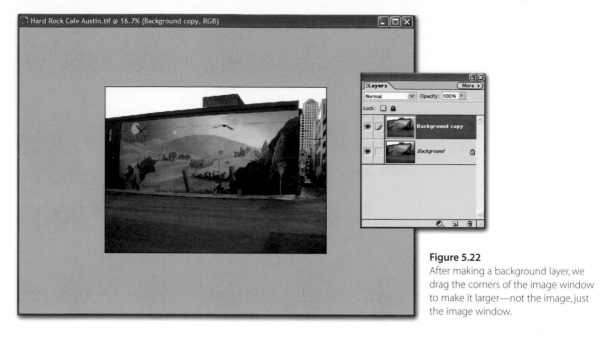

Figure 5.22
After making a background layer, we drag the corners of the image window to make it larger—not the image, just the image window.

3. Turn the grid on (View, Grid). Move the corner handles until the sides of the mural are roughly aligned with the grid. Because of the barrel distortion, they'll bend out a bit in the middle. Don't worry about that right now. When it's aligned, double-click it and, after a few moments, the image appears, like the one shown in Figure 5.23.

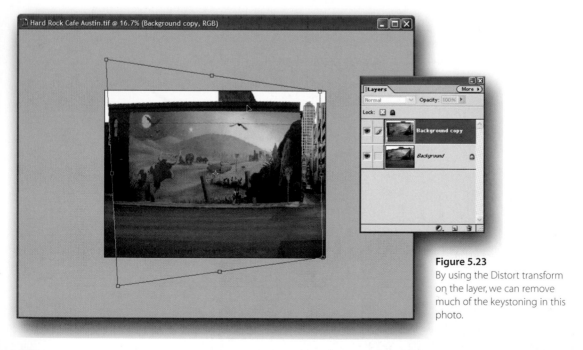

Figure 5.23
By using the Distort transform on the layer, we can remove much of the keystoning in this photo.

4. To remove the barrel distortion, we first need to flatten the photo (Layers, Flatten Image). Next, we use the Pinch filter. Just select Filter, Distort, Pinch, and make the setting 11 percent, as shown in Figure 5.24. This filter action removes much of the barrel distortion, but not all of it.

Figure 5.24
The Pinch filter is great for reducing barrel distortion in photos taken with wide-angle cameras.

5. To minimize the remaining appearance of the barrel distortion on the top edge of the roof, we select the Rectangular Marquee tool and create a rectangle selection on top of the building that excludes the chiller on the roof and the part of the roof edge. After it is selected, we hit the Delete key, and it is gone. Now that we're done with the selection, we remove it by using Ctrl-D. Figure 5.25 shows the result.

Figure 5.25
Using a rectangular selection provides a way to remove the chiller from the roof and make the roof's edge horizontal.

87

6. Because the photo was taken on an overcast day, the sky looks blank. Using the Magic Wand tool, the sky is selected. Using Edit, Paste Into, I put a replacement sky into the photo. I strongly recommend taking many photos of clouds just for use in situations such as these. Now, we crop the photo to remove some of the material at the edges. Figure 5.26 shows the result.

Figure 5.26
After you crop this photo to remove some of the material at the edges, it's time to replace the sky.

7. All that's left to do is use the Clone tool to remove the power line that's in front of the mural, and remove the bird that flew in front of the camera when I took the photograph. I estimate that the entire job took me about 10 minutes, and we ended up with a nice photograph of the mural of Austin's own Hard Rock Café, as shown in Figure 5.27.

Figure 5.27
After a little cleanup with the Clone tool, we have a finished photo of the Hard Rock Café with the distortion minimized.

Some Closing Thoughts About Composition

When you work with photographs, don't lose the content of the photograph while you try to create "perfect" composition. By this, I mean that we usually photograph people to capture a moment in time, whether it's an event (such as a wedding, birthday, graduation, and so on) or just capture an expression of who or what you want to represent. Sometimes, the best photograph is one that reveals something of who the person is, even if it violates the rules of good photo composition. I included an example of this concept here.

In Figure 5.28, we have a perfectly good crop from a crowded photograph. The bride is hugging a close family friend. The cropping isolated the subjects and they filled the frame, but was it the best crop? In Figure 5.29, I recropped the photograph so it shows the bride's best friend watching as the bride hugs her best friend's mom. The crop shown in Figure 5.29 produced a better picture, even though it was necessary to blur both the foreground and the background. Someday, if I ever have the time, I plan to replace the tablecloth with an empty one, which would be less distracting still.

Figure 5.28
This photo has good composition and the subjects fill the frame, but is it the best crop?

Figure 5.29
Adding the daughter on the right made for a better photo, even though the cluttered table had to be blurred.

The bottom line to all this: Be creative! Just because you thought you knew how you were going to compose the photo when you started doesn't mean that you have to do it that way. You can change your mind, and better yet, try it several ways—it doesn't cost you anything except your time, and that time is paid back with interest because of the experience you gain every time you experiment.

Summary

In this chapter, we covered a broad range of topics that make photographs look more professional. In the old days of darkrooms, little could be done to correct distortion produced by the camera lens. Now, we have learned that it is possible to reduce or remove this distortion to improve composition. We also discovered that although Photoshop Elements provides a command that can straighten out a crooked scan, it should be used only as a last resort because it degrades the image ever so slightly.

In the next chapter, we get into one of the most elusive topics in digital-image editing—color correction. When you get into this chapter, you discover that it's actually possible to remove that nasty blue cast that digital cameras love to add to bright-daylight photos and how to make people's faces look more life-like.

Fine-Tuning the Color

One of the biggest disappointments people experience with digital cameras is having color that appears lifeless or seems off from what it should be. In this chapter, we discover that adjusting color isn't rocket science. In fact, with the tools built into Photoshop Elements, it's easy to get perfect color.

Correct Color Versus Desired Color

When working with color photos, it's important to determine what you want from the finished print. Do you want the colors to be accurate, or do you want the colors to look good? It might surprise you to know that accurate colors don't always look great. To illustrate this important point, consider the photo of a tropical plant's leaf taken on a bright and sunny day in Texas. The Nikon Coolpix 5000 camera recorded the image shown in Figure 6.1. For all intents and purposes, this photo is an accurate representation of what the color of the plant looked like on that bright (and hot) day. Figure 6.2 shows the same photo after I use Photoshop Elements to enhance the color information that was present in the photo. So, you must decide what's more important to you: color accuracy or the overall appearance of the finished work.

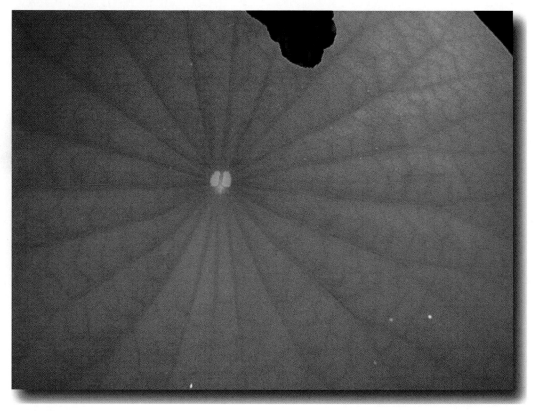

Figure 6.1
This digital photo of a tropical plant's leaf is an accurate representation of what this leaf looked like on a bright and sunny day in Texas.

Figure 6.2
The colors in this photo are not an accurate representation of how the colors actually looked. Which of the two photos do you like better?

Color Casts and Their Causes

Most of the color problems that people have with their digital photographs involve a *color cast*, which is a subtle but dominant color that's introduced into the photo. The favorite color cast of a sunny, cloudless day is blue. This is because the camera's sensor is partially being influenced by the blue reflection of the clear sky and partially because some camera sensors are tricked by large amounts of bright daylight.

Figure 6.3 was taken on a bright and sunny day. The bluebonnets growing on this abandoned rail spur had vivid colors that were in sharp contrast to the rusted rails. Originally, when I opened this photograph on my computer, I was disappointed. Even the automatic color correction of Photoshop Elements had no affect on the blue cast that dominated this photograph. But don't loose hope—you can almost always restore the color (see Figure 6.4).

Figure 6.3
A strong blue cast made what should have been a great photo of bluebonnets near a rusty rail lifeless.

Figure 6.4
It took some work, but by using the tools in Elements, I restored this photo's vivid colors.

More Than Just the Blues

If blue was the only color cast that affected digital cameras, we would all be much happier. Unfortunately, several sources of different-colored light exist. Figure 6.5 shows a horrible picture that I took at a wedding. This photo was taken in a small chapel that had no windows, so it was lit almost entirely by florescent lights. Yes, the photo actually came out this green. I didn't make it greener. In fairness, this is an old photo. It was taken in 1997 with HP's first PhotoSmart digital camera. Thankfully, digital cameras have greatly improved since then.

Figure 6.5
This photo, taken with one of the first consumer digital cameras, proves that florescent lights can make almost any image green.

Some light sources induce a desirable color cast. When your subject is illuminated by incandescent light, the resulting colors shift toward the warm colors (which is always more appealing). Although the photo shown in Figure 6.6 has a definite reddish-orange color cast, it would detract from the photo to remove it through color correction.

Figure 6.6
A combination of incandescent and natural lighting bathes this room in warm light, which gives it an appealing look.

Correcting Color Casts

Now that you understand color casts better, let's see how we can get rid of them. The first place to begin is the automatic color-correction tools that are found in Photoshop Elements.

Figure 6.7 is a photograph that I took of the U.S. Capitol building just as it came out of my camera. By selecting QuickFix from the Enhance menu, I applied Auto Levels and Auto Contrast. The result of this action is shown in Figure 6.8. Wait—did you notice that I didn't apply Auto Color Correction? Why not? Actually, I did apply it (after Auto Levels and Auto Contrast) and it didn't change anything; in fact, it added just a hint of blue into the photo, so I clicked Undo in the QuickFix dialog box and I was done.

More times than not, applying Auto Levels and/or Auto Contrast is all that you need to do. Does this mean that Auto Color Correction doesn't work? Not at all. It just means that you need to use this tool on a trial-and-error basis and that, after you apply any automatic correction, you need to look at the result and decide if it helped or hindered the color-correction process. Although Auto Color Correction didn't work on that particular photo, it does work well on others.

Figure 6.7
Here's a classic photo of the U.S. Capitol building straight out of the camera. Although it looks okay, it can look much better.

Figure 6.8
Applying Auto Levels and Auto Contrast brought some much-needed life into this photo.

Automatic Tools Vary in Their Effectiveness

Just to show how much these tools can vary in their effectiveness, I included a photo I took of my friend and editor, Megg, at her reception the night before her wedding in early 1999. Again, the light source included florescent lamps and the camera's flash. I applied both the Auto Levels and the Auto Contrast with no effect, as shown in Figure 6.9. Next, I applied Auto Color Correction. What a difference it made (see Figure 6.10).

Figure 6.9
The sickly color in this image was unaffected by either Auto Levels or Auto Contrast.

Figure 6.10
Applying Auto Color Correction removed the color cast and made this photo look much better.

So, can we draw the conclusion that Auto Color Correction works only with the florescent green color cast? Sorry, the only way to tell if these tools work is to try them out. If that sounds like too much work, this little tidbit might make your life easier: The Auto Color Correction in Photoshop Elements worked equally well on most of the photos that were taken at the reception that evening.

Helping Automatic Tools Do a Better Job

When any automatic tool is applied to an image, the contents of the entire image are evaluated by Photoshop Elements and then the correction action is applied based on the information that was extracted from the photograph. In some cases, all this information might cause a poor automatic adjustment to be made. In other situations, the proper application of color correction to one range of colors might cause another range of colors to look worse. In both cases, it is sometimes necessary to isolate one part of a photograph from the other part by using a selection. Adobe defines the operation of a selection as the following: "When you want to edit a particular area of your image without affecting other areas, you select the area you want to change." Photoshop Elements has numerous tools for creating selections. To demonstrate the benefits of isolating some color corrections by using a selection, I'll use the Magic Wand tool and the Selection brush.

Selective Color Correction

I was running on one of the many trails we have in the Hill Country of Texas (yes, I sometimes take my camera with me when I run) when I saw these great sunflowers standing tall against the blue Texas sky. I took quite a few shots, but was disappointed when I looked at the resulting photos. The sunflowers I photographed had bright vivid colors and the sky was a hard but clear blue. The image shown in Figure 6.11 was a great disappointment to me when I first saw it on my computer monitor. When I applied Auto Color Correction, it didn't look any better.

Figure 6.11
This should have been a great photograph of a sunflower against a bright blue sky, but the color was anything but that.

Next, I tried several manual correction tricks that I knew without any success. By that time, I realized that when I got the color in the sunflower correct, the blue sky got worse and vice versa. Here is my solution for this problem:

1. Isolate the sunflower from the sky by using a selection. In this case, this is easy enough to do because the sunflower and the sky are such different colors. I set the Tolerance setting on the Magic Wand tool to a very high setting (70), clicked the sky, and most of it was selected. I then chose Similar from the Selection menu, and all the sky was selected, as shown in Figure 6.12.

Figure 6.12
I used the Magic Wand tool to isolate the sunflower from the blue sky.

Applying Auto Contrast brightened up the blue sky without negatively affecting the sunflower (see Figure 6.13).

Figure 6.13
Applying contrast only to the blue sky brings out the hard blue that I saw on the day I took the original photograph.

2. Now invert the selection (by hitting Ctrl-Shift-I) so that only the sunflower is selected. In the Enhance menu, I chose Adjust Color, from which I selected Color Variations. I must be honest with you: This isn't my favorite tool. The previews are too small to accurately judge the color changes. Still, after playing with the adjustments to the midtones and highlights in the Color Variations dialog box (see Figure 6.14), it did a good job making the sunflower's colors appear more vivid.

3. Before removing the selection, I applied a larger than normal amount of Unsharp Masking to the sunflower. Applying sharpening to an object that has just been beefed up with contrast usually results in the generation of noise, which looks similar to film grain. Figure 6.15 shows the final photograph.

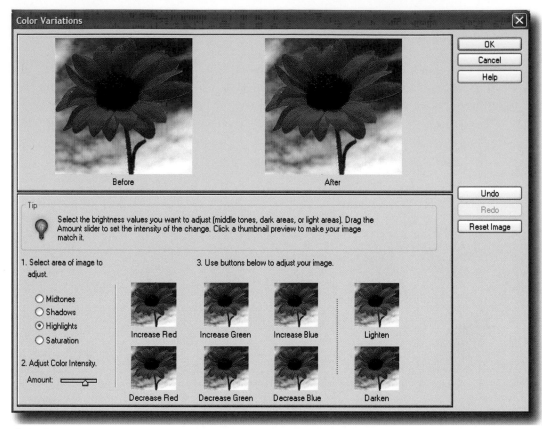

Figure 6.14
The Color Variations dialog box enables you to selectively add or subtract primary colors from shadows, midtones, or highlights.

Figure 6.15
By applying contrast and color variations, I restored this photograph almost to its original color.

The Color Cast Command

By definition, the Color Cast command removes any color casts from an image. Located in the Enhance menu under Adjust Color, selecting Color Cast opens the Color Cast Correction dialog box (see Figure 6.16) and changes your cursor into an eyedropper. All you need to do is click any part of a photo that's black, white, or gray. All these colors are neutral; therefore, any variation to a neutral color must be a cast. The challenge facing a user is finding a truly neutral color.

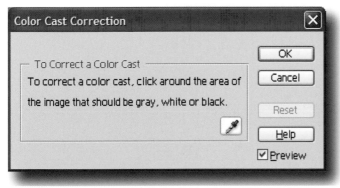

Figure 6.16
Using the Color Cast Correction dialog box is simple. Selecting a color with which to define the color cast isn't as easy, however.

Figure 6.17 is a photo of the carved back of a chair on a sunny day. I liked the composition of the stained glass and the blue sky in the background. When I opened the photo on my computer, I wasn't surprised that it had a bluish cast. Applying the Auto Color Correction helped, but because it's an automatic program, it only guessed which of the white colors were supposed to be neutral.

Figure 6.17
The blue cast created by the sunny day reflected in the glass diminishes the overall effect of this photograph.

After the Color Cast dialog box opens, there are several areas from which to choose. My first instinct was to put the eyedropper on the reflection in the glass at the top of the photo (just to the right of the center). These bright spots are typically nearly pure white. It created a change that wasn't as good as the results I got from the Auto Color Correction. Next, I clicked the white building that's reflected in the glass. I got a much better result (see Figure 6.18).

Figure 6.18
The Color Cast options successfully removed the bluish color cast from this photo.

TIP

I found that the Color Cast command works best after you apply Auto Levels or Auto Contrast.

Although the Color Cast command can be a great tool for removing color casts, remember that it requires that the photo have a neutral color in it that you must find. So, although this command isn't necessarily my first choice, when it works, it works great.

Summary

I hope you discovered that color correction is probably the one best action that you can apply to your digital photos to improve their appearance. Every photo shoot is different. In fact, the light source can change right-smack dab in the middle of your picture taking and twisting the colors out of whack. When you correct colors in your photographs, don't fall into a rut by always applying the same color-correction tools to every photograph. Try several different corrections to see which one looks best.

Now that we know how to correct color in a photograph, in the next chapter, we discover all the things that can go wrong with lighting (not the color of the light, but the amount) and what tools are available in Elements to correct it.

7 Correcting Lighting Problems

In the previous chapter, we discovered that light sources can produce different effects in regards to color. In this chapter, we discover how to deal with many of the lighting issues that face photographers and what tools are available in Photoshop Elements to correct these problems. But, before we discover how to correct lighting problems, it's helpful to understand any terms that describe them and then learn a few things that cause the problems. Let's face it: If you can prevent the problems in the first place, it isn't necessary to correct them later.

Understanding Lighting Problems

Whether we take photographs using a film or a digital camera, we need light to take pictures—it's that simple. The problem with lighting is that, many times, it seems there is either too much, too little, or it is coming from the wrong direction. This results in photos that are overexposed (washed out), underexposed (too dark), or the subject is either lost in the shadows (backlit), or has distracting cast shadows on his or her face. If that wasn't bad enough, we then can add a flash to the equation and usually end up with a subject that has big white splotches on his or her face (blowouts). If we stand too far away from the subject, our photos turn out totally black. Some sailors aboard my ship used to take pictures of the moon with a flash. That's not too smart.

Basic Light Problem Solutions

Several tools in Photoshop Elements are specifically designed to correct lighting problems in photos. It might surprise you to know that some of the automatic tools we used in the previous chapter for color correction also work well for resolving lighting problems: Auto Levels and Auto Contrast. The following sections give examples of the most basic lighting problems with photographs and offers solutions to these problems.

Shedding Light on Photos that are too Dark

For me, this is the problem that most people (and I) have most often. The reasons for an underexposed photo are many: the flash didn't work (batteries), the flash was turned off, a finger covered the flash sensor, or the subject was too far away. Regardless of the reason, the result is a dark photograph, similar to the one of my friends, shown in Figure 7.1—my flash was turned off.

Figure 7.1
This photo came out too dark because I forgot to turn on the flash.

First, crop the photo to remove anything that will not be in the final photo (see Figure 7.2). Because the automatic tools in Photoshop Elements evaluate the entire photograph, the tools always work better when you first remove any unnecessary part(s) of the photo.

Figure 7.2
Cropping away unnecessary parts of the photograph needs to always be done before applying any lighting corrections.

After cropping the photo, using trial and error, I applied each of the automatic tools located in the Enhance menu (Auto Levels, Auto Contrast, or Auto Color Correction). I also could have selected QuickFix and tried out these tools to see which produced the best effect. In Figure 7.3, you can see the affect when Auto Levels is used, but for the record, the other two tools produced almost the same results. At this point, you can see who's in the photo, but we can do better than that.

Figure 7.3
Applying Auto Levels enables us to see who's in the photo, but it still needs more work.

From the Enhance menu, under Adjust Lighting, is the Fill Flash command (Shift-Ctrl-F). Changing the Lighter slider to a value of 12, as shown in Figure 7.4, brings out additional detail in the photo.

Figure 7.4
The application of the Fill Flash command brings out more of the detail in the photo.

The photo still has many problems. Shannon's hands and arms are blurred. The table looks like they were having lunch—oh wait, they were having lunch. The waitress in the background needs to be either cloned or blurred out of the scene, which is described in Chapter 3, "Adjusting and Enhancing Photos." After applying a little contrast (+5), this photo is as good as we are going to get it for this chapter (see Figure 7.5). Now that you've seen Fill Flash in action, it's time to consider some of its limitations, and get familiar with other light-restoring operations.

Figure 7.5
The finished picture isn't perfect by any means, but at least we can recognize who's in it.

Bringing Light into the Darkness

Dad used to say, "There is no such thing as a free lunch." That phrase, born during the great depression, was hammered into my head when I was growing up. Trying to restore light into an underexposed photograph is like trying to get that proverbial free lunch. The result of extracting detail out of shadows always results in a grainy appearance (called *noise*). If the area of the shadows is really dark, the degradation of the detail hidden in the shadow can be extreme.

The photograph shown in Figure 7.6 illustrates this concept. I took this photo looking out from the inside of a lovely bed and breakfast in the Hill Country. Because the light measurement of the camera was reading the light streaming in through the window, it set the exposure so high that the detail inside the room was completely lost.

Figure 7.6
The light from the window fooled the camera and, as a result, the curtains and the window are properly exposed, but details in the room are lost in the shadows.

109

Applying any of the automatic tools to the entire photo would produce unsatisfactory results, so using the Polygon Selection tool, a quick selection is made about the window and then inverted so that everything except the window is selected (see Figure 7.7).

Figure 7.7
By selecting everything but the window, we can see the detail in the shadows without washing out the window.

By applying the maximum amount of Fill Flash (see Figure 7.8), we discover a lot of detail in the photo that wasn't previously apparent. Although it's good to see that the detail was captured, it's so noisy that it is of questionable value.

Note the elderly woman sitting at the table. The application of Fill Flash turned her hair into kind of a fright wig. Photoshop Elements doesn't have a tool that allows selective removal of a tool application. But there are a few workarounds that you can use to restore her to a less frightening appearance. Probably the easiest way to do this is to make a layer from the background (Layer, New, Layer from Background). Apply Fill Flash to the new layer. Next, use the Eraser tool at a low-opacity setting and paint over the area you want to restore. The more you erase of the new layer, the more transparent it becomes, and more of the original background layer reappears.

Another way to accomplish this is to use the Selection Brush tool (A) and paint a selection around her, after which you must invert it (Ctrl-Shift-I) and then apply Fill Flash. Although this works, it takes longer to do because you must first apply Fill Flash to see what the effect is before undoing it and applying a selection.

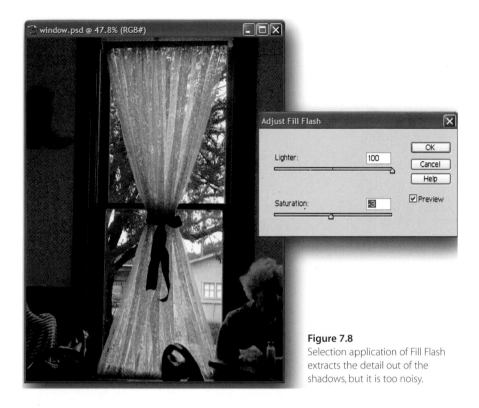

Figure 7.8
Selection application of Fill Flash extracts the detail out of the shadows, but it is too noisy.

Figure 7.8's example represents an extreme case of detail buried deep in the shadows. This next example shows the recovery of detail from the shadow region in a better light (groan).

The photo shown in Figure 7.9 is of a wedding cake taken with the external flash turned off (sigh).

Figure 7.9
This extremely dark photo of a wedding cake would be considered unsalvageable if it was not for Photoshop Elements.

To restore this photo, I applied Auto Levels and then a relatively heavy setting of Fill Flash (+30). The result is a better-looking photo, but it still needs some work (see Figure 7.10).

Figure 7.10
Auto Levels and Fill Flash seem to bring out all the details, but this photo isn't finished yet.

The finishing touches on the cake were done by first applying the Dodge Tool (O) to lighten the edges that Fill Flash didn't affect (just like a real flash). The Dodge tool affects the pixels in one of three ranges (Shadows, Midtones, and Highlights), depending on the settings in the Options bar. For most corrections similar to this, the Midtones range works best.

Next, I applied some contrast (Enhance, Adjust Brightness/Contrast), and increased the saturation by using Hue/Saturation (Ctrl-U). As it often happens, increasing the contrast and the saturation makes the noise in the photo painfully apparent. To correct this, I took the Blur tool (R) and applied it to the background and to everywhere that looked noisy. Figure 7.11 shows the final photo.

Figure 7.11
This final photograph looks much better than the image we started out with in Figure 7.9.

Selective Highlights and Shadows

Many times, the subject of your photo might be in a shadow caused by a building, or a shadow caused by the sun being in the wrong position relative to your subject. You can selectively highlight or darken an area by using one of two brush tools: the Dodge and Burn tools. The names are leftover from the days when we did all this magic in a real darkroom. It seems so long ago.

Figure 7.12
The Dodge tool (left) and the Burn tool (right) are located in the Toolbox.

Basically, the Dodge tool lightens the area on which it's painted, and the Burn tool darkens the area. Both tools are located in the Toolbox (see Figure 7.12).

These tools are actually more complicated than what I just described. They don't just darken or lighten the area where you apply them, they do it based on their range settings. Each one can darken or lighten shadows, midrange, or highlights, depending on what is selected in the Options bar for the tool.

Look at the cactus shown in Figure 7.13. In this photo, we want to enhance the spines. By selecting the Dodge tool and changing the affect range to Highlights in the Options bar, we can paint over the spines. They are the only thing that is affected because the colors in the rest of the cactus are in the midtones, or the shadow part of the spectrum (see Figure 7.14).

Figure 7.13
Here's a great photo of a small cactus, but for publication, its spines need to be highlighted—and only the spines.

Figure 7.14
Applying the Dodge tool that's set to affect only highlights brightens up the spines, but not the rest of the cactus.

In case you do not think that you will need to enhance cactus spines any time soon, here's a real example of a task that I had just recently completed. In the brochure, the photograph of the gold leaf letter for the building didn't stand out (see Figure 7.15). I put a selection around the glass with the gold lettering and applied the Dodge tool to the highlights and the Burn tool to the shadows. After I finished, the lettering above the door stood out much more (see Figure 7.16).

Figure 7.15
The gold leaf lettering in this photograph doesn't stand out as much as the owner wanted it to.

Figure 7.16
Applying the Dodge tool set to affect only highlights and applying the Burn tool to the shadows really
makes the lettering stand out.

Real Fill Flash

Whenever a bright light comes from behind a subject, you need to force the camera
flash to fire when the photo is taken. Even outside, especially on a bright sunny day, the
use of Fill Flash prevents shadows across people's faces.

The Darker Side of Washouts

So, with all the detail that we can recover from the dark reaches of a shadow area, it
seems natural that areas of a photo that are washed out (also called blowouts) can have
their detail recovered in a similar manner. Actually, in most cases, you cannot recover
image detail from areas that are blown out. What happens when a flash reflects in someone's glasses or off of a shiny nose is that the area of the blowout becomes pure white;
there is no image detail in it. In Figure 7.17, the white stone in the upper right is completely washed out and, although the original stone had texture to it, it was so bright
that the digital camera did not record the information.

Figure 7.17
The blowouts in this image cannot be restored.

Avoiding Blowouts

Blowouts can be avoided, but it can be a little tricky. You need to set your camera's light metering to spot or something similar so that it is reading the amount of light at the spot with the least amount of light. The result will be blowouts of the rest of the photograph. This is OK if the part of the photo that you are photographing using the spot setting on your meter is the part that you want to capture. You can always replace a blown out sky at a later date.

Another trick, which requires a tripod, is to set the camera's light metering for the darker area, take the photograph, and change the camera light meter setting to capture the brighter part of the image without moving the camera. Take a second photograph and then combine the best of both pictures into one photo.

Dealing with Red Eye

Red eye is a major problem for anyone taking photos with a flash. We all have had one photo or another ruined by red eye (see Figure 7.18). Red eye is caused by the flash reflecting off of the retina of the person you are photographing. I think it's made more frustrating by cameras that have an anti-red eye feature (that rarely works as advertised). For the record, a few things that help reduce red eye are using an external flash or taking the photo in a well-lit room. Also, it helps if the subject is sober—no kidding.

It is my experience that some people are prone to red eye, and no matter what you do, you get the demon eye. So, to remove red eye, we turn to the Red Eye Brush tool.

Figure 7.18
Here is a classic red-eye photo, which also proves one of my pet theories—your susceptibility to red eye is hereditary.

After selecting the Red Eye Brush tool from the Toolbox, I change the brush size so that it is a bit larger than the pupil of the eye. (This seems to be the best size.)

For the best work, zoom in really close (800%) at this point (see Figure 7.19).

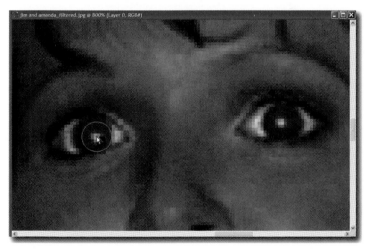

Figure 7.19
Although she doesn't look really pretty at this zoom level, if you want to do a good job of removing red eye, you must be up close and personal.

Next, I pick the color that will be removed by clicking the red color in the image. (This assumes that the first click from the Sampling pop-up menu is selected; it is by default.)

The important part is to pick the custom replacement color. This is the color that the eye is supposed to be. Click the Replacement Color swatch in the Options bar, and pick the color that you want to use for the correction.

TIP

This is not the time to change the subject's eye color. Always do your best to correctly match the eye color or viewers who know the subject will look at the photo and think that something's not quite right with it, but they won't be able to tell you what it is.

Set the Tolerance value. This setting determines how similar in color the replaced pixels must be with the original sampled ones. Theoretically, a low percentage replaces only adjacent pixels within a narrow range of color values similar to the pixel that you click. A high percentage replaces adjacent pixels within a broader range of color values. It has been my experience with this tool that I need to use a relatively high value (usually greater than 70), but experiment with it and discover what works best for you.

WARNING

If the subject has light, pinkish skin, the Red Eye Brush tool might become confused regarding what is red eye and what is skin color. If this happens, you need to Undo (Ctrl-Z), crank down the Tolerance value, and try again. Worst case, you need to draw a rough selection around the eye to prevent the Red Eye Brush tool from removing both the red eye and the eyelid.

Click the parts of the red eye that you want to correct and drag if necessary. Any pixels that match the target color are colorized with the replacement eye color.

While you are working at this detail level, it's a good time to use the Dodge tool and whiten both the whites of the subjects' eyes and their teeth. Figure 7.20 shows the finished photo. I probably spent more time on this red eye removal than necessary, but I have known this bride her entire life, so I felt that I couldn't do anything less. I also did some touch-up work on her dad because I have known him for about 30 years, and Jim needs all the help he can get.

Figure 7.20
With the help of the Red Eye Brush tool, the red eye is gone and the whites of the eyes are whiter. The father of the bride still looks old, but even Photoshop Elements has its limits.

Summary

In this chapter, we learned that, many times, photographic detail that's lost in the shadows can be recovered. Although it can be extracted from the shadows, it might be too noisy to use. Also, we discovered that photographs with large patches of white (blowouts) contain no image detail to recover.

The next chapter looks at techniques that make your photos stand out from the crowd.

8 Putting on the Final Touches

In previous chapters, we discovered various ways to correct mistakes in lighting and color. We explored ways to improve a photograph's composition by cropping and other techniques. In this chapter, we cover what I call the "frosting on the cake." The two photos shown in Figure 8.1 are the before-and-after images that were the result of using the procedures outlined in this chapter. This collection of finishing touches, presented in no particular order, isn't about secrets of the photo masters revealed (or whatever hackneyed title is often tacked on to such material to make it sound impressive). But it is about what you need to know to make your photographs look better than the rest.

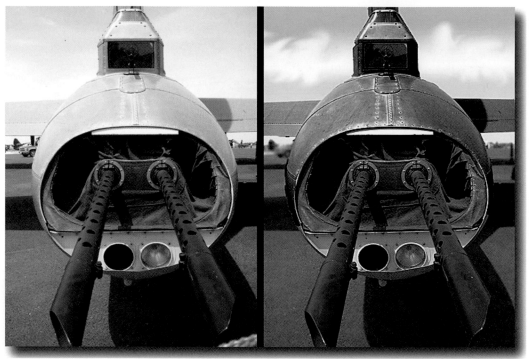

Figure 8.1
On the left is the rear gunner position of a WWII B-17 bomber taken on a bright sunny day with a good digital camera. On the right is what the photo looks like after the techniques covered in this chapter are applied.

What's Wrong with This Photo?

In Figure 8.1, the photo shown on the left is washed out and, as a result, there is no blue left in the sky (it was a classic Texas blue sky) and the green pane of the bomber is almost nonexistent. I used a Nikon Coolpix 5000 to take this photo, which, at the time I took this photo, was the top-of-the-line consumer digital camera. So, what went wrong? The answer: Nothing went wrong. When I took the picture, the sun was so bright that the canvas shroud at the base of the machine guns was covered in dark shadows. I had to make a choice—if I used the normal setting, the sky and green paint of the aircraft would look fine but, in the resulting photo, it would appear that the machine-gun barrels were sticking out of a black hole. Also, the window near the top of the photo would be pitch black. The other choice I had was to set the camera for spot metering (meaning that it would read the light level where I pointed it, regardless of other light sources) and let the other parts of the photo appear washed out.

In Chapter 7, "Correcting Lighting Problems," we learned that details can be extracted out of the shadows, but the results can be noisy (grainy). I also told you that, when part of an image goes pure white or nearly white (a blowout), all image detail is lost. In this case, I took a sample shot using spot metering on the base of the gun barrels. When I looked at the photo (in the shade), I realized that the sky and plane weren't blown out, they were washed out—that's a major difference. For the record, if I had had my tripod with me, I could have set up the camera and taken two photos from the same exact position (one with regular light metering and the other with spot metering) and combined the two photos by using Elements. Needless to say, I wasn't lugging a tripod around on the tarmac in the 90-degree heat, so the "before" photo in Figure 8.1 was the result.

To turn this photo into a professional-style photo, we need to apply several different procedures and introduce some new tools.

Divide and Conquer

The very first step when attempting to selectively restore parts of an image is to define the individual parts of the photograph using selections. In this photo's case, I created selections for the following:

- The sky (both above and under the wings).

- The planes fuselage, not including the gunner's window on top.

- Everything but the plane. Each selection was made using the Magnetic Lasso tool (which is explored in Chapter 12, "Rearranging and Replacing Objects in Photos"). Each selection was saved using the Selection, Save option.

Now let's learn about tonal adjustments.

Introducing Tonal Adjustments

The Levels command and Brightness and Contrast fall into the tonal adjustments category. We already applied tonal adjustments through the use of the automatic tools Auto Levels and Auto Contrast. For most photos, these automatic tools do an excellent job of tonal adjustment, except when they cause the color to shift in an undesirable direction. In the case of the original photo in Figure 8.1, application of both of these automatic tools had no affect on the photo (see Figure 8.2). When the automatic tools aren't working, you need to see what the manual versions of these tools can do.

Figure 8.2
Applying Auto Levels and Auto Contrast has little affect on this photo, so something else must be used.

Brightness and Contrast

At this point, we won't use the Contrast and Brightness controls, but we need to get familiar with them before we learn about Levels. The Brightness and Contrast controls are located in the Enhance menu under Adjust Brightness, Contrast. The Brightness and Contrast controls always appear to be located together, regardless of who makes the software, because the effect of each control impacts the other. For example, when the contrast of an image is increased, the photo sometimes gets darker so that, at times, it is necessary to increase the brightness to compensate for the additional contrast.

Contrast increases or decreases the difference in brightness values between adjoining pixels in an image. Figure 8.3 is a photograph of Jonathan (my son) that already has Auto Contrast applied to it. In Figure 8.4, I applied a large amount of contrast (+20) to the image and it held up well. More importantly, the image looks more vivid.

Figure 8.3
This photo, taken on an overcast day, looks better after I applied Auto Contrast, but there's still room for improvement.

Figure 8.4
Applying contrast at a setting of 20 (which is pretty high) brightens up the image.

Contrast is a great way to liven up any photograph. If there's one problem with contrast, it's that it is tempting to apply too much. My recommendation for the best way to evaluate how much contrast to apply to a photograph is to use the Preview check box. Click it on and off while watching the photograph. You're looking to see if subtle details are lost when the contrast is applied. Some detail will always be lost when you apply contrast; the question you must ask yourself is, "Is the loss in detail offset by the overall improvement to the photo made by the additional contrast?" We will be using contrast when we are nearly finished with our bomber photo.

Levels

An advanced way to control contrast and brightness in an image is to use the Levels command. Although this is a typical command in image photo editing, it has different names in other applications. I've seen it called histogram equalization, equalization, and contrast enhancement (to name only a few).

Contrast and brightness are applied equally to every pixel in an image. The Levels command operates in a different manner. Where the Contrast and Brightness controls are simple, when you open the Levels dialog box (see Figure 8.5), it looks downright complicated. Many users open it once, take a quick look at it, and close it after vowing that they will never open it again.

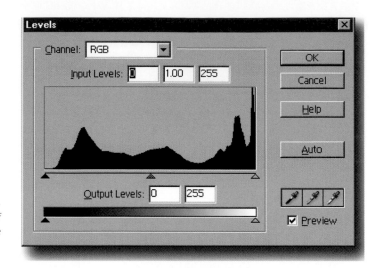

Figure 8.5
The Levels command looks compli-cated, but after you get the hang of using it, it will become your favorite adjustment tool.

Referring to Figure 8.5, look at the chart in the center (ignore the rest of this dialog box at this point). This is a histogram. It is the graphic equivalent of a census of the image that it represents. The histogram is divided into thirds; shadows (left), midtone (mid-dle—what else?), and highlights (right). The more pixels there are at a particular brightness level, the higher the chart is in that region. When we look at the histogram for the B-17 gunner photo (see Figure 8.6), we can see many pixels in the midtone and highlight region, but almost none in the darkest end of the shadow region.

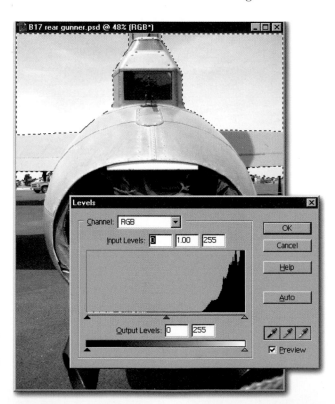

Figure 8.6
With only the sky selected, it's appar-ent that the sky is composed of pixels in the highlights region, which means it is so bright we cannot see any color.

To demonstrate further, I loaded the sky selection and opened Levels again (refer to Figure 8.6). Now, the histogram shows only the pixels that make up the sky. You can see that the sky is washed out, and it has only pixels in the highlights region. Notice the three triangles under the chart. As I move the left and the middle sliders to the right, the range of brightness of the highlight pixels is remapped, making some of them darker and allowing us to see the blue sky and the clouds again (see Figure 8.7). After I apply Levels and open up the command again, I can see that the pixels are now spread over a wider range of brightness (see Figure 8.8), which is why all the vertical lines are so far apart from each other. The only drawback to redistributing the pixels is that the sky becomes a little noisy (grainy). We remedy the noise a little later in this chapter.

Figure 8.7
Pushing the black point (left) marker and the midtone marker (also called the Gamma marker) to the right redistributes the pixels over a wider range and restores the color.

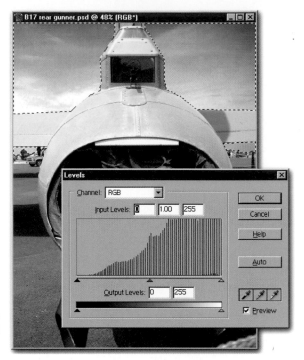

Figure 8.8
Reopening the Levels command
shows how the pixels in the sky have
been redistributed over a wider tonal
range.

Restoring the Paint Job

Using the selection that covered only the fuselage, we do the same thing and the color of
the paint reappears after the brightness of the pixels is redistributed over a wider range
(see Figure 8.9).

Figure 8.9
Applying levels to the selected area of
the aircraft fuselage restores the ugly
green paint job that was so popular
with WWII bombers.

Blurring the Background

At this point, we want to emphasize the aircraft by slightly blurring the background. By inverting the selection (Ctrl-Shift-I) that was on the aircraft, we have now selected everything but the aircraft. By applying a Gaussian Blur (shown in Figure 8.10) at a mild setting (2.0), we achieve the soft out-of-focus look. The same blurring also removes the noise from the sky that was created by applying Levels to it.

Figure 8.10
Applying a Gaussian blur makes the background appear slightly out of focus.
This helps draw viewers' attention to the plane.

More Background Modification

The shadows being cast by the plane are dark. Although they are blurred, I opened up the Brightness and Contrast dialog box and reduced the contrast and increased the overall brightness (see Figure 8.11).

Figure 8.11
Increasing the brightness and reducing the contrast of the background emphasizes the plane.

Sharpening the Plane

Similar to contrast, sharpening is a necessary tool that can, and does, get overused. Because we spent some amount of effort softening the background, it wouldn't make much sense to sharpen it up again. Inverting the selection, I applied the Unsharp Mask (the name seems weird, but it's a term that has been around the publishing business long before we started playing with computers). Located in the Filter menu under Sharpen, after selecting the Unsharp Mask, I applied a relatively mild setting of 70 percent at a 1.5 Radius (see Figure 8.12). Applying a setting greater than that results in the small reflections on the skin of the aircraft blowing out and producing many tiny hot spots all over the aircraft's skin.

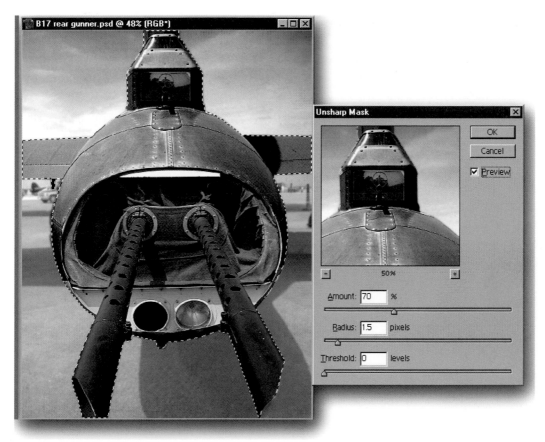

Figure 8.12
The Unsharp Mask filter brings out detail in the airplane, but use caution so you don't apply too much and produce blowouts.

Some Cleanup Items

Just a few items remain to tidy up before we put this jewel into a picture frame. That piece of orange rope in the lower-right corner was removed by using the Clone tool (S). Doing this was relatively simple; the Clone tool source point was selected and the Aligned check box in the Options bar was unchecked. It took only a few seconds to clone that orange rope out of sight.

The last thing was to take the Dodge Brush tool and paint inside the tail gunner's windows. This lightened the windows enough to give it more of a transparent appearance.

Framing Our Masterpiece

After we have the photograph of the tail gunner's position on the B-17 ready for framing, we need to frame it. It's much easier to frame pictures in Photoshop Elements than it is at the local hobby superstore. And it's free.

Matting the Photograph

To futhur emphasize our subject; we need to put a matte around the photograph. While this is easy enough to do, a little thinking ahead will save us some time later on in the framing project. You can apply the steps in this section to any image to produce some great frames.

First, we select the entire image (Ctrl-A) and then save the selection (choose Select, Save Selection, New). Next, open the Canvas Size command (choose Image, Resize, Canvas Size). Check the Relative check box, the desired width (.5 inch, in this case) is selected, and click OK. The selection that was on the image is lost (which is why we saved it). Loading the selection, we then invert it (Ctrl-Shift-I). Now only the new area we added to the photo is selected. From the Filter menu, under Texture, Texturizer is selected, and from the Texturizer dialog box, select Canvas (see Figure 8.13). Because this is a large image, I make the Canvas setting at a scale of 200 percent.

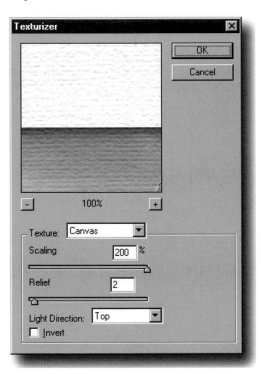

Figure 8.13
The Texturizer dialog box provides many different textures and settings from which you can choose.

TIP

Experiment with different textures. Don't fall into the rut of "the name has to match the texture you're looking for." I came close to choosing Burlap for this photo, but I settled on Canvas because it looked the best.

Although it appears that the texture is being applied to the entire image in Figure 8.13, it's applied only to the selected area. With that application, we almost have the appearance of a Bristol board paper matte but something's missing (see Figure 8.14).

Figure 8.14
With the application of the Texturizer effect, the matte border almost looks real, but something's missing.

If you ever worked with matting, you know that it is usually pretty thick stuff. To create that illusion, we need to make the photo look like it's placed inside a thick matte cutout. With most programs, this takes several steps, but in Photoshop Elements, it's relatively easy. Invert the selection that was used to add the texture to the matte. From the Effects palette, double-click the Recessed Frame effect. Figure 8.15 shows the results.

Figure 8.15
The Recessed Frame effect instantly creates the appearance of a photograph being recessed into a matte cut.

The last step is to add the actual frame. Photoshop Elements offers you several choices, but none of them are all that exciting. Still, because this is a frame for a photo of military hardware, a conservative black frame matches all the frames I ever saw during my hitch in the U.S. Navy.

Removing the selection (Ctrl-D), open the Effects palette, and this time double-click the Foreground Color frame. The little thumbnail shows that it has a blue frame but, in reality, the frame color is made in the current foreground color. Figure 8.16 shows the finished and framed photograph.

Figure 8.16
In only a few steps, we added Bristol board matting and created a nice black frame for this photograph.

Summary

In this chapter, I showed you some ways to add a little extra something to your photos. Learn to use the Levels command to redistribute the pixels in an image and salvage lost color or other photographic features. When you want to emphasize a subject, applying a light Gaussian Blur to the background can subtly make the subject matter stand out (don't make it so blurry that they appear to be coming out of a fog).

In the next chapter, we discover that Adobe has put many really cool features in Elements for playing with text.

9 Cool Tricks with Text

I'm guessing that the most popular use for a program such as Photoshop Elements is to do cool stuff with all the photos you have accumulated over the years. Or maybe you purchased a digital camera, and you suddenly have access to a multitude of newer images to work with, in addition to your photos from a traditional camera. So when I had to write a chapter on text, I decided to first tackle the Text tool from the point of view of adding text into a photo. Let's start with something simple—meaning simple text—and work up to more complicated effects.

Adding and Editing Text

The easiest place to start learning how to do tricks with text in your photos is simply finding out how to add text and how to edit that text after it's in your photos.

Plain Old Basic Text

The first example starts with a digital image taken on graduation day. As Figure 9.1 shows, this image captured the subject nicely, but it has many flaws overall. The background has tons of distracting furniture and the photographer makes an unexpected appearance in the mirror. I confess—the photographer is me, and like most people armed with a camera, I don't always plan out a photo perfectly. This leads me to the photo's biggest flaw—the blurred object in the foreground (bottom) area of the image. I was standing on the stairs, too close to the railing, and in my rush to take the picture, I didn't notice that the railing was making an appearance.

Figure 9.1
This is a typical image that many of us might instantly view as a mistake. But don't dismiss this gem so quickly.

The reason I chose this image is because of its flaws. Although you might think this is a bad thing, it's actually a perfect candidate for a simple fix—cropping. What has this got to do with text? Well, as long as we're cropping, we might as well turn the space surrounding the cropped image into white space. Then, we can make use of this white space by adding some simple text. By doing that, this photo becomes a perfect image for a card.

Before we begin the first exercise, it must be noted that I'm a huge believer in having my Layers palette *always* visible while I work. The first exercise walks you through finding your Layers palette, if you haven't already found it before getting to this point. Leave the Layers palette in your workspace throughout this chapter because I will make the assumption that it's easily within your view through the remaining exercises. By the time you finish this chapter, you might understand why I find this palette the coolest thing since sliced bread.

The Layers palette enables you to place text and images on separate layers. Think of layers as analogous to the sheets of clear acetate that are used with overhead projectors. If you have an object drawn on one layer (or sheet), you can move it around independently of the objects drawn on the other layers (or sheets). This allows for great flexibility and power while working with your images:

1. Open an image that you would like to use to follow along in this project (or download the `GradPic04.jpg` from this book's web page on the New Riders Publishing web site). Go to the Window menu and choose Layers to view the Layers palette. If the palette is docked in the Palette Well, it might help you to drag the Layers tab out of the Palette Well so that you can view and work with this palette during this exercise (see Figure 9.2).

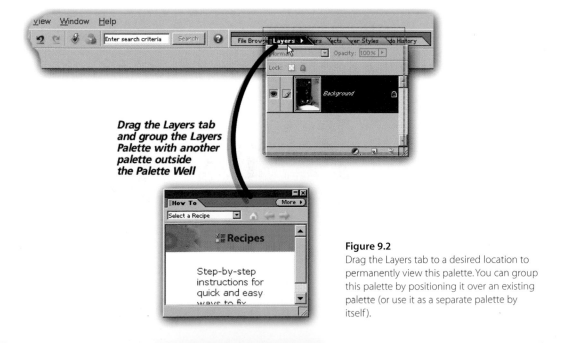

Drag the Layers tab and group the Layers Palette with another palette outside the Palette Well

Figure 9.2
Drag the Layers tab to a desired location to permanently view this palette. You can group this palette by positioning it over an existing palette (or use it as a separate palette by itself).

135

2. We want to create a new Background layer on the Layers palette that will be filled with white color. But, before we can create a new Background layer, the current Background layer needs to be made into an ordinary layer. To do this, hold the Alt key and double-click the Background layer (on the Layers palette). The Background layer has now been given a new title of Layer 0 (see Figure 9.3).

Figure 9.3
Turn the Background layer into Layer 0.

3. Press D to make the default colors black and white. White needs to be the background color. Click the Create a New Layer icon at the bottom of the Layers palette. Go to the Layer menu and choose New, Layer From Background. This fills the layer with your background color (in this case, white), and makes this layer a Background layer. This layer automatically moves to the bottom of the palette (see Figure 9.4).

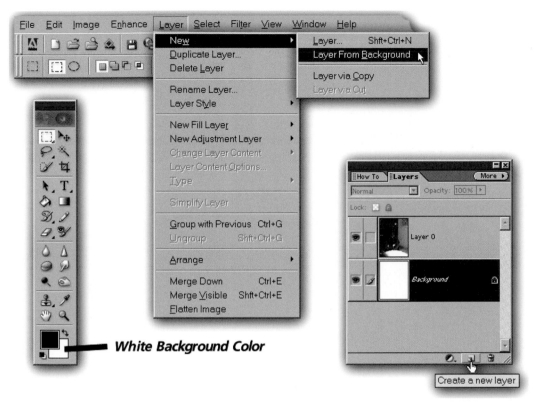

Figure 9.4
The New, Layer From Background command turns Layer 1 into a new Background layer, fills it with the background color (in this case, white), and automatically repositions the layer at the bottom of the Layers palette.

4. Click Layer 0 to make this the active layer. Choose the Rectangular Marquee tool and make a selection to crop around the graduate and the cat. (Don't include any of the railing that appears at the bottom of the photo.) If you need to move or reposition the selection as you create it, hold the spacebar as you drag a marquee selection. After you're satisfied with the selection, press Ctrl-Shift-I to invert the selection. (This includes everything surrounding the original selection.) Press the Delete (Backspace) key (see Figure 9.5). Press Ctrl-D to deselect.

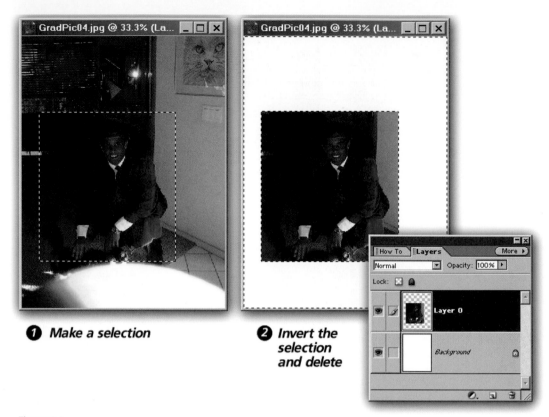

① Make a selection

② Invert the selection and delete

Figure 9.5
Make a selection to crop the image and clear the image surrounding the cropped portion.

5. Press V to activate to the Move tool. Center the image near the lower half of the document window. Switch to the Eyedropper tool and sample a bright orange color from the chair (behind the graduate). Switch to the Horizontal Type tool. On the Options bar, choose Arial Black or a similar thick font. Set the font size to about 20 point, and click the Center Text icon. Click in the document window near the center top area and type **Congratulations**. Press Enter to move to the next line and type **on your**. Press Enter again and finish the last line by typing **Graduation!**. Hold the Ctrl key to toggle to the Move tool and reposition the text if necessary (see Figure 9.6). After you're satisfied with the text, press Ctrl-Enter to commit the text to a layer (or click the Check icon on the Options bar).

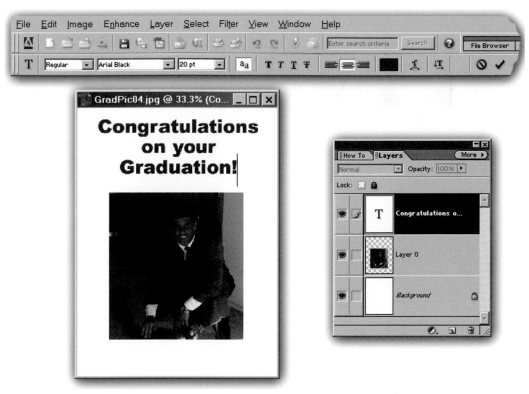

Figure 9.6
Create the text for the image by using the Text tool.

6. Let's add a few more details to make this image more dynamic. Drag the text layer to the Create a New Layer icon at the bottom of the Layers palette. This creates a duplicate layer of the text. Click the original text layer (which is below the text layer copy) to make it the active layer. With the Text tool still active, click the color swatch on the Options bar and change the color to black (R:0, G:0, B:0). Click OK. Switch to the Move tool and press the down arrow on your keyboard once, then press the left-arrow key once. This creates a poor man's bevel effect, but it can be effective when simplicity is the agenda (see Figure 9.7).

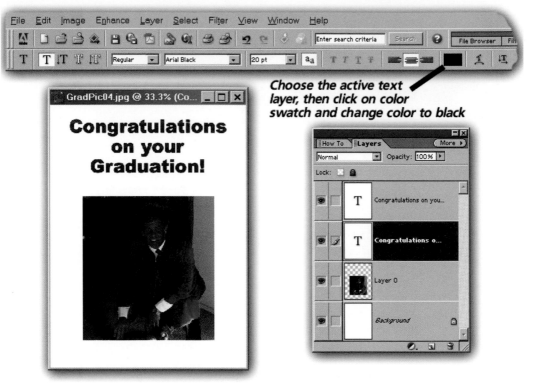

Figure 9.7
Add another layer of text and change the color to black. Nudge the black text layer down and to the left by using the arrow keys.

7. Let's create a black border frame for the picture. Click Layer 0 to make it active, and click the Create a New Layer icon at the bottom of the Layers palette. Ctrl-click Layer 0 to load the image selection. Press D to make the foreground color black. Go to the Select menu and choose Modify, Expand. In the Expand dialog box, type 20 (pixels) and click OK. With Layer 1 still the active layer, press Alt-Delete to fill the selection with black. Don't worry that it hides the image because we take care of that in the next step (see Figure 9.8).

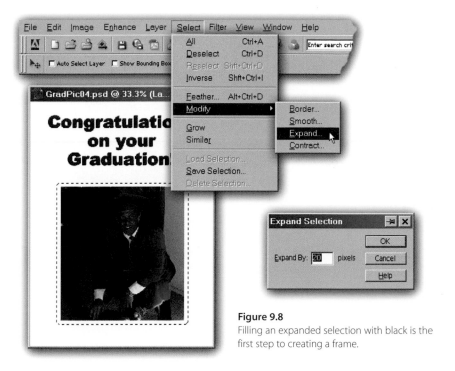

Figure 9.8
Filling an expanded selection with black is the
first step to creating a frame.

8. Ctrl-click Layer 0 again to load the original selection. Go to the Select menu and
choose Modify, Contract. In the Contract Selection dialog box, type 10 (pixels);
click OK. With Layer 1 as the active layer, press the Delete key. Press Ctrl-D to deselect (see Figure 9.9).

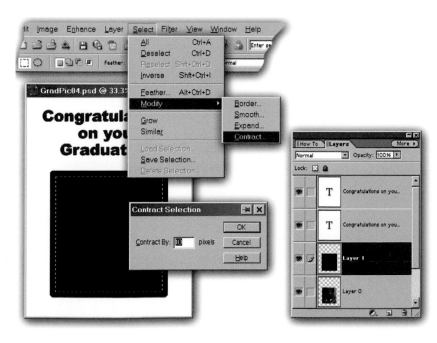

Figure 9.9
Contract the selection
and delete the center
area to create a frame.

9. Let's add a rough edge to the frame. With Layer 1 still active, go to the Filter menu and choose Brush Strokes, Spatter. In the Spatter dialog box, type 16 for Spray Radius, and 9 for Smoothness (see Figure 9.10). Click OK. You might want to experiment with the settings and choose your own.

Figure 9.10
Use the Spatter filter to add a rough edge to the frame.

10. Finally, the frame might show some white fringing. To fix this, switch to the Magic Wand tool and click inside the black-frame area to load the frame as a selection. We use the Magic Wand so we load only the black areas of the frame (and not the white fringe areas). Go to the Select menu and choose Modify, Contract. Type 3 (pixels) in the Contract Selection dialog box and click OK. Press Ctrl-Shift-I to invert the selection. Press the Delete key to remove the fringe (see Figure 9.11). Press Ctrl-D to deselect. Go to the File menu and choose Save As, and then save the file to your hard disk as a PSD file (to pre-serve the layers). Also, you can go to the Layer menu and choose Flatten Image if you want to save a copy as a JPEG to send to friends.

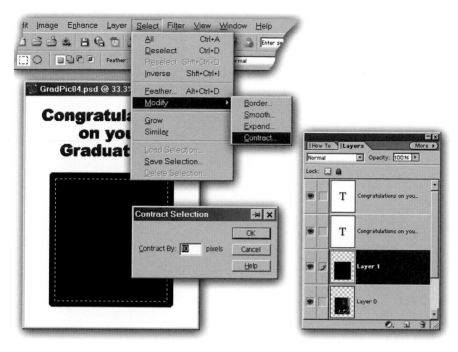

Figure 9.11
Make a frame selection of black pixels. Contract the selection, invert the
selection, and delete the white fringe.

This exercise contained more than just using the Text tool. That's because the goal of this exercise was not only to show you how to add the simplest of text, but to give you a sense of how to prepare an image and assess if you need a space for text. Many images might be too busy and can compete with the text for visual attention. When this happens, you make design decisions to create an area for text so that the message is clearly seen without any distraction.

Editing Text

Editing text is relatively straightforward. If you want to change the text, simply choose the Text tool, click in the text area where you want to make changes, and then add or delete the necessary text. The Esc key cancels out any changes you make to your text. (In other words, if you change your mind and decide you don't like the changes, the Esc key is your best friend). The Enter key on the numeric keypad (or Ctrl-Enter) accepts any changes that are made to text. If you prefer to click icons instead of using keyboard shortcuts, the universal No icon and Check Mark icon at the top right of the Options bar performs the same tasks of "reject" or "accept" changes (respectively).

Now, let's say that you don't want to edit the text message itself, but changes need to be made involving the font, font size, font color, and so on. Again, you can click in the text area and drag the Text tool to highlight the text you want to change. But, did you know that if you want to make these types of changes to the entire text on a layer, you don't have to go through the hassle of highlighting all the text on that layer. Instead, just click the layer itself (from the Layers palette) and, with the Text tool active, make the changes on the Options bar. Your changes are applied universally to all the text on that layer only. Keep in mind that at times it might be necessary to press Enter to apply the changes. For example, if you type in a font size on the Options bar, press Enter to apply the new font size.

Here's one last item that could conceivably throw you for a loop if you're new to this program. In the last exercise, there were two layers of text. Both layers are identical in message content, and the text (from both layers) is close to the same area in the image document. If you click and attempt to edit the black text, you discover that the program keeps inadvertently editing the orange text. Why? The layer that contains the orange text is on top of the black text, and the program automatically chooses to edit the closest text layer near the cursor location (in this case, the top layer). How can you bypass this problem?

Open the GradPic04.psd image from the last exercise (or create some text in a practice document and duplicate the text layer to follow along). On the Layers palette, click the Eye icon at the far-left column, next to the top text layer. This turns the visibility off for the orange text and prevents the layer from being edited. Switch to the Text tool, click in the text area of the image, and delete a word. Because this is just practice, experiment with editing on this image's black text layer. Press the Esc key to cancel the edits (again, this was just practice). After you're done, on the Layers palette, click the far-left column of the top text layer to turn on the visibility for this layer. The image again shows all the layers in the document window (see Figure 9.12).

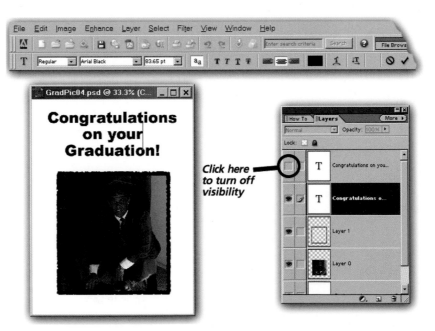

Figure 9.12
Turn off the top text layer to edit the text layer below it.

Introducing the Custom Shape Tool

The Custom Shape tool is located in the Toolbox, just left of the Text tool. If you click this tool and hold the mouse button, you can see many different tools available on the Flyout menu (these tools also appear on the Options bar).

Let's give a quick run down of the tools within this group. First, there's the Shape Selection tool (which simply looks like an arrow). As its name implies, it selects a shape that has been created (simply by clicking the shape with this tool active). This tool also enables you to adjust the size or position of any created shapes.

Additional tool options within this group enable you to create simple shapes with tools such as the Rectangle tool, Rounded Rectangle tool, Ellipse tool, Polygon tool (when selected, there's an option to specify how many sides are desired in the polygon shape), Line tool, and the Custom Shape tool. The Custom Shape tool gives you more complex shape options, so this tool is the focus of the following steps:

1. Press Ctrl-N to open a new document (or choose File, New). In the New dialog box (with the units set at pixels), type 400 for Width and Height because this project needs an ample size canvas. Set the Resolution to 72 ppi. Set Mode to RGB color, and Contents to White so that the new document has a white background. Click OK (see Figure 9.13).

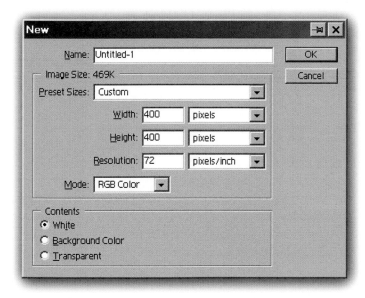

Figure 9.13
Use these settings in the New dialog box.

2. For this exercise, pick a light temporary color for creating the shape (choose any color). I chose light green from the Swatches palette (or click the foreground color and type the following numbers in the Color Picker dialog box: R:49, G:182, B:120), and click OK (see Figure 9.14).

145

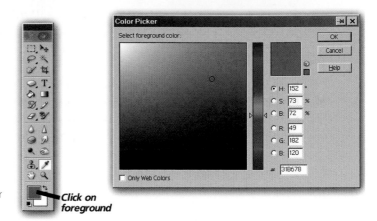

Figure 9.14
Pick a color to use for
the custom shape.

Click on foreground

3. Make sure that the Custom Shape tool is the active tool. Click the Custom Shape picker. Next, click the arrow in the upper-right corner of the Custom Shape picker and choose Banners and Awards from the list to view this set of custom shapes. Choose the Ribbon 1 shape (see Figure 9.15).

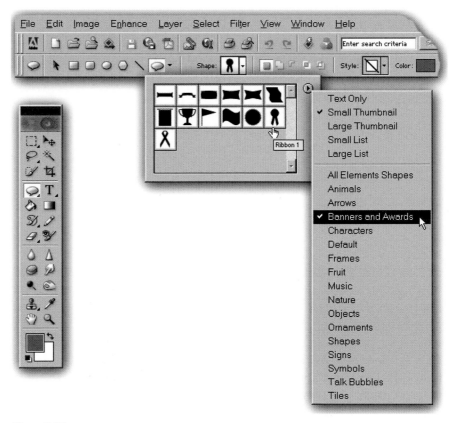

Figure 9.15
Choose the Ribbon 1 custom shape from the Banners and Awards options.

4. Hold the Shift key to keep the shape proportional while it's being created and drag in the document window until it fills up a fair amount of the canvas space. If you need to reposition the shape as you drag, hold the spacebar; this enables you to move the object around while still dragging with the mouse. After the shape is the desired size, release the mouse button. If you still need to reposition the shape, hold the Ctrl key to toggle to the Shape Selection tool, and drag the shape to the desired location (in this case, the center of the document window). Press Ctrl-Shift-S to save the document to your hard disk. Type **Ribbon** for the title and save the file in the native Photoshop format (as a PSD file). Leave the document open for the next exercise (see Figure 9.16).

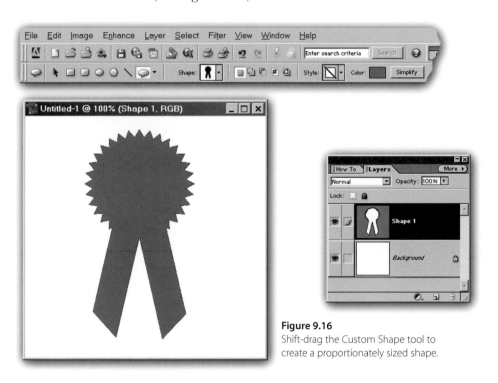

Figure 9.16
Shift-drag the Custom Shape tool to create a proportionately sized shape.

If the Custom Shape tool intrigues you, many web sites provide free Photoshop downloads. Custom Shape files are often found at these types of sites. After the Custom Shape file is downloaded, simply put the new file in the Elements 2.0/Preset/Custom Shapes folder on your hard drive and the new shape file will be available to view the next time you launch Elements. The Adobe web site is a good starting point and a great resource to discover some sources for downloads (http://share.studio.adobe.com/Default.asp). This site does not have a section specifically labeled for Photoshop Elements, but if you follow the links for Photoshop, you will discover these custom shape files work equally as well in Elements as they do in Photoshop.

Warping and Unwarping Text

Elements has a really cool feature called *Warped Text*, which is located on the Options bar when the Text tool is active. By default, this option is set to None when the Warped Text dialog box is selected, because we typically type text without this feature. If you click the arrow to reveal the Style drop-down list, you can see a long list of ways you can warp your text.

If you choose a warp style and decide that you don't like it, simply pull up the Warped Text dialog box again and choose None to unwarp your text. Sound simple enough? Let's see how this works. We'll use one of the more common styles for this project:

1. The `ribbon.psd` file should still be open. Choose the Text tool. Click the color swatch on the Options bar at the top right. Choose a nice blue in the Color Picker dialog box (R:0, G:6, B:129). Click OK (see Figure 9.17).

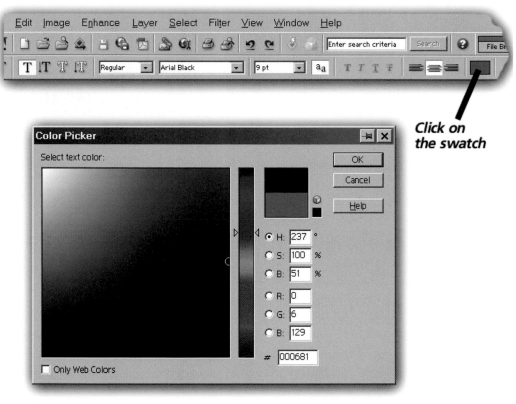

Figure 9.17
Choose a text color.

2. Choose Arial Black for the font (or any plain thick font will work). Type 15 pt for the size (the font size might vary and might need to be adjusted depending on the size of your custom shape; don't worry about that now). Click anywhere in the document (we'll adjust the position of the text later), and type **FIRST PRIZE** (see Figure 9.18). Press the Enter on the numeric keypad to commit the text to a layer (or click the Check Mark icon on the Options bar).

Figure 9.18
Type FIRST PRIZE in the document window.

3. On the Options bar, click the Create Warped Text icon (located to the right of the color swatch). In the Warped Text dialog box, click the Style drop-down menu and choose Arc, and move the Bend slider all the way to the right (setting it at +100%). Click OK. Hold the Ctrl key to toggle to the Move tool and position the text as shown in Figure 9.19. If the size of the text needs adjusting at this point, type in different numbers for point size and experiment to find a size that fits inside the shape as shown in the figure.

Figure 9.19
Give the text an Arc warp and make any adjustments to the text's point size and location.

4. Let's add a big number 1 to the center of the ribbon shape. With the Text tool still active, click in the center of the shape, type the number **1**, and press Enter on the numeric keypad to commit the text to a layer. On the Options bar, change the font to Times New Roman, change the font style to Bold, and the font size to 100 pt (this point size might need to be adjusted to fit the size of your shape, so experiment with point sizes if necessary). If needed, hold the Ctrl key to toggle to the Move tool and reposition the number to the center of the shape (see Figure 9.20). Press Ctrl-S to save your changes. Keep this image open for the next exercise.

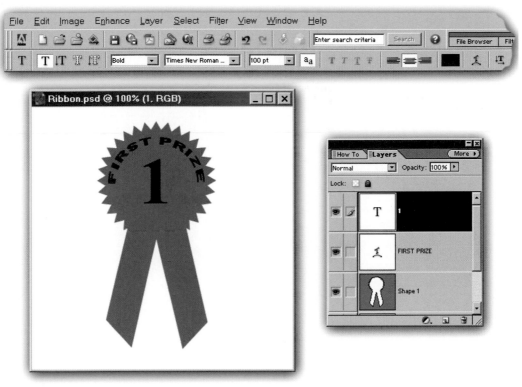

Figure 9.20
Add a large number 1 to the center of the ribbon shape.

Adding Styles for Great Effects

It's time to add some pizzazz to this image. Earlier, I explained that the color chosen for the custom shape was temporary. This is because the next exercise uses Layer Styles to add style to the custom shape. When using Layer Styles, the color settings for the style overrides any color that you previously chose for the object. Keep in mind (when you see how easy it is to use the Layer Styles) that these little gems can be applied to any kind of layers (even text layers). So, you can also use these styles to experiment with text. But, for this exercise, we'll apply the Layer Styles to our ribbon shape and use another trick to make the text blend into the style that's applied.

1. The Ribbon.psd file should still be open. On the Layers palette, click the Shape 1 layer to make the ribbon layer active. Click the Layer Styles tab in the Palette Well. (If you don't see this palette listed, go to the Window menu and choose Layer Styles.) Click the drop-down list and choose Wow Plastic (see Figure 9.21).

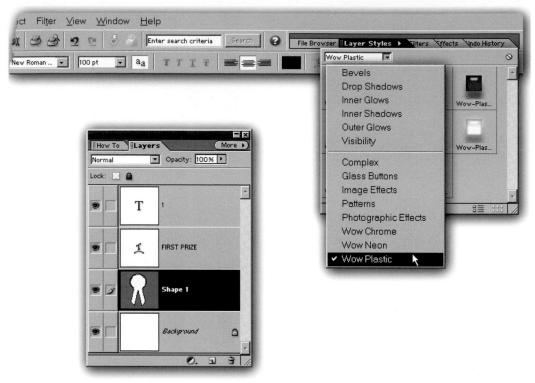

Figure 9.21
Choose Wow Plastic in the drop-down style list to view these style choices.

2. The Shape 1 layer should still be the active layer. Click the Wow-Plastic Dark Blue style from the Layer Styles palette. That's all there is to it (see Figure 9.22). The ribbon turns into visual eye candy. Note that, when you apply a style to a layer, an "f" mark appears next to the layer title. If you double-click the "f" mark, a dialog box opens to show you the style settings. If you're feeling adventurous, play with the sliders to see how they affect the image. (You can always click the Cancel button if you don't like the changes.)

Figure 9.22
Click the Shape 1 layer from the Layers palette and click the dark blue style in the Layer Styles palette to get an instant "wow"–effect.

3. Let's change one more setting on the text layers to make the text appear like it's a part of the total plastic effect. On the Layers palette, click the FIRST PRIZE text layer to make it active. Click the drop-down menu near the top-left of the Layers palette and change the mode from Normal to Overlay (see Figure 9.23). Click the 1 layer and change the layer mode from Normal to Overlay for this layer, too. Press Ctrl-S to save your work. Leave the file open for the next exercise.

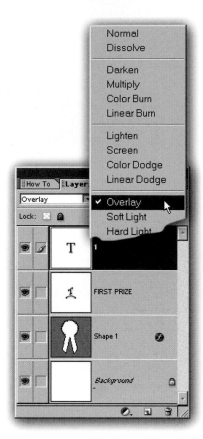

Figure 9.23
Change the blending modes on the text layers to Overlay.

Making Semitransparent Text and Transforming Text

The next exercise is purely optional. Its only goal is to show you the power of your Layers palette and how you can use the features available on the palette to benefit the way you work (and to understand how to make future project goals easier).

What if you want the text to be more transparent? Or what if you want to rotate the ribbon and all its accompanying parts, such as the text? Well, the Opacity setting can help for the first part. Linking layers combined with the Transform tool can accomplish the second goal.

1. The Ribbon.psd file should still be open. On the Layers palette, click the FIRST PRIZE layer to make it active, and lower the Opacity setting (located at the upper-right area of the Layers palette) to 75 percent. Click the 1 layer and repeat this step for the Opacity setting (see Figure 9.24).

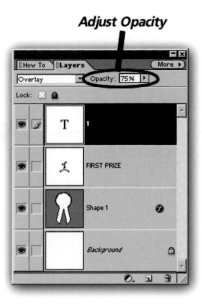

Figure 9.24
Lower the Opacity setting on the Layers palette to give the text layers a more transparent appearance.

Let's say that you want to rotate the ribbon and you want the text to rotate with it. You don't want to have to rotate the text separately and then have the additional hassle of repositioning the text into the ribbon. The solution is to link the layers so that Elements treats the layers as a group.

2. On the Layers palette, click the 1 layer to make it active. (Which layer you start with as the target layer isn't important; I arbitrarily chose the layer at the top, in this case.) Then, click in the column to the left of the FIRST PRIZE layer and the Shape 1 layer to link these layers to the active layer. A chain icon appears in the boxes (located next to the Eye column) to indicate that the layers are linked. Press Ctrl-T and a Transform bounding box appears (or go to the Image menu and choose Transform, Free Transform). Move the cursor outside one of the corners of the bounding box, and when a bent arrow appears, click and drag to rotate the ribbon (see Figure 9.25). When you're satisfied with the rotation amount, press Enter to commit the transformation. (The Esc key cancels the changes you made.)

Even after rotating the text (on the text layers), the text is still editable. You can still use the Text tool to click in the text and change the content, font, and so on.

Figure 9.25
Link the layers on the Layers palette and use the Transform command to rotate the layers as a group.

If you don't like any of the changes, use the Undo History palette in the Palette Well to undo any unwanted changes before you save the file.

It is important to note that there are other advantages or instances when you want to link layers. What are they? Well…what if you want to move the ribbon into another image with the text included? Simply link the layers (refer to the previous exercise). Open another document, photo, or image. Switch to the Move tool, click in the desired document (in this case, the ribbon.psd document), and drag to the other document. All the linked layers move with the target layer (see Figure 9.26).

Figure 9.26
Link the layers and drag the ribbon into a new document. Everything linked moves with the target layer.

Outlining Text

Let's create another document and quickly throw some text into it to demonstrate how to outline text. Actually, Elements (and many other programs) use the term *stroke*.

1. Press Ctrl-N to open a new document. In the New dialog box, type 500 (pixels) in Width, 200 (pixels) in Height, Resolution at 72 (pixels/inch), RGB Color for Mode, and White for Contents (see Figure 9.27). Click OK.

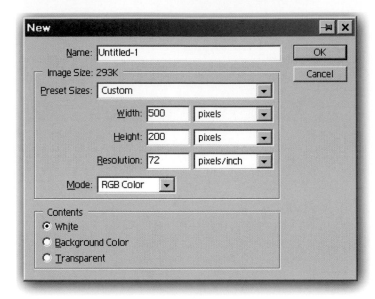

Figure 9.27
Use these settings to create a new document.

2. Let's try using a deep red color for the text. Click the foreground color swatch of the Toolbox and pick a deep red color (or type in the Color Picker dialog box R:123, G:0, B:0). Click OK. Switch to the Text tool and set the font to Arial Black and 100 pt for font size (or use any thick heavy font and adjust the font size to your satisfaction). Click in the document window and type **STROKE**. If you need to reposition the text to center it within the document window, hold the Ctrl key to toggle to the Move tool and drag to reposition the text. After you're satisfied with the text, press the Enter key on the numeric keypad (or click the Check Mark icon on the Options bar) to commit the text to a layer (see Figure 9.28).

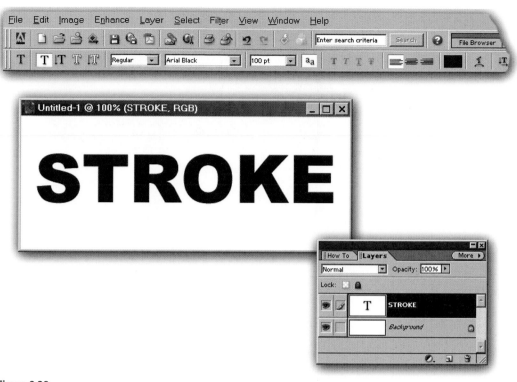

Figure 9.28
Use the settings shown in the Options bar for the Text tool and type the text in the document window.

3. If your Swatches palette is not showing, go to the Window menu and choose Color Swatches. Hover your cursor over the gray colors near the top of the Swatches palette until the tooltip displays which gray color is 50 percent gray. Click this gray swatch (we'll use this color for the stroke). On the Layers palette, click the Create a New Layer icon at the bottom of the palette. Now, Ctrl-click the STROKE (text) layer to load a selection of the text. With Layer 1 as the active layer, go to the Edit menu and choose Stroke. In the Stroke dialog box, type 2 px for Width, and set Location to Center (if you feel adventurous, experiment with different settings or widths). Click OK. Press Ctrl-D to deselect (see Figure 9.29).

The Location option in the Stroke dialog box determines if you want the stroke color to appear outside your selection marquee, at the center of your selection marquee, or inside your selection marquee.

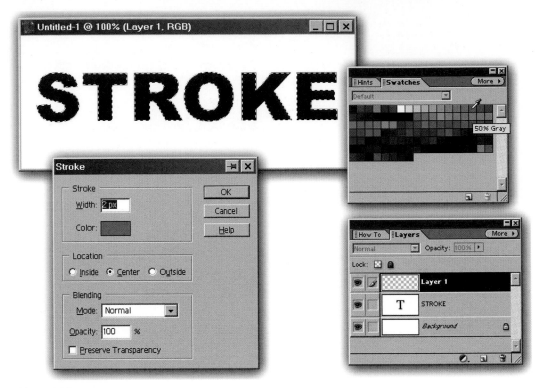

Figure 9.29
Choose a stroke color and use the Stroke dialog box to decide how thick you want to make the stroke.

4. The cool thing about putting the stroke on a separate layer is that you can now choose any position for your stroke. You can leave it where it is (surrounding the outer edge of your text), or give it an off position for an interesting look. Here's what I'm talking about: Switch to the Move tool and press the down-arrow key on your keyboard three times to nudge the stroke down three pixels. Now, press the right-arrow key three times to nudge it to the right a little (see Figure 9.30). This gives the text and stroke a fun look—don't ya think?

Figure 9.30
Nudge the stroke off center slightly for a different and unexpected design look.

Keep in mind that you can make a selection of any object (not just text) and apply a stroke. Hopefully, you've learned that it's also an advantage to create separate layers for each new item added to your image. By getting into this habit, you give yourself the flexibility to move objects around independently of the other objects in the document. Also, you have the freedom to delete a layer that you are unhappy with (simply by dragging it to the Trash icon at the bottom of the palette). Or you can rearrange layer order to move an object in front or behind another. In Figure 9.31, see what happens if the STROKE layer is dragged to a position above Layer 1 (on the Layers palette). The layer order can create a slightly different image effect.

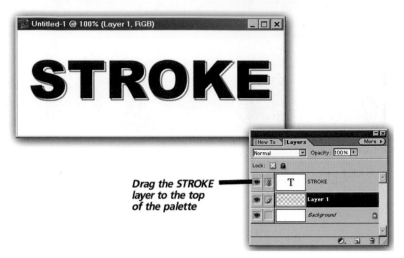

Figure 9.31
Drag the STROKE layer to the top to rearrange layer order.

Summary

This chapter's goal was to provide basic text-handling concepts and to develop skills to increase your confidence when tackling personal projects. We covered how to add and edit text, and how to customize and add effects to it. Somewhere along the way, maybe you even discovered that "Oh wow" factor while working with this program.

10 Cool Photographic Techniques

One of the great things about Photoshop Elements is all the cool stuff you can do to photos or other images by using the built-in filters. This chapter is all about getting your creative juices flowing. We discover that it's quick and easy to create some great-looking images after you learn how it is done (see Figures 10.1 and 10.2). We also learn a bunch of tricks to make ordinary images turn into jaw-dropping masterpieces. Enough chitchat, let's go to it.

Figure 10.1
The original photo taken of a cut rose in the kitchen.

Figure 10.2
Applying a few artistic filters produces a painted rose.

WARNING

My conscience compels me to warn you that after you begin to creatively apply the Artistic filters in Photoshop Elements, you can become addicted and might spend hours, days, or even weeks in front of your computer going from one effect combination to another. You have been warned.

Creating Painterly Masterpieces

My favorite creative expression with Photoshop Elements is applying *painterly effects*. This effect turns photos into images that look like they were painted. I enjoy applying this effect to photographs and using them as covers for note cards.

The most important factor affecting the final result when applying the painterly effect has to do with the size of the original image in relationship to the filter that you are using. Most of the painterly effect filters in Photoshop Elements use a fixed-size brush when applying their painter effects; therefore, when the image is large, the effects produced are small. Sometimes, they can be so small that they're not noticeable. Likewise, if the image is small to begin with, the photo can become unrecognizable after the filter is applied. Here are some examples of this.

Figure 10.3 shows the original photo of a caboose (the photo is over 8 inches wide at 300dpi). When the Watercolor filter is applied to it at its default setting, the effect is almost not noticeable (see Figure 10.4). When I use the Resize command and change the resolution from 300dpi to 72dpi and reapply the same filter, the results are so heavy that I can no longer read the logo on the caboose (see Figure 10.5). The reason why the size of the image alters the effects of most painterly filters is because the filters apply their effects using a bitmap shape that is a fixed size. When the image is small, the bitmap shape is relatively large, and when the image is large, the shape is comparatively small; hence, there's little to no effect.

Figure 10.3
A large original photo of a caboose. (When did they stop painting them red?)

Figure 10.4
Applying the Watercolor filter to this large photo has little visible results.

Figure 10.5
With the image resized to make it much smaller, the same Watercolor filter makes the name on the caboose unreadable.

Evaluating the Effects of a Painterly Filter

A tricky part of working with painterly effects is the effect that the zoom setting has on the preview. Many times after applying the filter, it might appear that the filter has had little to no effect. As previously mentioned, this might be because the image is so large that the effects are minimized. But, before jumping to that conclusion, make sure that you are viewing the results at 100 percent (called Actual Pixels in the View menu). Figure 10.6 is a digital photograph of a water lily viewed at a zoom of 33.3 percent, and Figure 10.7 is the same flower after the Watercolor filter was applied to it. It appears that there were some minor changes, but the image still looks more like a photograph than a watercolor painting. When the zoom is changed to Actual Pixels, the watercolor effect becomes more apparent (see Figure 10.8).

Figure 10.6
Here's the original photo of a water lily viewed at a zoom setting of 33.3 percent.

Figure 10.7
Applying the Watercolor filter to this photo doesn't seem to have much effect when it's viewed at this zoom level.

Figure 10.8
Changing the zoom level to 100 percent (the Actual Pixels setting) enables us to view the effect that the Watercolor filter has on the photo.

As a rule, most of the painterly effects work better when the original image has high contrast and vivid colors. Figure 10.9 shows a Texas bluebonnet against a contrasting background. The application of the Artistic filter Watercolor produces the desired effect (see Figure 10.10).

Figure 10.9
The original photo taken of the Texas state flower: the bluebonnet.

Figure 10.10
The vivid colors of the original image enable the Watercolor filter to create a good painterly effect.

Other Painterly Effects

All the examples until now involved the Watercolor filter. I don't want to leave you with the impression that watercolor is the only painterly effect in the Artistic filter library. Here are some examples of other filters that produce excellent painterly effects.

Figure 10.11 was taken at Pioneer Farms in Austin, Texas (where else?). It is the bedroom of a log cabin built back in the mid-1800s. Although the photo looks fine, by using Poster Edges in the Artistic filers menu (at the default setting), the image appears more rustic (see Figure 10.12).

Figure 10.11
The log cabin's interior is almost too perfect for the subject matter.

Figure 10.12
Applying the Poster Edge filter gives the photo a more rustic look.

The photo of a blacksmith shop in Figure 10.13 is okay, but we can improve it by using the painterly effect filter Poster Edges. I must confess, I use this filter often. In this case, the filter wasn't used to make the photo look like a painting, but to enhance the overall image and make it suitable for placement in a brochure. The application of the Poster Edges filter adds punch to the photograph without adding enough of an effect to distract viewers (see Figure 10.14).

Figure 10.13
This photo of a blacksmith shop has good overall composition, but the similarity of the colors makes the image appear flat.

Figure 10.14
Although still retaining the appearance of a photograph, the application of the Poster Edges filter adds a little oomph to this photo.

Using Filters to Cover Up Poor Photos

Like it or not, in spite of your best efforts, some photos coming out of your camera are less than perfect. If it makes you feel better, I'm considered a good photographer and I am pleased if I get one great photo out of every 50 I take. Many times, the problem with your photos is out of your control. For example, the carpenter in Figure 10.15 was in a dimly lit room with light streaming in from behind him. Dim lighting further complicated focusing with a digital camera. As it turned out, the only way to get the shot was to brace the camera against a barn wall and accept the blurriness that accompanies a photo taken at $1/8^{th}$ of a second. The result was a blurry photo, but that doesn't mean we can't use it.

Figure 10.15
Normally, a photo like this could never be salvaged, but with the Artistic filters, we can perform a little pixel magic.

The first step is to enhance the soft photo prior to applying any of the painterly filters. This is much like putting on stage makeup: It looks grotesque up close, but it looks great from where the audience sits. In Figure 10.16, an obscene amount of Unsharp Masking (Filter, Sharpen, Unsharp Mask) is applied (200 percent at a 4-pixel radius) and then an equally obscene amount of Contrast (+40) is applied. It's grotesque at this point, but it will look better, I promise.

Figure 10.16
Although the amounts of sharpening and contrast are way over the top, the photo was in such poor condition that it looks better.

Next, the Rough Pastels filter (Filter, Artistic, Rough Pastels) is applied to the image. It gives the photo the appearance of being created by hand using oil pastels. Figure 10.17 was captured at 100 percent zoom (the Actual Pixels setting).

Figure 10.17
Applying the Rough Pastels filter disguises many of the photo's defects with its painterly effects.

Because this man is working at a turn-of-the-century farm, we can apply one final, but optional, touch to make the photo really fit into a brochure about this place: Select the Hue/Saturation control (Ctrl-U), and check the Colorize check box to create a sepia-tone print that looks like it belongs in the old west (see Figure 10.18).

Figure 10.18
The Colorize feature of the Hue/Saturation command gives the photo an antique appearance.

The photo in Figure 10.19 was taken in The Pantry Café—one of the oldest eateries in Los Angeles. I used to eat there when I was a kid—over 45 years ago! The photo (shown in Figure 10.19) was shot with the *Slow Synch* setting, which means that the camera's shutter was open a long time to get the darker parts of the dimly lit café, and it fired the flash to fill in the rest of the picture. Of course, when the shutter (I know a digital camera doesn't really have a shutter) was open for a relatively long time, all the hustle and bustle of a morning breakfast in a diner was a blur. So, is it a bad shot? Not if you have filters to turn it into a painting!

Figure 10.19
In a busy café, everything is blurred during the breakfast rush.

Figure 10.20
Applying the Watercolor filter and then the Poster Edges filter on top of that, produces an interesting painterly effect.

Combining Filters

I want to show you another example of combining filters to enhance a painterly effect. In Figure 10.21, I applied the Paint Dubs filter (Filter, Artistic) to the photo of Steve and his daughter, Stephanie. Next, I duplicated the background into a layer and applied Rough Pastels (Filter, Artistic) to the layer on the top. In the Layers palette, I changed the Blend mode to Overlay, which resulted in a great painterly effect without losing any image detail.

To wrap up this painterly session, we need to consider framing our work—with frames.

Figure 10.21
A combination of two painterly filters applied through layers resulted in a great photo of a dad and his daughter.

Framing Your Work

When you go to all the trouble of creating the effect of an image being painted, it sometimes helps to frame the final work of the effect. Photoshop Elements has a collection of frames that are helpful in this regard. To be honest, I have seen better collections than the ones in this product, but I'm not complaining—they came free with Elements.

If you say the word frame, most people think of a wooden rectangle that supports and surrounds a painting or photo. The Frame effects (Window, Effects, Frames) in Photoshop Elements (see Figure 10.22) provide some basic frames and some frames that are effects that give the rough-edged appearance of a painted work along the edges of an image, similar to the edge of the Pantry Café photo (refer to Figure 10.20). Although the actual frames are somewhat plain, there's a cute one that makes the photograph appear like it has photo corners on it (see Figure 10.23).

Figure 10.22
The Effects palette has many categories of effects. When Frames is selected, thumbnails of all the frame effects are displayed.

Figure 10.23
One of the frame effects makes the photo appear to have photo corners on it.

Other Painterly Options

Several other programs use the plug-in architecture of Photoshop Elements to provide additional painterly effects. One of them, Virtual Painter, costs almost as much as Elements, but it does a fantastic job of creating the illusion of a photo being painted with natural media, such as oils or watercolor. A big advantage of Virtual Painter is its variable brush size that changes to accommodate the physical dimensions of a photo. I included several examples of art that I created using this plug-in (see Figures 10.24, 10.25, and 10.26). This program is available at www.jasc.com.

If you are seriously into painting, you might consider these two other programs: Deep Paint (www.righthemisphere.com) and Procreate Painter (www.procreate.com). Deep Paint is a plug-in for Photoshop and Photoshop Elements, and Painter is a standalone application that acts so much like natural media that it's spooky.

Figure 10.24
The capitol of Texas has great doorknobs, so after I shot a photo of one, I applied a painterly effect to it.

Figure 10.25
A photo of Bull Creek Falls became a painting when I applied Virtual Painter's watercolor effect to it.

Figure 10.26
I applied Virtual Painter's Color Pencil setting to this panorama I made. I was surprised how well it came out.

Selective Color Removal for Effect

A cool trick to draw attention to something in a photo is to remove all the color in the photo with the exception of the subject of attention. In Photoshop, this is extremely easy to do. Just select Desaturate (which removes all the color information, but the image remains a color image) and then use the History brush to paint the color back. It isn't that hard to do the same thing in Elements; you just have to do it in a different way.

We'll test out this technique on a photo I took of some bluebonnets growing on a very unused spur (see Figure 10.27).

Figure 10.27
Bluebonnets are a common sight in Texas, so here's a way to draw attention to these beauties.

With the photo open, we create a new Adjustment layer—Hue/Saturation. When the dialog box opens, we move the Saturation slider to the extreme left. Figure 10.28 shows the result.

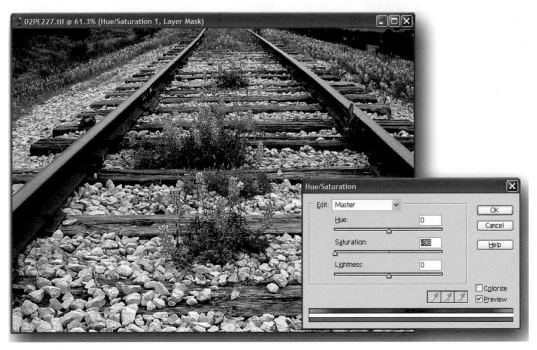

Figure 10.28
Applying a Hue/Saturation adjustment layer and moving the Saturation slider to zero removes all the color.

Select the Brush tool (B) and, with the color set to black (default), begin painting the flowers on the photo. The color begins to reappear. Magic? No. If you open the Layers palette, you can see that there's a Layer mask that is associated with the Hue/Saturation adjustment layer. Everything on that mask that's painted black is no longer visible to the adjustment layer and, therefore, its color can be seen again (see Figure 10.29). If you miss a spot, no problem; any area painted with white is seen by the adjustment layer and the color goes away.

Figure 10.29
Painting on the photo's adjustment layer with a black paintbrush restores the color everywhere on the image that is painted.

Summary

You can do so much more using filters that several books could be written about it and the topic still wouldn't be adequately covered. The important thing to remember is, when it comes to painterly effects, you must match the size of the image with the effect of the filter. It takes some practice, but I'm sure that you will get it. However, I am anxious to move on to the next chapter and discuss my favorite subject these days…the creation and editing of panoramas.

11 Creating Stunning Panoramas

Before I began using Photoshop Elements, I had limited experience creating panoramas. This was because making them without using a program specifically designed to create them was a major effort. After I began using Photoshop Elements' Photomerge feature, I was hooked. One of the challenges for me in writing this chapter is to remember that not everyone makes panoramas or photo montages. So, I promise not to get too carried away—maybe. But, after you read this chapter, you might get inspired!

Photomerge in Elements 2.0

Adobe made several improvements to Photomerge in Photoshop Elements 2.0. The most important improvement is the way that Photomerge handles memory. In the previous version, panoramas were generally limited to 2MB; if the image you were creating got much larger than that, the dreaded warning dialog box shown in Figure 11.1 appeared. Be aware that you can still run out of system resources and still be unable to complete the panorama, but for that to occur, you need to be using immensely large images. Other than that, about the only other changes are that Photomerge has been somewhat streamlined. If you used the original version, you had several options from which you had to select at the start. Thankfully, those options have been removed.

Figure 11.1
Even with the improved memory management in Photomerge's newest version, you can still run out of memory.

Taking Pictures for a Panorama

Of all the features and projects that can be accomplished by using Photoshop Elements, making a good panorama requires preparation on the photographic side. I spent the past six months learning how to do it, and I am just now beginning to get the hang of it. Don't let that last sentence scare you, however. Taking photos to be used in a panorama isn't *that* hard—it just takes some getting used to.

What You Need to Take Panoramas

Probably the most important item that you need to take panoramas is a tripod. Having said that, some of my best panoramic shots were taken without using a tripod; the panoramas came out because of my using a tripod substitute or just by dumb luck.

The second item you need to have is a camera that can lock the automatic exposure (AE) settings. This isn't critical either, but it helps. When you begin taking a series of photographs, if the camera is continually adjusting between the individual panels (photos), you end up with light and dark lines of demarcation, as shown in Figure 11.2. Because the idea is to create the sense of the photo being one continuous picture, it takes away from the effect.

Most digital cameras that I have worked with have an AE lock feature. If yours doesn't, it doesn't mean that you can't take panoramas; it just means that doing so will be a bit trickier.

Figure 11.2
If the camera's AE setting isn't locked, it can produce dark and light panels in the panorama.

General Rules for Taking Panorama Photos

Here are a couple of rules and general guidelines that might help you take good panorama photos.

Don't Get Too Close

When taking panoramic pictures, you want to get as far away from the subject as reasonable. The closer you are to the subject, the wider the setting on your zoom lens; this produces greater barrel distortion on each panel. If there's too much distortion, even Photomerge cannot avoid weird-looking gaps between each panel. So, get a good distance away from your subject and set your zoom lens so that it is at a less wide angle and more telephoto-like.

Controlling Overlap

Overlap is the next thing that you must consider. *Overlap* is like vitamins—you need just enough to get the job done. With too much overlap, the file becomes huge and the program doesn't do a good job in automatching the panels together. How much is enough? Most photographers agree that 20–30 percent overlap is about right. So, how do you calculate the overlap? It helps if your tripod has degree markings. My tripod doesn't have any markings (it's a really cheap tripod), so I use a method that seems to work. When I take the initial photograph, I note some point of reference in the LCD frame of my digital camera. As I rotate the camera (more on that in a moment), I try to make sure that the reference point remains in the right or left third of the frame (depending on which way I turn it).

When you turn the camera, make every effort to have the camera lens rotate around an imaginary axis. When I first started taking panoramic photos, I held the camera and turned my body. By doing that, I changed the angle of the camera in reference to the scenery that I was photographing. It is less important when the subject is a great distance away, but it becomes important when the subject matter is close.

We cover additional tips later in this chapter. Now, it's time to make a simple panorama.

Creating a Simple Panorama

For the first panorama, let's make a simple one from two photos. If you downloaded the files for this chapter, we will be using `right plane.jpg` and `left plane.jpg`:

1. In the File menu, select Create Photomerge. The dialog box that appears enables you to select the photos used in the panorama (see Figure 11.3). If any photos are already open in Photoshop Elements, they appear on this list. I strongly recommend that you have all of your images closed because any open photo uses memory resources. Click the Browse button and select the `right plane.jpg` and `left plane.jpg` files. The order of the files in this box is not important. Click OK.

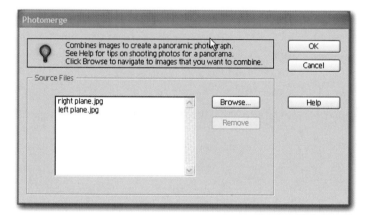

Figure 11.3
The images to be included in the panorama are selected from the Photomerge dialog box.

2. Photomerge works on the image for a few moments. How long this takes is a function of the size and number of the photos and the horsepower of your system. Because there are only two small photos in this example, the next (huge) dialog box appears relatively quickly (see Figure 11.4).

Figure 11.4
Use the Photomerge control dialog box to edit the panorama.

3. Because this image has only two photos, there's no need to be concerned about using the Perspective setting. Click the Advanced Blending button and click OK. The dialog box closes and a new untitled image window opens, similar to the one shown in Figure 11.5. Make a note of two errors in this panorama. First, it is a layer without a background; we correct that momentarily. Second, look carefully at the bottom-left portion of the yellow cowling and you can see that the pieces don't exactly match up. Why? Because I took these photos without a tripod and the position of the camera changed between photos.

187

Figure 11.5
Photomerge seamlessly (almost) made the two halves of the plane into a single image.

4. Flatten the panorama (select Layers, Flatten Image) and select the Crop tool (C).

5. To fill in the gaps, I used a combination of things. By creating rectangular selections, I was able to move large sections of grass and sky around using the Move tool (V) while holding the Alt key. (We learned about this in Chapter 5, "Dealing with Composition Problems And Distortion.") I then used the Clone tool (S) to cover up the edges and fill in the small spaces. When it was all filled in, I used the Crop tool to remove some of the rough edges, as shown in Figure 11.6.

Figure 11.6
An easy panorama made by using Photomerge and two photographs.

Creating a Panorama from Three Photos

Now, let's get fancier and make a panorama from three photos. If you want to try your hand at this, the files have been made available for download from this book's web page on the New Riders Publishing site:

1. By choosing File, Create Photomerge, we will be using the files labeled river right.jpg, river center.jpg, and river left.jpg. Use the Browse button to locate the three files and click OK. Figure 11.7 shows the Photomerge dialog box after it has stitched the pieces together.

Figure 11.7
This panorama is made by using three photos. It has some interesting challenges to overcome.

2. Photomerge has accurately stitched the three photos together in Normal mode. Because these three photos represent a medium-sized arc, the resulting panorama has flattened the perspective a bit. So, clicking the Perspective button causes the panorama panels to be distorted to restore the perspective of the original scene, as shown in Figure 11.8. If the screen had been really wide, the amount of distortion applied to the ends would have been much greater.

Figure 11.8
The Perspective feature distorts the ends of the panorama slightly to compensate for the curvature of the scene.

3. Because these photos are well balanced with regards to their overall lighting and color, it isn't necessary to select the Advanced Blending option, but if you like, go ahead. It just takes a bit longer to process the image when you finally make the panorama. Click OK. After a few moments, Elements creates the initial panorama, as shown in Figure 11.9.

Figure 11.9
The initial panorama from the three photos requires some work.

4. Several things need to be done next. First, from the Layer menu, choose Flatten Image. Next, crop the image. Some might think that it's a good thing to crop out the small piece of tree on the left side, but I left it because it helps frame the complete picture. Finally, from the Enhance menu, choose Auto Color Correction, which works well on this photo, as shown in Figure 11.10.

Figure 11.10
After you flatten, crop, and correct the color, the panorama looks pretty good.

5. I previously mentioned that locking the AE of your camera prevents the visible lines between the panels. Unfortunately, you'll notice the down side of this technique. The trees on the far right are really in the dark. Fortunately, Elements possesses some great tools to solve this problem.

6. In the Layers menu, choose New Adjustment Layer, Levels. When the Levels dialog box appears, change the settings to what's shown in Figure 11.11.

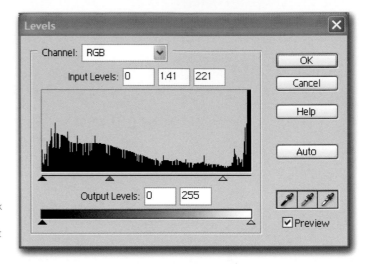

Figure 11.11
Using these settings makes the dark part of the panorama lighter. Unfortunately, it washes out the rest of the picture.

7. At this point, the panorama looks washed out. Now comes the cool stuff. The background image on the bottom remains unchanged because we are looking at it through the Levels adjustment layer. To prove it, open the Layers palette (F11) and click the eyeball icon on the top layer. The old photo is still there. Click the eyeball again to make the layer visible again. We need to find a way to remove the adjustment layer that's over the part that isn't too dark.

With the adjustment layer still selected, select the paintbrush and, assuming you have black selected as the paint color, begin painting the washed-out area. The color from the background can be seen again and, if you look carefully at the adjustment layer in the Layers palette, you can see that the mask portion of the layer is black wherever you painted the image (see Figure 11.12). At this point, paint all the washed-out area black. I also changed the opacity of the brush to about 40 percent and painted some of the trees on the right, just not the tree trunk (which was the darkest). If, after you paint something black, you must restore it, no problem. Change the brush color to white (X) and by painting the image, you restore the effect of the Adjustment palette.

Figure 11.12
Using the Brush tool, we are able to selectively apply the effect of the Levels adjustment layer to the dark side of the photo.

8. To wrap up this panorama, I applied a contrast setting of 9 and applied Unsharp Masking at a setting of 70 percent at a 1-pixel radius. The finished work is shown in Figure 11.13.

Figure 11.13
The finished panorama took only a few minutes to create.

A Challenging Panorama

Until now, we have panoramas from either two photos or from photos of natural settings that have few image-matching problems. What happens when you have photos that contain hard geometric lines? Let's find out.

The next panorama is made from three photos taken inside the historic Driskell Hotel in Austin, Texas. An image containing many subjects with hard lines and patterns can present some unique challenges, all of which can be overcome using Photoshop Elements:

1. When the files `Hotel Left`, `Hotel Right`, and `Hotel Middle` are loaded using Create Photomerge, they sometimes will automatch incorrectly, as shown in Figure 11.14. When this happens, it is a simple matter to grab the individual photos with the Move tool and drag them to the thumbnail gallery above the main workspace, as shown in Figure 11.15. It isn't necessary to move them all up there—just enough so that you have room to move and match the pieces.

Figure 11.14
Sometimes, the automatching feature of the Create Photomerge command gets confused and needs help.

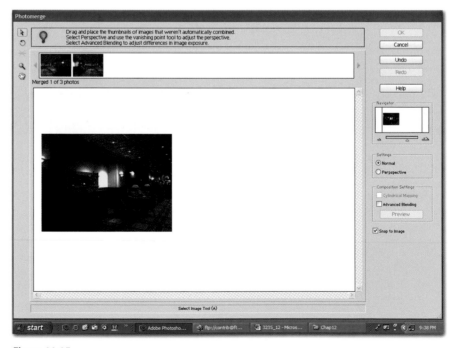

Figure 11.15
By dragging the photos to the preview area and bringing them back one by one, most times it's possible to assist automatching and have it work great.

2. The next problem is that the normal stitching of the Photomerge cannot correctly compensate for the distortion of the wide-angle lens and the close proximity of the subject as shown by the part of carpet pattern that doesn't match (see Figure 11.16). Another problem of the image is that it has too much overlap.

Figure 11.16
Using the Normal setting causes a mismatch where the carpet and ceiling in the different panels meet.

3. If you change the setting from Normal to Perspective, the program attempts to distort the end panels so that the perspective of the different panels match, as shown in Figure 11.17.

Figure 11.17
Looking like a bow tie, the Perspective setting looks weird, but the carpet and ceiling panels of the panorama match better.

4. When the Perspective button is enabled, another option becomes available: Cylindrical Mapping. This option flattens the image, much like you would flatten out a map of the earth to display it. The result with the hotel panorama also looks a little weird (see Figure 11.18), but it produces a smooth transition between panels.

Figure 11.18
Cylindrical Mapping reduces the transition, but as we will see, it exacerbates another distortion.

Figure 11.19 shows the panorama created using the Cylindrical Mapping setting after it is cropped. Notice the bending distortion in the carpet and the ceiling. Sometimes, the content of the image does not give you the option of using Normal mode. Figure 11.20 shows the resulting mismatch of the floor pattern using the same panorama content, but with Normal selected instead of Perspective.

Figure 11.19
The Cylindrical Mapping flattens the panorama but introduces a fish-eye type of distortion in the middle of the image.

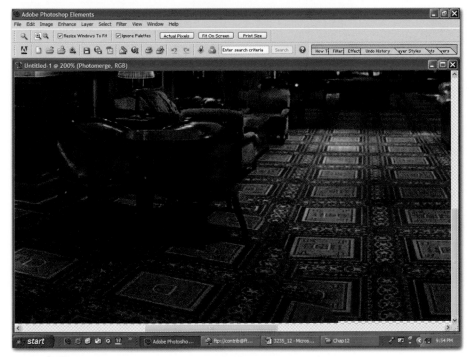

Figure 11.20
Here is a close-up of the type of mismatch that can occur when either of the two perspective options is not used.

Panorama Examples

I wanted to show you some of the projects that I have created with the newest version of Photomerge in Elements 2.0.

Figure 11.21 doesn't look much like a panorama, but it was created from three photos. The sky, which was behind me when I took the photo of the Capitol building, is also a panorama. It took only a few minutes to replace the overcast sky that was behind the Capitol with the other image.

Figure 11.21
Not all panoramas have to be wide and narrow. This one is a combination of two panoramas (each with three photos). One is the Capitol and the other is the sky.

Of course, some panoramas are very wide and narrow. There is a small town in Texas, called Smithville, whose claim to fame in recent times is that it was the town where the movie *Hope Floats* was filmed. One of the charming aspects of this tiny hamlet is that several buildings in the town still have billboards that date back to the 1940s, similar to the one for the Star Biscuit Company (shown in Figure 11.22). It was made from five photographs using the Normal setting. When a panorama gets this wide, Perspective gets completely confused and wildly distorts the panorama's ends.

Figure 11.22
This old building is a marvelous combination of textures and time periods. This panorama was made from five photos.

Multiple Panels Overlaid

The challenge I had with the Falls on Bull Creek panorama was that diffused light from the overcast sky had made the falls dark. The solution was to take two sets of panoramic photos. I shot the first set using the sky as the light source. The second set of photos I took by using the spot setting on my camera so that the exposure would be adjusted correctly for the waterfall portion, even though the sky would be overexposed (washed out). I created two separate panoramas from the photos and then merged the two panoramas together using layers in Elements. Figure 11.23 shows the final result.

Figure 11.23
This photo was made from two sets of photos taken at two different exposure settings.

How Big Can You Make Them?

When it comes to making panoramas, this it the most frequently asked question. There isn't a really good answer to that. Because I like to make panoramas that print flat, I limit my photos to take in no more than 180 degrees. Figure 11.24 is a monster of an image that was made from seven photos.

Figure 11.24
This monster panorama, made from seven photos, was a whopping 60MB in size while I was working on it.

First Panorama

The panorama shown in Figure 11.25 was the result of incredibly good luck. We were on the hill overlooking the Acropolis on one of the clearest days in almost a decade. I had my 2 megapixel Nikon Coolpix, and there was an old concrete cylinder on which to rest the camera for the panorama. This was the first panorama that I ever created—after this, I was hooked.

Figure 11.25
Without a tripod, and using a relatively small digital camera, I took the photographs used to make this panorama.

Summary

I could write another 30 pages on this subject, but I have it on good authority that most of the readers are not as interested (read: obsessed) with panoramas as I am. But, maybe this chapter has given you the bug...

Now that we know how to stitch photos together, it's time to learn how to add and remove material (people, places, and things) from photographs.

12 Rearranging and Replacing Objects in Photos

Rearranging objects in a photo is one of the most popular things users like to do with Photoshop Elements. We all have some favorite photos of ourselves or of a loved one that also includes someone we don't want in the picture. Before digital photo editing, removing the "jerk" from the photo was crudely resolved with a pair of scissors. Figure 12.1 shows a classic example I created almost six years ago. It was my first experience using the Clone tool. When I was able to seamlessly (well, almost seamlessly) remove the guy from the photo, I was hooked. I have been removing, adding, and generally rearranging people and objects in photographs ever since. In this chapter, we learn how to use the many Photoshop Elements selection tools to isolate the part of the photograph that needs to be removed or moved. Because these tools are critical to this type of photo editing, we spend more time learning how and when to use them.

Figure 12.1
Breaking up might be hard to do in real life, but with Photoshop Elements, it's not that hard to make people disappear.

Harnessing the Power of Selections

Until now, we used selections to isolate color or other image corrections to a specific area of a photograph. We also used selections for creating special effects, such as a soft-focus background. Most of these selections were simple. To select a complex shape, such as a person or a pet, requires more precision. This is why Photoshop Elements provides a large assortment of tools that enable us to precisely select the portion of the image that we want to work on and protect other parts of the image. To be able to use these tools effectively, we will spend more time than usual learning just how selections work and how to use them.

Understanding Selections

As previously mentioned, Photoshop Elements has a large number of different tools whose only purpose is to define the part of the image on which we want to work. The defined area is called a *selection*. All the tools used to make the selections are know as *selection tools*, with names such as Magnetic Lasso and Magic Wand. If this is your first time using Photoshop Elements, don't let the large number of selection tools and their strange-sounding names overwhelm you. We learn this one step at a time, beginning with a look at what a selection actually is.

The concept of selection is something that we all have used at one time or another. I have heard many analogies to the selection. Here are a few: If you have ever used a stencil, you have used a selection. The stencil enables you to apply paint to the part of the material while protecting the rest of the material. Another example of a selection that's closer to home (literally) is the use of masking tape to mask off parts of a room on which you don't want to get paint—which, for me, would be the whole room. Selections in Photoshop Elements act just like a stencil or masking tape when it comes to applying any effect to an image. So, let's look at the most basic of the selection tools: the Marquee tools.

Introducing Marquee Tools

The Marquee tools shown in Figure 12.2 appear at the top of the Toolbox. They can be used to create selections in the shapes of rectangles and ellipses. If you access the Options bar, you can also create unique selections in fixed shapes.

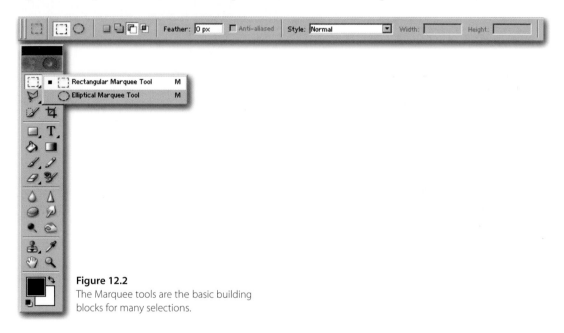

Figure 12.2
The Marquee tools are the basic building blocks for many selections.

Although we used these tools in previous chapters, let's see how these basic selection tools can create some neat stuff. For the upcoming exercise, I recommend that you download the file Sunflower.jpg from the New Riders Publishing web site. After you do that, let's jump right in and create a visual effect by producing small glass balls filled with sunflowers. To make them, we use the Elliptical Marquee tool:

1. Open the file named Sunflower.jpg.

2. Select the Elliptical Marquee tool in the Toolbox by placing the cursor over the Marquee Tools button and clicking the small black triangle in the lower-right corner of the button to open the tool selection.

3. Place the cursor near the center of the photograph (not the sunflower). Click and hold the left mouse button and, while still holding the button, press and hold both the Shift and the Alt keys. Drag the mouse outwards to form a circle roughly in the position that's shown in Figure 12.3. Release the mouse button and then release the keys. The edge of the selection is marked by flashing black and white marquee that has come to be called "marching ants."

Figure 12.3
The selection created is a perfect circle surrounding the sunflower.

4. Choose Edit, Copy (or Ctrl-C). Only the contents of the photo inside the selection will be copied to the Clipboard.

5. Choose Edit, Paste (or Ctrl-V) and the selection marquee disappears. Open the Layers palette to see the new layer. Because we will need the selection that was lost when we used the Paste command, choose Select, Reselect and the marquee returns. We need this selection to be in place before we apply the next filter or the shape of the sphere will distort.

6. Select Filter, Distort, Spherize and use the default setting of 100 percent, as shown in Figure 12.4.

Figure 12.4
The selection enables the Spherize filter to be applied to the top layer without distorting the shape.

7. Turn off the visible selection marquee (Ctrl-H) to make it easier to see what we are doing next. Select the Dodge tool (O) from the Toolbox and, in the Options bar, select a soft brush that is 100 pixels and ensure that the range is Midtones at 50 percent Exposure. To make this look like a glass sphere, we must lighten the edges. The one I am working on is shown in Figure 12.5.

TIP

The trick to this effect is to apply just the edge of the brush inside of the selection edge. As human viewers, we expect there to be more light reflected near the top upper-left part of the sphere, so apply additional stokes of the Dodge tool here.

Figure 12.5
Applying the Dodge tool along the edges defines the edge of the selection.

8. Select the Move tool (V) and, while holding the Shift key, click and drag the upper-right handle of the glass ball and make it smaller so that it looks like the one shown in Figure 12.6. When it's the correct size, double-click it to apply the resizing (called a *transform*).

9. Now for the fun part. Deselect any selection that remains (Ctrl-D). In the Layers palette, select the background and apply the Polar Coordinates filter, which is located in the Distort category of the Filters menu at its Rectangular to Polar setting (the default) (see Figure 12.6).

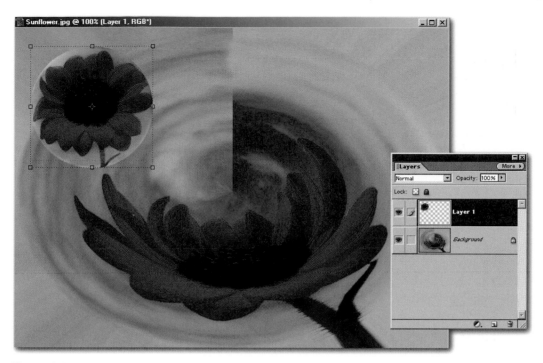

Figure 12.6
The finished sunflower in a glass ball on its layer is now independent of the background.

10. At this point, we have accomplished all we need to demonstrate the technique of selecting an image and using the Clipboard to make it into a layer. I finished the image by using the Smudge tool (F) to remove the hard vertical line that's produced by the Polar filter. The Smudge tool smears pixels like dragging a finger through wet paint. To smear the hard line out of existence, I set the brush size large and dragged it across the line from right to left and then back. Next, I selected the sunflower ball and, with the Eraser tool (E) set to a low opacity (17 percent), I partially erased the background of the sunflower ball so that viewers could get the impression that they were looking through the glass. Figure 12.7 shows the finished image.

Figure 12.7
This exercise looks like something Salvador Dali would have loved to create.

Using Marquee Tools: Some Tips and Tricks

So, what did we just do in the previous exercise? You used several keyboard combinations, which I didn't explain at the time. Here's what you were actually doing when you used those keys:

- **Shift key**—When enabled *after* the mouse button is pushed, the Shift key forces (constrains) the Ellipse tool to a circle and the Rectangle marquee to a square. If you don't do this, it is nearly impossible to get a square- or a circle-shaped selection.

- **Alt (Option) key**—Depressing this key *after* the mouse button is clicked makes the marquee produced by the tool expand outward from the center. If you didn't have this option, it could take forever to get the selection centered.

TIP

At any point while creating a selection (without lifting your finger off the mouse), depressing the spacebar enables you to reposition the selection marquee by dragging it around with your mouse. Release the spacebar and you continue to create the marquee selection.

The Marquee tool modifier keys are unique in that the action they perform is relative, depending if they are pressed before or after the mouse button is clicked. If the modifier key is pressed before the mouse button, the action changes.

The Marquee Tool Options Bar

If this is your first time working with Photoshop, the Marquee tools might seem to be limited. After all, how often will you need to select a square, rectangle, ellipsis, or circle? In fact, you can create about any shape imaginable using these tools if you learn how to use some of the features found in the Options bar, shown in Figure 12.8.

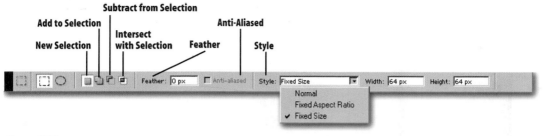

Figure 12.8
The Options bar gives the Marquee tools more capability.

The Marquee tools interact with existing selections in four different ways. The default setting for the Marquee tools is New Selection. When it is selected, any time you make a selection, it replaces the current selection (if one exists). The ones you will use most often are the Add To and Subtract settings. Their operations are obvious, I hope. By using the Marquee tools in combination with these modes, it's possible to make almost any irregular shape imaginable. The last setting, Intersect with Selection, is unusual in that, when it is dragged over an existing selection, only the part of the selection that is under the new selection remains. Don't worry about it; you won't use it very often.

Feathering the Selections

Until now, we have been considering selections that have a hard and defined edge. The circle mask used in the previous exercise had an anti-aliased option, which feathered (smoothed) the edges of the circle we made (it also works with rounded rectangle selections). Many times can arise when you want to make a selection that has a soft edge. When you are removing someone or something from one photograph into another by using a feathered selection, the subject being moved blends into the picture more smoothly. Be careful with the amount of feathering you apply to the mask. Usually, just a few pixels are sufficient. If you put in a large amount of feathering, the object looks like it has a glow or is furry.

I created Figure 12.9 using a selection I made with the Magnetic Lasso tool (which we learn about in the next section). After making the selection, I applied three different settings of feathering and copied the image to the Clipboard with each of the three different featherings from the original photograph. Of the three copies of Michelle, the one on the left was made using a selection that was not feathered; the middle image used a feather of 3 pixels; and the one on the right had a Feathering value of 9. The feathering effect produced by any particular setting is controlled by the size of the image. For example, the original photograph of Michelle was taken with a Nikon Coolpix 990; as a result, the image is relatively large. On a larger image like this, a 3-pixel feather has less of an effect than the same feather setting would have on a much smaller image. Although the higher feathering setting in the image on the right loses tiny detail in her hair, it gives it a desirable softening effect. But remember that this smoothing effect on the hair isn't always a good thing.

Figure 12.9
Feathering produces much softer edges when a subject is copied out of a photograph.

Although many things can be done with the Marquee selection tools, they represent a really basic tool. When you need to create an irregular-shaped selection, consider the Lasso tools.

Rounding Up the Lasso Tools

The Lasso tools, which are located under the Marquee tools in the Toolbox, are a collection of three different tools that you can use to draw both straight-edged and freehand edges when making an irregularly shaped selection. The three tools (shown in Figure 12.10) are

- Lasso tool

- Polygonal Lasso tool

- Magnetic Lasso tool

Unlike the Marquee tools, which produce closed shapes, the Lasso tools let you draw a meandering path around a subject and, when you are done, you either let go of the mouse or double-click it (this depends on the tool you are using). Photoshop will make a straight line back to the starting point to complete the selection.

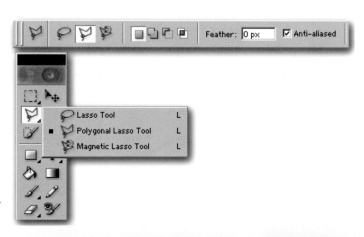

Figure 12.10
Unlike the other Marquee tools, the Lasso tools enable you to define any irregular shape that you can draw.

The Lasso and Polygonal Lasso Tools

All these tools act in a similar fashion. In the grand scheme of things, the Lasso tool is designed to draw freehand selections and the Polygonal Lasso tool creates a selection made out of many straight lines. Well, in truth, the Lasso tool can act like a Polygonal tool when the Alt key is held; in the same manner, the Polygonal tool operates like a freehand tool when the Alt key is held. So why have both a Freehand and a Polygonal tool? It's a great mystery.

The Magnetic Lasso

The Magnetic Lasso tool is similar to its two Lasso-tool cousins, except it has the capability to automatically detect the edge (in most cases), which can save you so much work. And (do I need to say it?) if you hold the Alt (Opt) key, it becomes a Freehand tool just like the Lasso tool.

As previously mentioned, the idea behind the operation of the Lasso tools is for you to take your mouse and outline the part of the image you want selected. Most folks use one of the Lasso tools to isolate a part of a photograph so they can copy it into another image. Because you are essentially drawing an outline with a mouse, ask yourself this simple question: Can I sign my name with a mouse? If your answer is yes, you need a date. If your answer is no, and you are going to be creating many selections, seriously consider buying a graphics tablet. The industry standard for graphic tablets is Wacom Technology (www.wacom.com). These tablets used to be expensive, but now some models can be purchased for less than $100. Does this mean that you can't use Lasso selection tools without a graphics tablet? Of course not; it's just much easier if you have one. With that matter settled, let's consider some ideas on how to make better selections.

Getting the Best Selections (In the Least Amount of Time)

Whether doing art layout for work or for community projects (read: free), I have spent the past ten years making selections and the resulting composite images. In that time, I developed a short list of "dos" and "dont's" that I'll share with you to help you make great selections.

Do Make a First Rough Cut Selection

If the image is large enough so that it does not fit on the screen when you view it at 100 percent (Actual Pixels setting), shift the zoom level to Fit On Screen using either Ctrl-0 (zero) or double-click the Hand tool in the Toolbox and make a rough selection. It doesn't matter which selection tool you use. You just want to get as close as you can without spending too much time doing it. This selection gets you in the ballpark.

Zoom and Move

Set the Zoom to Actual Pixels. Use either Ctrl-Alt-0 (zero) or double-click the Zoom tool in the Toolbox. I know, the image no longer fits on the screen, but it doesn't matter. There are several ways to move around when you're this close, but probably the best way I know of is to press the spacebar and your currently selected tool becomes the Hand tool (as long as you keep the spacebar depressed). This is a lifesaver when you are drawing a selection and you find that you have come to the edge of the part displayed on the screen. When that happens, press the spacebar, drag the image to expose more of the subject on the screen, and when you let go of the spacebar, you return to your selection just were you left it.

Adding Some and Taking Some

Using the Add To Selection and Subtract From Selection modes begin to shape the selection to fit the subject you are trying to isolate. Here is a trick that saves time when doing this. First, instead of clicking the buttons in the Options bar, use the key modifiers to change between modes. Pressing the Shift key changes the selection mode to Add To and the Alt key changes it to Subtract From. Just remember that these modifier keys must be pressed *before* you click the mouse. Second, in the Options bar, pick Add To as a mode so you need only to use the modifier key when you want to subtract from the selection.

Get in Close

On some areas, you might need to zoom in at levels even greater than 100 percent. (Photoshop goes up to 1,600 percent, which allows you to select microbes and stray electrons.) Now and again, you must return to Fit To Screen just to keep a perspective on this entire image. Speaking of keeping a perspective, all the time you are improving the selection, keep in mind the ultimate destination for the image you are selecting. Here are some examples of factors that should affect the degree of exactness you want to invest in your selection:

- How close are the background colors of the image you are selecting and the current background colors? If they are roughly the same colors, investing a lot of time producing a detailed selection doesn't make much sense because a feathered edge works just fine.

- Will the final image be larger, smaller, or the same size? If you are going to be making the current image larger, every detail will stick out like the proverbial sore thumb. So, any extra time you spend to make the selection as exact as possible will pay off big. If you are reducing the size of the subject, many tiny details will become lost when it's resized, so again, don't invest too much time in the selection.

- Is this a paid job or a freebee? Creating a complex selection is a time-consuming process. I once spent nearly half a day on a single selection.

Let's Lasso Somebody

I can run on about these tools for many more pages, but I am not going to. I'm going to get some coffee while you make what is possibly your first freehand selection. This involves a groomsman named Jon in a cluttered church office wearing a ridiculously overpriced rental tuxedo. If his mother is going to frame this photograph, the background must be replaced with something less cluttered:

1. Download and open the picture labeled TuxedoJon.psd. I made this sample image much smaller than the original so it wouldn't gag your system.

2. Choose the Magnetic Lasso tool and get as close as you can to the edge of his tuxedo. Click and drag a line around him until it looks like the one that's shown in Figure 12.11. If you have any problems with creating the selection with the Magnetic Lasso tool, see the sidebar, "Controlling the Magnetic Lasso." After you are finished, Jon will be selected, but because we need to select the background, invert the selection by using Shift-Ctrl-I.

Figure 12.11
We can quickly select Jon from the background by using the Magnetic Lasso tool.

3. If you want to do this exercise without all the work, I included a selection I made inside the PSD image. To load the selection, choose Select, Load Selection. When the dialog box appears, change the values to match those shown in Figure 12.12 (make sure to check the Invert check box).

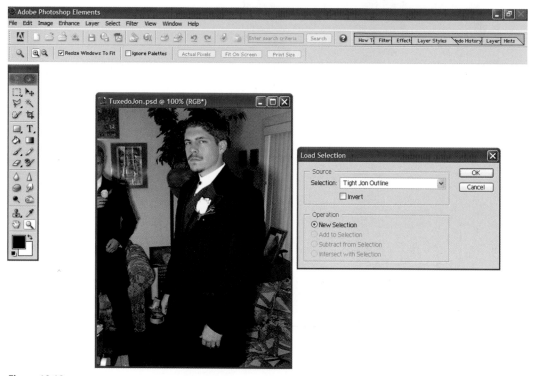

Figure 12.12
You can load a saved selection, which saves a lot of time.

4. One of the ways to emphasize the subject is to blur the background using Gaussian blur. In this case, the problem with this approach is the background is so cluttered that, by the time you get it blurred enough to do the job, it looks sort of surreal. On top of that, Jon and the couch on his right are the same distance from the camera so it doesn't look right. Let's replace the background with a different one. Download and open the file Background.jpg. When it opens, select the entire image (Ctrl-A), copy the image to the Clipboard (Ctrl-C) and close the image. (Don't save the changes.)

5. With Jon's photo selected, choose Edit, Paste Into. Wow! The photograph has replaced the previous cluttered one! Select the Move tool (V) in the Toolbox, and move the background image around to position it, as shown in Figure 12.13.

Figure 12.13
The new background is less cluttered than the original.

Using a selection allows for a background replacement without losing the original background.

Controlling the Magnetic Lasso

The Magnetic Lasso tool is a great timesaver when it comes to making selections. Essentially, as you move the tool along an edge that you want to select, the tool is constantly looking for and creating a selection along the edge. On a high contrast, well-defined edge, it works better than advertised. On edges that are poorly defined, in that the colors inside and outside the edge are very near the same color, it needs some help from you.

Using the tool is relatively simple. Click once on the point where you want to begin the selection. This point is called a *fastening point*. Now, move the tool (slowly and without holding the mouse button) along the edge. Fastening points appear along the edge of the selection as the computer tries to automatically determine where the edge is. At some point, the computer will guess wrong. When it does, stop and press the Backspace key. Each time you press this key, Photoshop removes the last point on the selection. Continue to do this until you get to a point on the selection that is on the actual edge.

You can try it again, but usually, when the Magnetic tool is guessing wrong, there's either a low-contrast edge or there is something nearby (not on the edge) that is pulling the tool away from the edge.

At this point, you have several choices. You can change the settings in the Options bar, click your way through it (I'll explain in a moment), or temporarily change Lasso tools. I rarely recommend changing the options settings. So, here is what I recommend you try. When you hit a rough patch, if the edge is irregular (lots of ins and outs), you can click each of the points that define the edge, which puts them close together. Another option is to temporarily switch to the Lasso tool by holding the Alt (Option) key and dragging the mouse along the edge with the mouse button depressed. If the edge that is confusing the Magnetic Lasso tool is basically composed of straight lines, you can temporarily switch to the Polygonal tool by holding the Ctrl key and clicking from point to point.

TIP

In images where the subject being selected is close to the color of the background so that it blends with the shadows or background, the Magnetic Lasso tool might not be the best tool to use. To get a good selection, the Magnetic Lasso tool needs a fairly distinctive edge with which to work.

Saving and Loading Selections

In the previous exercise, you had the opportunity to load a selection rather than create it yourself. After making that particular selection (which only took about five minutes), I saved it as part of the Photoshop file. If a selection is not saved as a selection, it is lost as soon as the file is closed, even if the file is saved as a Photoshop PSD file.

The Alpha Channel

So, how do you save a selection? If you invest a lot of time making a selection, it seems reasonable that you would want to save it. The process is simple, but before I tell you how to do it, I must introduce a term that you might have heard before: the *alpha channel*. Sounds like the name of a science fiction-oriented program channel on your local cable TV. The alpha channel is not a channel at all, but the name assigned by Apple (who created it) for additional storage space in a graphics file format called Tagged Image Format File (TIFF). Why is it called alpha channel? The truth be known. When Apple created the concept of the channel, it wasn't sure what it was going to be used for until Adobe latched on to it and made it into the general purpose storage for selections (and what all that has become). Although it is still technically referred to as an alpha channel to differentiate it from the red, green, and blue channels, Adobe and the rest of those working in the graphics industry just call it a channel. How many alpha channels can fit into a Photoshop Elements file? Good question—how big of a file can you live with? For all practical purposes, there's no limit to the number of additional channels that can be included in a TIFF or Photoshop file.

Saving a Selection

After spending much time creating a selection, as a rule, you'll want to save it. Choose Select, Save Selection. This action opens the dialog box that's shown in Figure 12.14. If the image already has an existing channel, you can add your new selection to the existing ones, or more than likely, you will be saving to a new channel. Choose New and give the channel a descriptive name. In the case of the one in Figure 12.14, I used the one of Michelle that you saw back in Figure 12.9. Three selections were already stored in the image, but there's always room for a new one. You must save the image as a Photoshop (PSD) or a TIFF (TIF) file to save the channel information. If you don't, Photoshop gives you a single obscure warning that some features will not be saved in the format that you have chosen.

Figure 12.14
The Save Selection dialog box.

Loading a Selection

The next time you open the file, the selection won't be on the image. To get it, you must choose Select, Open, and pick the name of the alpha channel that you or someone else tucked away into the image. This might surprise you, but many stock photography

NOTE

If you save a file in any format other than TIFF or Photoshop (PSD), any selection information that is part of the file will be lost.

companies offer selections in their photos. Two different companies that offer photographs with selections that immediately come to mind are Photospin (www.photospin.com), which is a great online photo subscription service, and Hemera (www.hemera.com), which offers large collections of photo objects on CDs (lots and lots of CDs).

Magic Wand Tool Magic

The Magic Wand tool is great for making selections of areas containing similar colors. The problem with this tool is not the tool itself, but the fact that many users have no idea how it works and, therefore, are disappointed when the "magic" doesn't work. So, let's figure out how this tool works and then do some cool stuff with it.

The first fact to learn about the Magic Wand tool is—no magic! (Were you surprised?) Until now, all the selection tools we used involved either closed shapes or lassos that surround the subject to be selected. The Magic Wand tool acts a little like dropping a stone into a calm pool of water. The selection, like ripples of water, spreads outward from the starting point. It continues radiating outward, selecting similar (and adjacent) colored pixels until it reaches pixels whose color/shade is so different from the starting point that they can't be included. If you complete the next exercise, the Magic Wand tool will make more sense.

An Exercise in Pane (Window Pane, That Is)

In this exercise, we use the Magic Wand tool (W) and a few other Photoshop Elements features to create a photo composite from two photographs. In this case, I have an excellent exterior photo taken on a bright summer day in a rural Texas town, but I cannot see inside the building. I also have a good photo I took of a stairway in Ybor City in Florida. Our job is to combine the two images into a photo that can be used in a brochure to make people aware of problems with urban decay in the inner city:

1. Download and open the file named Old Windows.jpg and select the Magic Wand tool (located in the Toolbox).

2. Ensure the Contiguous check box in the Options bar is checked and change the Tolerance setting to 30. Click in the center window pane. The selection instantly expands to select all the black pixels in the pane, as shown in Figure 12.15. Because the Contiguous check box was enabled, the selection had to stop at the edge of the window pane.

Figure 12.15
The Magic Wand tool quickly selects all the black pixels in the single window pane.

3. To select the rest of the window panes, choose Select, Similar. Now Photoshop Elements selects all the pixels in the image that are within the Tolerance setting. Because no other black pixels are in the image, all the pixels in the window panes are selected (see Figure 12.16).

Figure 12.16
The Magic Wand tool quickly selects all the black pixels in this photograph.

Tips on Using the Magic Wand Tool

One of the first things you might run into when working with the Magic Wand tool is this: You click in an area and the Magic Wand tool will not produce a uniform selection, but will instead create many little selections. These little selection "islands" are caused when the difference between the color value of the starting point is greater than the color value of the pixels that make up these islands. You can resolve this issue in several ways. You could click all the individual points with the Magic Wand tool until they are all gone. However, that is not the most efficient way to do it, and I am embarrassed to admit how many times I have done just that. Here is the right way to do it: If the colors you are selecting are really different from the rest of the image, you can either choose Select, Similar or try increasing the Tolerance setting and try reselecting the same area. The problem with both of these approaches is that, many times, the selection begins to appear in the part of the image that we do not want selected. If the selection goes too far into the part of the image that you don't want selected (especially at the edge), here's another trick you can try. Did you know that when you use the Similar command, Photoshop uses the current Tolerance setting to determine which pixels can be included in the selection? This means that after you do an initial selection with the Magic Wand tool, you can lower the Tolerance setting to a low value, such as 4 to 8, and when you use Similar, it adds only colors that are much closer to the original starting point. Still, sometimes the selection islands are there because areas of vastly different colors exist. In this case, select a Marquee tool, hold the Shift key (Add To Selection), and drag a selection shape over the islands. That should resolve the issue.

4. Download and open the file named `Old Stairs.jpg`. Select the entire image (Ctrl-A). Copy the image to the Clipboard (Ctrl-C). Close the file without saving any changes.

5. With the Old Windows image selected, choose Edit, Paste Into. The photograph of the stairs now appears to be viewable through the window panes, as shown in Figure 12.17. With the Move tool, you can move the stairs photograph around. So far, this exercise is similar to the exercise we did with Jon in the tuxedo, so let's get creative.

Figure 12.17
Using the Paste Into command, we are able to put stairs into the window.

Replacing an Overcast Sky

Taking photographs on an overcast day is always a mixed blessing. Because of the clouds, the illumination is diffused—that's good. Because of the clouds, the horizon on a landscape photograph is uninteresting at best. Using the Magic Wand selection tool enables you to replace most overcast skies with an artificial one that you either create using Photoshop or using another photograph of a sky with clouds taken on a clear day.

Here's how it is done:

1. Download and open the file Rest in peace.psd. Choose the Magic Wand tool (W) in the Toolbox. Change the Tolerance setting to 70. This high setting ensures that all the areas around the branches will be tightly selected. (If you want, you can load the selection that is contained in the file.) Uncheck the Contiguous box in the Options bar. Click the tool on the sky in the upper-right quadrant. The initial selection made by the Magic Wand tool also selected some flowers and other parts of the photo besides the sky (see Figure 12.18). We'll fix that in the next step.

Figure 12.18
The Magic Wand tool selects all the overcast sky and more.

2. Choose the Rectangle Marquee tool and, in the Options bar, choose the Subtract From Selection button. Click and drag a marquee over all the area in the lower part of the photograph that doesn't contain any sky. Now only the sky is selected. In Figure 12.19, I selected the Selection Brush tool (which produces a red overlay when Mask Mode is selected in the Options bar) to show the finished selection. Personally, I find the selection marquee distracting, so you might want to turn it off (Ctrl-H).

Figure 12.19
With only the sky selected, you can replace it with another sky.

3. Open the file clouds.jpg. Select the entire image (Ctrl-A) and copy it to the Clipboard (Ctrl-C). Close the image without saving it.

4. Back to the original image. From the Edit menu, choose Paste Into (Shift-Ctrl-V) and the contents of the Clipboard appear in the selection, as shown in Figure 12.20.

Figure 12.20
We have a new sky to replace the overcast sky in the original photograph.

5. We're not done yet—this is the cool part. Select the Move tool (V) and click the sky that you just added. You can drag it around the selection. In Figure 12.21, I moved it up as far as I could so the clouds matched the existing foreground better. When the replacement sky is where you want it, remove the selection (Ctrl-D). It becomes a permanent part of the image.

Figure 12.21
Using the Move tool, you can position the replacement sky inside of the selection.

Summary

In this chapter, we learned how to use the selection tools to isolate parts of an image so that we can remove or replace them with something else. We learned that although making a selection can be time consuming, it is possible to save the selection as part of the Photoshop Elements file format (*.psd) so that all the work you invested into the selection isn't lost. It might take you some practice to get good at making selections, but the time that you invest in this all-important skill helps you make better compositions and montages with your photographs.

Next, we jump into the art form that will make your photography very popular: retouching and repairing photographs. This is the neat stuff that makes those of us who are older look younger (which I greatly appreciate) and also tidies up physical imperfections.

13 Retouching Photographs

How to retouch photographs is the subject of many books. When I say that I'm going to retouch a photo, that very phrase conjures up thoughts of doing everything from making someone look ten pounds thinner to making a model look so different that even her own mother wouldn't recognize her.

In this chapter, we briefly explore four general areas. First, we're going look at some ideas for taking better pictures with our cameras. Second, we consider enhancing existing features. Next, we tackle the trickier topic of removing or concealing unflattering features on the subject. Finally, we look at adding objects into our photos.

Photo Tips for Better Pictures

One of the best changes you can make doesn't even involve Photoshop Elements. I am referring to suggestions to make the people in your photographs look better, which ultimately makes your work with Elements easier. When I looked up books on the subject of photography on Amazon.com, more than 1,000 titles were retrieved. Obviously, we are not going to cover all photography in this chapter. In this section, I want to touch on some basic suggestions and examples that might help you get better pictures and spend less time trying to fix them in Photoshop Elements. If you learn nothing else in this chapter except the following quote, you will have learned a lot.

"If your pictures aren't good enough, you're not standing close enough."
Robert Kapra
American Photographer, 1944

Decide on the Subject Before You Shoot

Two principal motivations exist for people taking photographs: to capture a moment in time (see Figure 13.1) or to prove that they have been somewhere (see Figure 13.2). Whatever the subject or theme of your picture, make sure that you have an idea of what it is you want to capture as you look through the viewfinder. If you don't, it shows (see Figure 13.3).

Figure 13.1
At a wedding, there isn't much question as to what the subject of the photograph should be.

Figure 13.2
This photo, taken on the set of *Rush Hour 2*, falls in the category of "I was there."

Figure 13.3
And the subject of this photo is what again?

Simplify the Photo

For a posed photo, simplifying the photo is so easy to do. Figure 13.4 is a photo of one of the many bikers in Austin (home of Lance Armstrong) that train in the Hill Country. The problem with this photo is that the background is cluttered. I could have spent some time (about 20 minutes) removing or replacing the background, or I could have just asked him to move ten feet over to the right, where I took the shot that's shown in Figure 13.5. Which do you think was easier?

Figure 13.4
The background in this photo is cluttered. Although Photoshop Elements can replace the background, doing so takes some time.

Figure 13.5
All it took to change the background was to ask the biker to move a few feet to the right, which he gladly did.

Composition

It is no longer necessary to have the subject in the middle of the photograph or facing the camera—that amendment to the U.S. Constitution was repealed. Figure 13.6 is our son Jonathan not facing the camera and standing off to the right so that I could capture the beautiful fall foliage of Baltimore.

Figure 13.6
Here are two subjects: my son Jonathan and the fall foliage. He is not in the center of the photo and he's not facing the camera.

Flash Photography

If you spend any time at all retouching photos, you will begin to believe that more photos are ruined by a flash than are achieved using a flash. That isn't true of course—it just feels like it's true. This section discusses the pros and cons of flash photography.

Pros of Flash Use

It provides extra light both indoors and outdoors (fill flash). It can be used to freeze action (assuming that it isn't a bright sunny day), which is especially handy with digital cameras that have a little trouble in this area because of their shutter delay.

Cons of Flash Use

There are two major downsides to using a flash. It can wash out color in the subject, and the big problem is it creates the dreaded red eye. Did you ever see anyone get red eye from an available light photo?

Rules of Flash Photography

We all have flashes built into our cameras, or if we are really into photography, we have an external flash. Because flash photography is unavoidable, here are Dave's rules for flash photography. I hope these rules help you create better photos with your flash.

Times to Use the Flash

Always consider using the flash on your camera in situations like these:

- To fill in shadows on outside shots.

- With red-eye reduction turned on, if the option is available.

- On most indoor shots, especially if you are using an external flash that has a tilt head that enables you to bounce the flash off the ceiling instead of pointing directly at your subject(s).

When to Not Use the Flash

There are only two situations when you shouldn't use your flash; both involve distance:

- On outdoor shots of distant subjects taken at night. Did you ever watch someone take a flash picture of a football game from the stands? I even watched as someone took a flash picture of the moon one evening.

- When you are very close to your subject—unless you don't like them. They should be at least six feet away and be off-center of the camera lens to lessen the chance of red-eye.

Much more could be said about this topic, but these aforementioned points are the most crucial.

Improving Appearances

One of the terrible things about a camera is that when you take a picture of someone, you capture everything about his or her appearance. This includes wrinkles, thinning hair, and other features that they might or might not want included in the photo. The great thing about a program such as Photoshop Elements is that you can alter the actual photograph in many cases and improve the subject's appearance. So, let's look at some examples and sort out the best way to deal with them.

Evaluating the Photo

Before you jump into a photograph, you should first evaluate it and decide what needs to be changed. Figure 13.7 is a photograph taken with one of the first digital cameras, which means that the photograph is noisy. When working with photos of people, noise has a tendency to sharpen all of their features—both good and bad. Several other things about this photo of my friend Megg also needs to be addressed. It needs cropping, and the angle of the camera when I took the photo was not good. As a general rule, it isn't good to take a photo looking up a person's nose because the result is that the nose looks larger than it actually is.

Figure 13.7
This photograph needs to be touched up in several areas.

Cropping for Composition

As previously mentioned, cropping is the first thing that needs to be done to this photograph. Because this is a photo of Megg and not the person on her right, who is a stranger to me, we need to use the Crop Tool (C) to remove her and the white area as well (see Figure 13.8). We need to crop the photo before we apply any automatic enhancement tools or the large white area will affect the operation and the outcome of the tool.

Figure 13.8
Cropping this photograph removes the other person, the large white doorframe and improves the overall composition.

After cropping the image, I applied the automatic levels, contrast, and color correction. None of them worked. The Auto Levels and the Auto Color Correction turned her blue and Auto Contrast cooled down her color temperature. This isn't an uncommon occurrence when working with photographs from early digital cameras. The best part is that her overall color in the photo doesn't require any serious adjustment.

Getting the Red Out

The next step to improving this photo is to remove the red eye. To do this, I used the Zoom tool and got really close on her eye. Using the Eyedropper tool (I), I sampled the color of her eye that wasn't the "demon-possessed" red color. Next, I used the Red Eye Brush tool (y) to remove the red eye, as shown in Figure 13.9.

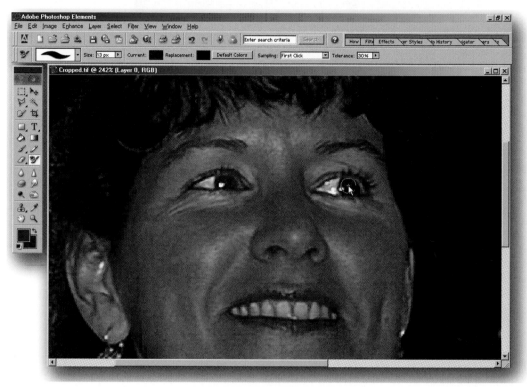

Figure 13.9
The next step to improving this photo is to remove the red eye with the Red Eye Brush tool.

Whitening the Eyes and Teeth

With her red eye gone, and because we are already zoomed in very close on her face, I will add a little extra white to her eyes and teeth. Selecting the Dodge tool, I changed the Options settings to Highlights at an exposure of 20 percent and applied it to add a little boost to her eyes and teeth. Be careful when you use the Dodge tool for this kind of work because it's easy to add way too much brightening and give the subject a surreal appearance. Remember that the object of retouching is to make the subject look better, not scary. Figure 13.10 shows a before and after of the eye and teeth job.

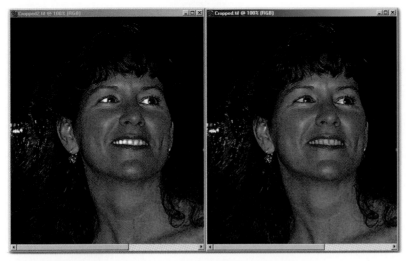

Figure 13.10
Can you tell which photo has had the removal of red eye and brightened white in teeth and eyes? The original is on the right.

Highlighting Her Hair

The next step involves highlighting her hair a little to separate it from the dark background. You can accomplish this in several ways. I could use the Dodge tool with the Midtones and the Shadow range, but the real disadvantage to this approach is that whatever changes are made are permanent. To make her brown hair lighter than the background without washing out the rest of her, I added a Level Adjustment layer. After making the initial settings, her hair looked okay, but the rest of her was slightly out—no problem.

To restrict the area affected by the Layer Adjustment layer to the hair, it was only necessary to paint the layer black where I didn't want the layer to have an effect. To make the really dark edges stand out, it was necessary to apply a hefty amount of Levels adjustment. As a result, I didn't want some areas of her hair highlighted as much as others. To accomplish this, I painted those areas gray. This allowed part of the highlight produced by the Adjustment layer to appear. So, in summary, areas of the Adjustment layer that are painted black have no affect on the image. As shades of black (gray) are painted, the layer has greater effect until you approach white or unpainted. These show the total effect of the layer. Figure 13.11 shows the lightened image, and on the Layers palette, you can see the area of the layer (actually, it is the layer's mask) that is painted to restrict the effect of the adjustment layer.

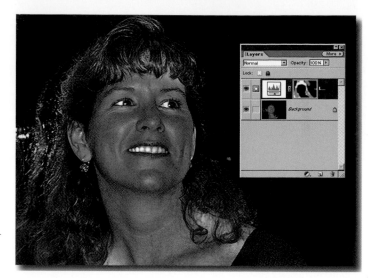

Figure 13.11
The Levels Adjustment layer that highlights her hair is restricted to the areas of the layer that were not painted.

Smoothing Out the Pixels

As previously mentioned, this photo was taken with one of the early digital cameras (a top-end 1-megapixel camera). The result was the subject's noisy skin. To remove this grain, I applied a small amount of the Smart Blur filter, which smoothed out her skin, but also smoothed out her hair. Next, I applied the Sharpen filter to her hair (see Figure 13.12).

Figure 13.12
Applying the Smart Blur filter followed by a little sharpening smoothes out her skin and adds emphasis to her hair.

Removing Reflections

Megg is standing by a mirror, so some of the flash on her hair is reflected on the left side of the photo, and a part of her face on the right side is barely visible. I removed both of these by using the Clone tool (see Figure 13.13).

Figure 13.13
The Clone tool removes unwanted reflections and a dimly lit face on the right side of the photo.

Resizing an Ear and Moving Hair

The angle at which the photograph was taken makes Megg's ear appear larger than it actually is. To correct this optical illusion, I used the Clone tool to make her ear a bit smaller. This is accomplished by clicking the source of the Clone tool right next to the edge of her ear and placing the Clone tool just inside the ear.

Also, I used the Clone tool to add a little more hair falling behind her neck, which was also exaggerated by the angle of the photograph. Figure 13.14 shows the result.

Figure 13.14
I used the Clone tool to reduce the apparent size of her ear and add some hair to de-emphasize her neck.

A Nose Job

The last item that was exaggerated by the camera angle is her nose. Using the Liquify command, which is located in the Filter menu under the Distort category, I applied the Pucker tool to her nose to make it a bit smaller (see Figure 13.15).

Figure 13.15
The Liquify command can make even cute noses look cuter.

Final Tweaking

Now that all the facial manipulations are complete, it's time to correct the color. Opening the Hue/Saturation menu (Ctrl-U), I tweaked the hue to balance out the color shift that was caused by the flash (see Figure 13.16). I also added more saturation.

Figure 13.16
Using Hue/Saturation corrects the color. This photo is just about complete.

The last thing that I added to this image was some shading under her chin and around her ears using the Burn tool (see Figure 13.17).

Figure 13.17
After all the pulling, tweaking, and assorted fiddling, this shows that even a poorly composed image shot with a so-so digital camera can be restored.

Further Editing Options

We just discussed retouching photographs using their existing elements. As we saw in Chapter 12, "Rearranging and Replacing Objects in Photos," occasions arise when changing a subject's background or some other aspect of the photo is also desirable. Magazines and ad agencies do this work all the time, usually with Photoshop. The same tools to swap backgrounds exist in Elements, so even the inexperienced photo editor or those on a budget can get into the game. These techniques are great for adding flair to your photographs, whether they're for screensavers, brochures, or for sending pictures to grandma.

One other retouching option is that of adding objects to a photo. Adding objects is relatively simple, but adding them in such a way that they look natural and believable takes some thought and technique.

Adding Objects

A great way to spice up photos of friends or family is by adding elements from other pictures that really do not belong. Think of a normal day and add an impossible situation: Elements makes it possible for you do that.

Take a look at Figures 13.18 and 13.19. The first photo was taken in the mountains of Montana at a church meeting. The second photo is, of course, a lion. On their own, each photo is pretty uneventful, and would appeal only to those with an interest in the involved subjects.

Figure 13.18
It seems like a normal Sunday morning, but our speaker is about to be thrown into a strange situation!

Figure 13.19
The lighting in the lion photo comes from the same general direction as the church meeting photo.

Before we get too far into this, however, I first want to point out something. The source and direction of light in both photos comes from the same general direction. That's important, especially for believability. We could certainly throw something into the photo whose reflections differ from the destination photo (in this case, the meeting), but the lighting will make the finished product believable. If you can match the lighting between the two, the believability factor shoots way up, even when creating an unbelievable situation.

If you want to follow this exercise in Photoshop Elements, download the files `Lion.jpg` and `Church Meeting.jpg` from this book's web page on the New Riders Publishing web site.

To start, we must extract the lion from his world. Do that by selecting the Polygonal Lasso tool (L). In the Lasso Tool Options bar, set a feather size of 1 or 2 (see Figure 13.20).

Figure 13.20
The Polygon Lasso tool lets us remove the lion from his habitat.

The feather is going to soften the edges of our selection, so when we extract and paste the lion into the other picture, it does not appear that the lion was clipped and pasted.

After the Polygon Lasso tool is selected, we can start creating the selection. Remember that the Polygon Lasso tool requires you to click the mouse on a starting point on the perimeter of the object that you want to extract. You then move the mouse to another point, click, move the mouse, click, and so on until you have an active selection around the entire subject (see Figure 13.21).

Figure 13.21
The Lasso tool enables us to select
the lion without selecting the background.

After the lion is selected, he needs to be copied and then pasted into the other image.
Ctrl-C copies the lion to the Clipboard (or simply go to Edit, Copy).

Now, make the second image active and go to Edit, Paste (Ctrl-V). The lion appears in
the second image, creating his own layer in the process (see Figure 13.22).

Figure 13.22
The lion just moved to Montana, but
he needs to be placed in a more natural position in the image.

Now that the lion is in his own layer, we can click the Move tool and place him wherever we want. In this case, I move him into the foreground, somewhere away from the podium and put his feet back on the ground (see Figure 13.23).

Figure 13.23
With his feet back on the ground, we can now begin working on the scale of the lion to make the image more realistic.

Now, we have another consideration. As he sits, he is probably the smallest and least intimidating lion in the world. By going to Image, Resize, Scale, we can stretch him out a bit (see Figure 13.24).

Figure 13.24
We can resize the lion to make him more intimidating.

After the size is agreeable, the final thing we need to consider is—you guessed it—the shadow. In order to make this believable, not only does the light need to be correct, but the shadow that's cast must also be correct. Creating a new layer beneath the lion's feet, spraying some black with the airbrush (see Figure 13.25), and setting the Layer Mode to Overlay takes care of this nicely. When we're done, we have merged two worlds that, though unlikely, now seem possible (see Figure 13.26).

Figure 13.25
We need shadow to increase the illusion.

Figure 13.26
Visit Montana, but please don't pet the wildlife!

Summary

The tools in Photoshop Elements are some of the best for photo retouching. Even when the automated tools can't clear up the problems, the manual tools have the capability to resolve almost any retouching challenge that you might come across. I need to advise you that, even with the great tools in Elements, retouching takes time. Until you get some experience, you need to experiment often. When you apply a correction, I encourage you to undo it and try a slightly different variation until you find the technique that looks best.

14 Restoring and Repairing Photographs

In Chapter 2, "Getting Pictures Into Your Computer," we discussed how to take a standard paper photograph and convert it to a digital image through a scanner. With the increased affordability of digital cameras, many people are now bypassing the film development route altogether and simply snapping digital shots for a quick and easy transfer to their computers. Unfortunately, it is not a perfect world (yet!), and so some errors in the processes involved for either photo type do occur. In this chapter, we discuss a few of those errors and, by this chapter's end, hopefully you'll have a handle on correcting those blemishes using Elements.

Determining the Problem

The place to start when restoring or repairing photographs is to determine the problem. Perhaps the photo has been hanging in a poker parlor for the past 40 years and has seen enough cigar smoke to choke Godzilla. It could be that your digital camera decided to pick up 256 shades of blue when you were snapping the perfect sunset. One predominant problem people face when restoring aged photographs is dust and scratching on the surface, along with age spots. Overexposure, underexposure, bad lighting, red eye, and insect spots can all carry over in the process of converting an image to a digital format, and even digital snapshots are not immune to error (see Figure 14.1). All is not lost! Chances are, if you have this book, you have Photoshop Elements. If that is the case, you are well on your way to restoring those photos and returning them to their former, or intended, glory (see Figure 14.2).

Figure 14.1
Some problems might be obvious, as the finger seen covering the lens in this photo. The blue cast may be more difficult to see, but can be corrected in a few easy steps using Elements.

Figure 14.2
Not only can both the finger be taken from the photo and the color be corrected,
but the chocolate on her shirt has also been removed.

How to Evaluate a Photo

As just mentioned, many errors in a photo are distinguishable with the naked eye. Errors
in lighting, color cast, and subtler inconsistencies are harder to catch at a first, second,
or even third glance. In cases such as these, we can use the tools Elements puts at our
fingertips to determine the problem and correct it accordingly.

For example, let's say that you have a photo that appears to be near perfect, but you
aren't quite sure. Figure 14.3 was one of those images that I couldn't quite pinpoint. At
times, a monitor can be slightly off, displaying errant color information. A quick way to
check your image to ensure tonal quality is to open the Levels dialog box and check the
Red, Blue, and Green levels for optimum color cast (see Figure 14.4). In the following
example, the Blue Levels are represented. Adjustments to the levels of all three (Blue,
Red, and Green), however, result in the image shown in Figure 14.4.

Figure 14.3
Some images might appear near perfect to the eye, but still require tonal adjustments.

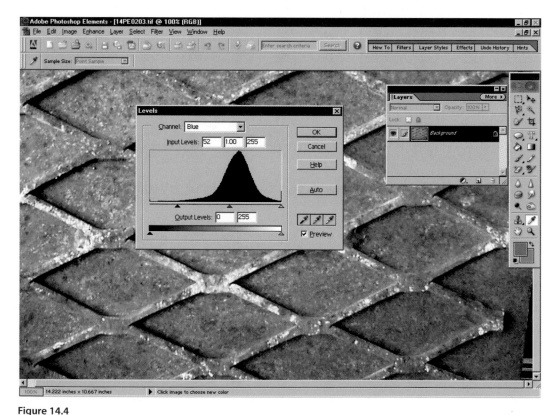

Figure 14.4
By moving the sliders of the color levels to the color endpoints, we can remove or add tonal information for a more natural-looking image.

Moving the sliders for each hue toward the beginning or end of the slope respectively equalizes the tones (see Figure 14.5). The slope represents the color value from its lightest point to its darkest, with the lowest points of color information known as *endpoints*. We can make intensity adjustments to three aspects of the image: shadows, midtones, and highlights.

Figure 14.5
Moving the Levels sliders to their endpoints renders a truer representation of color than the original photograph.

We cover this more in depth later in this chapter; for now, it's enough to know that not only is Elements a wonderful tool for fixing a problem, but it is also an excellent diagnostic tool for determining problems.

Establishing A Plan

After you have a stack of photos in need of correction, where do you start? Like all jobs worth doing, it is best to establish a plan of attack prior to manipulating pixels. Typically, big changes are best tackled first and cosmetics last. In the previous example with the little girl, the thumb was removed first (a fairly big change—turning an appendage into concrete). Next, the color was corrected. The final step was cosmetic, something this author hadn't thought of, but his wife certainly did—removing the chocolate from the little girl's shirt. If there is any set way in which to tackle corrections, I'm not aware of it, so I'll leave it to you to find your preferred angle of attack.

The idea is to find a stepped approach with which you are comfortable. Why? Productivity. Imagine tearing down an engine with no organization, without keeping track of what parts came off in what order, and so forth. Even a seasoned mechanic would be hard pressed to put the engine back together in a reasonable amount of time without a clear idea of what to tackle first. No two mechanics will approach a rebuild in exactly the same way, but each will find a method that they are comfortable with and that will be timely and effective enough to be profitable.

Understanding What Can and Cannot Be Repaired

Before you can begin repairing a photograph, you first must determine if the photo can be repaired. Again, look at the example of the girl in Figure 14.1. In that example, replacing the finger with sidewalk was relatively simple using the Clone Stamp tool. As the texture and color of the sidewalk remains somewhat constant in the upper left where the finger covers the lens, replacing that pixel information with captures of the sidewalk left a nearly unnoticeable change, especially if the viewer had not seen the original image. The chocolate was removed from the shirt in a similar manner on a smaller scale. The shirt was not actually cleaned, but the dark brown pixels were replaced with those taken from other areas of the shirt.

What if the finger had obstructed half of the girl's face? In this situation, the photo could not be salvaged. The pixel information simply isn't present to duplicate all the nuances of texture, lighting, and character required for such a feat.

In turn, however, some photos that appear unfixable can be repaired. This is especially true for photographs with extreme lighting (overexposure) or darkening (underexposure). Often, the human eye cannot detect subtle variances in hue, especially in extreme light or dark. Elements can detect those subtle shifts between similar pixels, and we can make corrections accordingly. As long as the tonal information for a photograph is available, it can be manipulated.

Figure 14.6 demonstrates a picture that cannot be repaired without total facial reconstruction. Too much of the primary subject is obscured. Figures 14.7 and 14.8 demonstrate that, though not perfect by any stretch of the imagination, some tonal information can be salvaged for underexposed or overexposed images. These are quick examples. A bit of pixel-pushing savvy, familiarity with the program, and experience working in restoration will definitely garner better results more frequently.

Figure 14.6
In situations where a major portion of the target image is obstructed or missing, the image cannot be restored.

Figure 14.7
Some images appear hopeless
because of lack of light.

Figure 14.8
Although far from perfect, some color and
lighting can be restored to this photo by
using Elements.

In some situations, we can salvage extremely dark or light images by averaging pixel
information using the tools provided by Elements.

Making Copies Versus Using Adjustment Layers

Before we actively dig in to tackling some real-world photo manipulation, let's take a
look at a pair of options we have for manipulating our images.

When we work on an image, it's a general rule of thumb to create duplicates of the back-
ground layer, select portions of the image for placement on other layers and so forth.
Elements, such as its big brother Photoshop, treats these layers as individual documents.
Imagine a stack of photos in a pile or a stack of transparencies for an overhead projector.
Layers are similar to these things—they're a stack of pictures. When editing or correcting
a layer, we are doing so with the rest of the layers separated (and thus, not affected).
When working with an image with specific objects on each layer, such as a collage,
manipulating the layers separately is ideal. We can apply effects specific to that layer,
without altering the objects on the other layers.

When dealing with photographs, however, we have another option that is usually preferable to manipulating each layer separately. Elements gives us the ability to create Adjustment layers.

An Adjustment layer does not contain pixel information; rather, it holds a value set by an adjustment command. For example, when we create an Adjustment layer that holds levels information, the layers beneath the Adjustment layer adopt that levels setting (see Figure 14.9). Figures 14.10 and 14.11 provide you with a before-and-after look at what happens when a Levels Adjustment layer is applied.

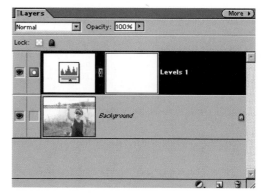

Figure 14.9
Layers beneath the Adjustment layer adopt the settings of the Adjustment layer. The Adjustment layer does not contain image data, but a value for the adjustment type.

Figure 14.10
An image prior to the Levels Adjustment layer being applied.

Figure 14.11
An image with the Levels Adjustment layer in place.

Here's the primary benefit to using Adjustment layers: We can experiment with color and tone without altering the image pixels. Think of it as a lens. We view the sky in altered hues through the lens, without altering the sky.

Another note about Adjustment layers: We can tell Elements to affect one layer and leave the rest alone, or affect every layer beneath the Adjustment layer.

Creating and Applying Adjustment Layers

To create an Adjustment layer, follow these steps:

1. Open your image (see Figure 14.12).

Figure 14.12
A sunset image with no adjustments.

2. Go to Layer, New Adjustment Layer.

3. Select the type of adjustment that you want to perform (see Figure 14.13). In this example, we use a Gradient Map to remove the color from the photo (not really…remember, an Adjustment layer doesn't affect the original image) and bring out the streaks and billows in a black-and-white rendering. A metallic gradient might be just what we need (see Figure 14.14).

4. Make your adjustment using the dialog box for the selected command.

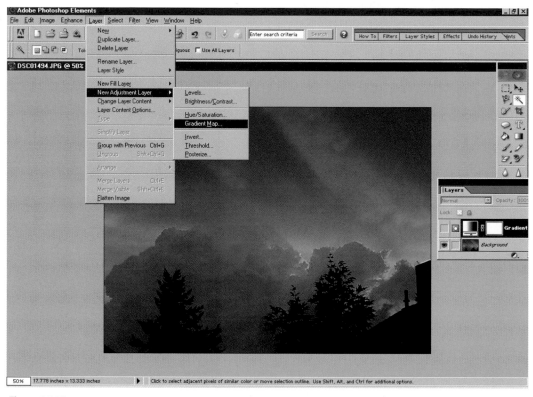

Figure 14.13
Applying a Gradient Map Adjustment layer.

Figure 14.14
Selecting a Gradient for masking.

Figure 14.15 illustrates the effect our Gradient Map has on the image. We can change these adjustments by double-clicking the Adjustment layer and altering the settings...all without damaging the original photo.

Figure 14.15
Here's the sunset image after the Gradient Map Adjustment layer is applied.

By using Adjustment layers, we can apply changes to Levels, Brightness/Contrast, Hue/Saturation, apply a Gradient Map, invert the color, adjust the Threshold, or posterize the layers below it.

Multiple Corrections: Figure 14.1 Revisited

It doesn't do much good simply to display what can be done with a photo without any explanation of how it was accomplished. Therefore, let's take another look at Figure 14.1 and walk through the process of fixing it up. Figure 14.16 shows the original figure again.

Figure 14.16
The original photo that we saw in Figure 14.1.

As you might have noticed earlier, this image can use some serious help. The following steps were used by the author to make it ready to email to grandma.

Step 1: Clone Stamp

A quick glance at the photo takes your eyes to its greatest error: the finger on the lens. Because this section of the photograph is not central to the subject, but lies in the background, the Clone tool can fix things up nicely:

1. In the Toolbox, select the Clone Stamp tool.

2. Select a brush size that enables you to cover the area as quickly and seamlessly as possible. In this example, a brush size of 100 was used. For more precise alterations, we need a smaller brush, as you will note when we clean the shirt. But for now, the larger size will do nicely.

3. Holding the Alt key, click in an area of the concrete close to the finger (see Figure 14.17).

4. Release the Alt key.

5. Begin filling the finger portion with concrete by clicking the mouse over the offending digit.

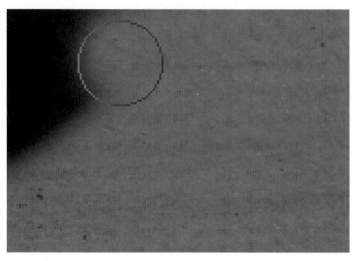

Figure 14.17
Although it appears we are erasing the finger, we are actually replacing it with a clone of the sidewalk.

6. You might need to capture the concrete again with the Clone Stamp. Continue copying and stamping until the entire finger is no longer visible (see Figure 14.18).

Figure 14.18
Choose a spot that will appear to seamlessly match the background.

Step 2: Removing the Stains

Because we are already working with the Clone Stamp, let's continue and remove the chocolate from the little girl's shirt:

1. Select a smaller brush to work on the stains (see Figure 14.19).

Figure 14.19
We can change the size of the sampled area just like changing the size of a paintbrush.

2. Alt-click a section of unstained cloth. Remember to do so close to the stained area to stay as true as possible to the tone and lighting as you can.

3. Start overlaying the stains with the Clone Stamp tool (see Figure 14.20). This might take some practice and even some brush size adjustments. Be patient…it will come together just fine (see Figure 14.21).

Figure 14.20
Just like the sidewalk, we can sample and stamp clean areas of the shirt over the dirt.

Figure 14.21
Look Ma…no stains!

Step 3: Adjusting the Color

The final step to fixing the photo is to restore a natural mix of hues to the image. As you can see, this one appears to have an abundance of blue. Using an Adjustment layer, let's see if we can't pull out some of those other hues that, when mixed with the blue, give us a more life-like rendering:

1. Go to Layer, New Adjustment Layer, Levels.

2. When the New Levels dialog box appears, just click OK.

3. Starting with the Red channel, move the left and right sliders to the endpoints of the red color information (see Figure 14.22).

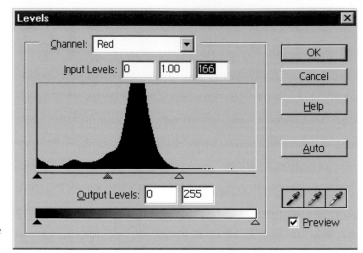

Figure 14.22
You can fix colors by moving the Levels sliders to the endpoints.

4. Repeat the process with the Blue and Green channels.

5. Keep an eye on your image and note the changes when you move the sliders. After you are finished with all three channels, your image should have a much healthier tone (see Figure 14.23).

Figure 14.23
Elements not only helps a photo look healthier, it can also be used to cover up evidence!

How to Remove Dust and Debris

Scanning does have a downside, especially when you transfer old photographs to a digital medium. Dust, scratches, and blemishes acquired with age make the transition difficult because the scanner has no way to distinguish between actual photo information and particles stuck to the photo or scratches on the finish. Don't worry, Elements includes tools and filters to tackle these problems easily (see Figure 14.24).

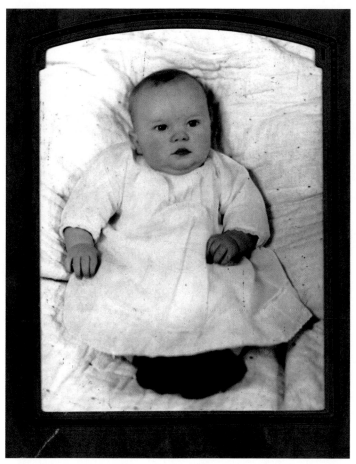

Figure 14.24
Older photographs often carry defects that can be cleaned quickly in
Photoshop Elements.

Using the Dust and Scratches Filter

Located under the Filters menu, a filter set called Noise can be used to either add noisy pixels to a photo or remove offending pixels that come with age or poor scanning quality. In the case of Figure 14.24, we want to remove numerous age spots, stains, and wrinkles (see Figure 14.25). Let's start with the age spots and dust:

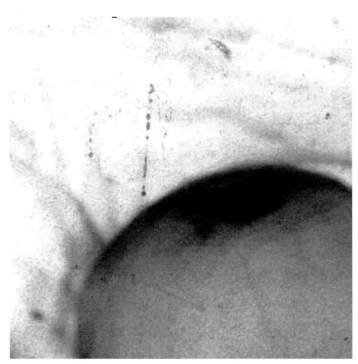

Figure 14.25
Age and stains damage
heirloom photos.

1. To remove spots and dust from the entire image in one swoop, go to Filter, Noise, Dust and Scratches.

2. By adjusting the Radius and Threshold sliders, we can eliminate much of the added noise in the image (see Figure 14.26).

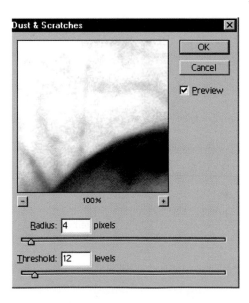

Figure 14.26
The Dust and Scratches filter
helps rejuvenate age marks.

A few problems might arise when trying to remove the noise from the entire image at once. The primary problem is that you might also remove image information that you might not want to lose. For example, reflections in the eyes, color variations around lips or hair, and so forth might take needed information with them when the photo's corrected (see Figures 14.27 and 14.28).

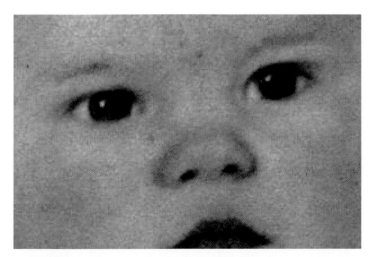

Figure 14.27
The image before applying the Dust and Scratches filter.

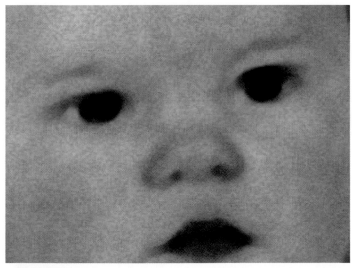

Figure 14.28
The Dust and Scratches filter might remove details that are better left untouched.

Isolating with Selections

In order to maintain pixel integrity for the majority of the photo, we can isolate the offending dust, scratches, and stains with selections and apply the corrections only to those areas.

As we saw in earlier chapters, Elements has the standard selection tools found in other Adobe products. These tools are found at the top of the toolbar, and consist of the Rectangular (see Figure 14.29) and Elliptical Marquee selection tools (and, of course, the Magic Wand tool). These tools enable you to select blocks or circular areas of the image (Rectangular and Elliptical), or selections in specific color ranges (Magic Wand). Although useful for some jobs, they aren't much help in photo restoration. The last thing we want is blocky or circular patterns on the photograph that we're trying to restore.

Adobe Photoshop Elements has another tool that's better suited for this type of work. It is called the *Selection brush*, and is also found in the toolbar. By choosing the Selection brush, we can literally paint the areas on which we want to run our filter (see Figure 14.30). By selecting a feathered brush type, we can prevent stark changes between the filtered and unfiltered areas for an overall better-looking image.

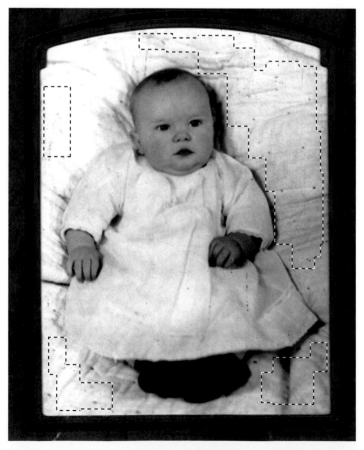

Figure 14.29
Selections made using the
Rectangular Marquee tool.

Figure 14.30
The Selection brush gives you more control over what areas you can select for editing.

Using The Selection Brush

Let's run through some quick corrections using the Selection brush and the Dust and Scratches filter.

Step 1: Making the Selections

1. In the toolbar, click the Selection brush.

2. In the Options bar, select the characteristics of your brush (see Figure 14.31).

Figure 14.31
The size of the Selection brush can be changed in the Options bar.

3. Begin painting your selections (see Figure 14.32). You might need to change brush sizes occasionally, especially when working around or on the primary subject (in this case, the baby).

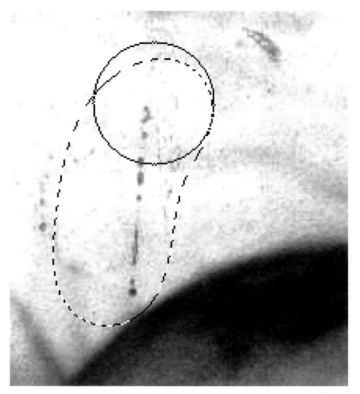

Figure 14.32
You can paint a selection over the area that we want to touch up with the Selection brush.

Step 2: Applying the Dust and Scratches Filter

1. After you are satisfied with your selections (see Figure 14.33), go to Filter, Noise, Dust and Scratches. A low radius/low threshold combination renders the best results: eliminating the blemishes without blurring the selected areas. Figure 14.34 shows the completed image.

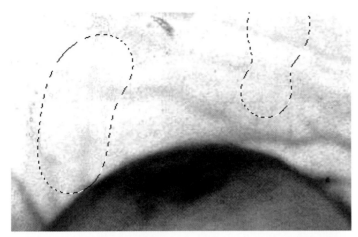

Figure 14.33
We can select multiple spots to edit more than one area of this photograph.

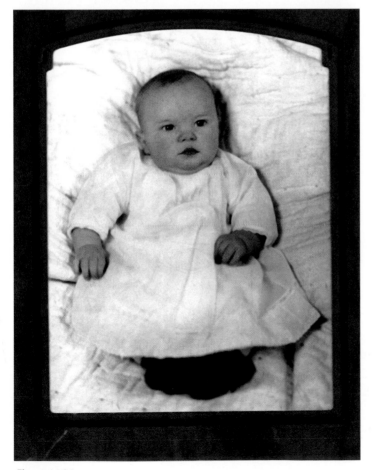

Figure 14.34
The Dust and Scratches filter, when applied to the trouble spots only, gives us a
cleaner-looking image.

Aligned Versus Non-Aligned Cloning

Earlier, when we were working with the Clone tool, the samples were taken in Aligned mode. We can also take samples and apply the Clone Stamp in Non-Aligned mode. We can switch between the modes in the Clone Stamp Options bar. What, exactly, is the difference between the two?

When we sample an area in Aligned mode, the Clone Stamp selects large portions of the image (see Figure 14.35). If you start at a point in the picture and just continue to apply the Clone Stamp, you would soon have a duplicate of the original photo, regardless of how many times you stop and resume painting (see Figure 14.36).

Figure 14.35
Sampling with the Clone Stamp tool in Aligned mode samples the entire image.

Figure 14.36
If we continue to use the Clone Stamp tool, entire sections of the image will be duplicated.

With the Aligned box unchecked, the Clone Stamp tool still samples the entire image, but it will place the original capture every time the Clone Stamp tool is applied (see Figure 14.37 and 14.38).

Figure 14.37
My son is enjoying a day at the park.

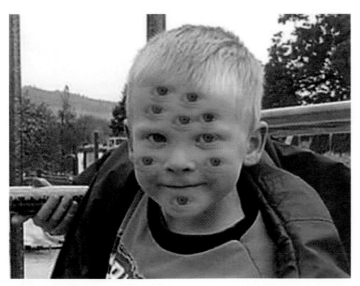

Figure 14.38
With the Aligned box unchecked, the stamp continues to place the same sample over and over again.

Restoring Faded Color

Let's take another look at the baby photo we worked on earlier (see Figure 14.39). By using techniques and tools that we've already mentioned in this chapter, we can restore a healthy glow to the child:

Figure 14.39
The baby photo.

1. With your image open, click the Selection brush. Choose a brush size that enables you to select the flesh-toned areas.

2. Paint your selection (see Figure 14.40). If you are using a feathered brush (which I recommend), don't worry about painting outside of the edges of the face.

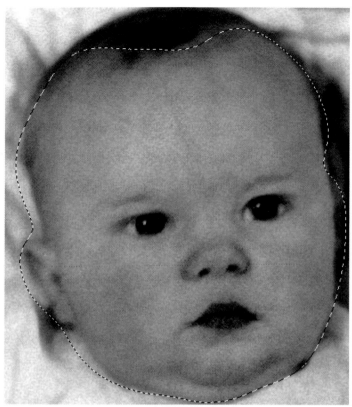

Figure 14.40
Create a selection where the color is to
be corrected.

3. Go to Layers, New Adjustment Layer.

4. Click the Hue/Saturation option.

5. Move the Saturation slider until a healthy glow is restored (see Figures 14.41 and 14.42).

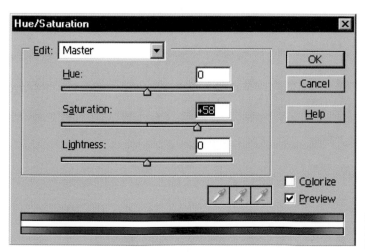

Figure 14.41
Increasing the saturation enhances
lost color.

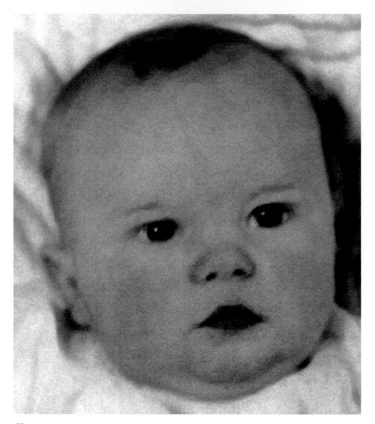

Figure 14.42
The baby has a nice, healthy glow.

6. Go to Select, Reselect.

7. Again, go to Layers, New Adjustment Layer. This time, select the Levels Adjustment.

8. Step through the Red, Blue, and Green channels, moving the sliders to the endpoints (as shown previously in this chapter).

9. Click OK. Your result looks like what's shown in Figure 14.43.

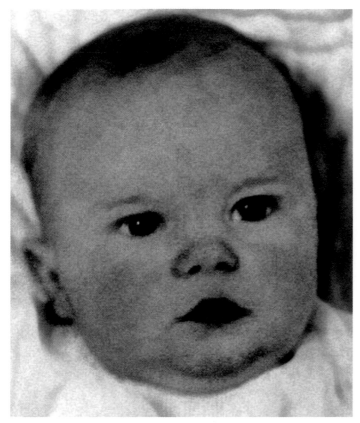

Figure 14.43
Elements is a great tool for restoring life to old images.

Summary

In this chapter, we took some positive steps to increase the quality of our cherished photos, both old and new. We used a car analogy before, and one applies here as well. When my car breaks down and I have no idea how to fix it, my first tendency is to tow it to the wrecking yard. That would be foolish if it required only a tune up. Much grief could be avoided by recognizing the problem, knowing my tools, and walking through the repair in a methodical fashion.

The same goes for photo repair and restoration. Having a handle on the tools, recognizing the problems, and a step-by-step approach can save those cherished moments in time. In the next chapter, we take a look at making those images available to the masses online, so you will want your memories to look their best.

15 Publishing on the Web

These days, using the Internet is just about the easiest way to share your photos. That might even be the main reason why you bought this book. Whether you want to send images through email, place scans on your own web page, or are preparing digital photos of items you have for auction on eBay, this chapter is for you.

To properly save images for the web, you want to achieve a balance of the highest possible quality with the lowest possible file size. Using Elements and the techniques found in this chapter make creating perfect Internet-bound images a snap.

Sizing Up an Image for the Web

Let's start by opening an image shot with a digital camera to uncover the best tricks to get optimum results for the web. The example image, named Park.jpg can be downloaded from this book's web page at www.newriders.com if you want to follow along. You can also use your own digital image if you have one handy.

When you open an image file in Elements, the program automatically displays the file at the largest size that will fit in the workspace of your computer. This means that you might be fooled by the actual size of the image at which you're looking. You might think the image is small because the image you see displayed on your monitor appears small, but in reality, the image is huge. Look at the title bar of the image shown in Figure 15.1. The title bar reads Park.jpg@16.7%. The number after the filename is the zoom factor. This image is relatively large; it is being displayed at only 16.7 percent of its actual size.

Figure 15.1
Looks can be deceiving. This image appears to be small when it's opened in Elements.

To see an image at actual size (100 percent), double-click the Zoom tool (the Magnifying Glass icon) or press Ctrl (Cmd)-+ to zoom out to 100 percent. Now you are able to see the actual pixels of the image, as shown in Figure 15.2. Elements enables you to zoom in even closer than 100 percent (all the way to 1,600 percent). The term *actual pixels* can be confusing to beginners because they might be expecting to see squares or blocks. At 100 percent, those don't show up. Usually, they don't appear until you zoom in to 200–300 percent. When you view the actual pixels, you are seeing every picture element that's used to make up the image, whereas at a zoom of 50 percent, you are only being shown 50 percent of the pixels that reside within the image.

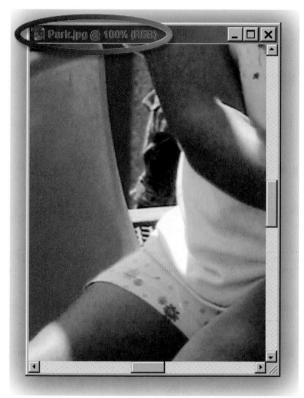

Figure 15.2
The Park image is zoomed in to see the actual pixels.

If you were to send a file of this size to someone else through email, the image that looks small within Elements on your computer might open on the recipient's computer differently. In fact, a person might open up the image to see your navel in extreme close up and have to spend days scrolling to find the billboard-size object that is your face. If you already attempted to send an image in an email and had similar results, now you know why. The image size is too large to view easily outside of Elements, so let's make this image less troublesome for sharing with others.

Making Images Web Friendly

You can reduce the image size in a couple of ways. There's cropping, which is discussed in detail in Chapter 3, "Adjusting and Enhancing Photos," and downsampling, which is explored in Chapter 4, "Sizing and Saving Your Photos." This image is direct from a digital camera. The file is 1,704 pixels wide and 2,272 pixels tall. Cropping needs to always be your first choice when looking to lower image size, followed by downsampling. That's because, sometimes, cropping away the excess junk might be all that's needed to end up with a manageable image size. With that concept in mind, the Crop tool is chosen from the Toolbox and dragged out, as shown in Figure 15.3.

Figure 15.3
Use the Crop tool to effectively reduce image size.

Press Enter to perform the crop. (If you make a mistake, press Ctrl (Cmd)-Z to undo the crop.) I probably could have cropped the image very close to Rachel's face, just showing from the waist up, but I'm planning to send this image to Rachel's grandma. I want Grandma to see how big Rachel is getting, so I purposely chose not to crop away Rachel's legs. OK, let's check our results.

When I open the Image Size dialog box (go to Image, Resize, Image Size from the menu), I see the cropped image is down to 1,296 by 1,476 pixels, which is better. However, the file's present size is still not one that most other people will be able to view easily, so I need to downsample the image to reduce the image size even more.

If you're following along with the downloaded image and the dimensions of your cropped image doesn't exactly match mine, don't worry!

The Image Size dialog box should still be open, so make sure the Constrain Proportions and Resample Image boxes are both checked, as shown in Figure 15.4. Next, in the Document Size area, enter a value of 72 pixels in the Resolution box and change the Height to 6 Inches. (Why did I pick the value of 72 pixels? Because all monitors are 72 pixels per inch.) If you accidentally make a bad mistake entering the values, you can hold the Alt (Opt) key and the Cancel button changes into Reset. After you have the correct settings, click OK.

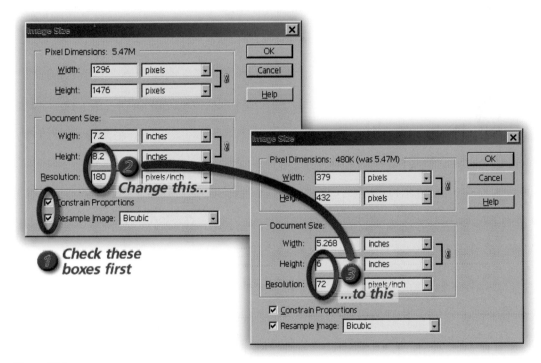

Figure 15.4
Adjust the Image Size settings to match those shown here.

Now you have an image that can be emailed to anyone without worrying whether the recipient will be struggling with a massive image of your nostril! Double-click the Hand icon in the Toolbox (this makes the image fit on your monitor as large as possible), and double-click the Zoom tool (the Magnifying Glass icon) to view the image at 100 percent, as shown in Figure 15.5.

Figure 15.5
This image is sized so that it can safely be sent to anyone.

All that's left to do is save the image for the web. Before you do that, let's talk about downsampling images for other images destined for the web. In the meantime, if you're following along with the downloaded image, you're not through just yet, so sit tight.

Reducing Images for Internet Auctions

Many people buy digital cameras not to shoot family and friends, but for the sole purpose of adding images to their Internet auctions. If that's also the reason you bought Photoshop Elements 2.0, you should have been following along closely until now, because you would need to do the exact same steps. The only place where you would want to deviate would be in the Image Size settings. For auctions, you want even smaller images than if you were sharing images with others through email.

I recommend the following settings for downsampling images for Internet auctions using the Image Size dialog box:

- For large images, enter a value of 5 inches in either the Width or Height box. (Enter this value in whichever box has the higher value to begin with.)

- For medium-sized images, enter a value of 3 to 4 inches in either the Width or Height box. (Enter this value in whichever box has the higher value to begin with.)

- For smaller images, enter a value of 1.5 to 2 inches in either the Width or Height box. (Enter this value in whichever box has the higher value to begin with.)

- For tiny images (sometimes called *thumbnails* because they are roughly the same size as a person's thumbnail), enter a value of .5 inches in either the Width or Height box. (Enter this value in whichever box has the higher value to begin with.)

Enter a resolution of 72ppi in all cases. Because the Constrain Proportions box must be checked in this dialog box, you have to worry about only changing the larger of the two dimensions. Elements will automatically change the other dimension to the appropriate setting. Great, huh?

Keep in mind that you can add as many images for auctions as you care to, so you might want to use these guidelines to make thumbnail-sized images, and medium and large images showing your item from different angles.

Don't limit using these settings to just auctions! These settings are good for more than just that. You can apply them to any web project—really! You can use these guidelines for creating online photo albums, images for your home page, or anything you can think of. The sky's the limit!

Making Images for Your Home Page

If you want to add images to your home page, you can make them any size you want, within reason. In this scenario, the only thing you really want to be aware of is file size. If your web page takes too long to download, people just surf to the next spot that strikes their fancy. For this reason, many webmasters have had a rule of thumb that a web page should be no more than 60 to 75KB per page, although with many people now having broadband access (specifically cable modems or DSL service), the number might be extended to as high as 100KB now.

Until this point, I talked about image size, as opposed to file size, but there is a correlation between the two. Common sense tells you that when you reduce the number of pixels within a file, an added benefit will be smaller file size. That's because less data is needed to describe the contents of the smaller file.

An additional way to reduce file size is through compression. Both common file formats for the web (JPEG and GIF) use compression, but each format uses a different method. (See Chapter 4 for more info about file formats and compression.) Because the Park image is a photo, you'll want to use the JPG format. You could use File, Save As, and choose JPG as the file format, but then you are presented with a bunch of buttons, sliders, and gizmos, as shown in Figure 15.6. Because JPG is a lossy file format (which means that image information will be permanently thrown away after the file is saved in order to make the file size smaller, as discussed in Chapter 4), it's much better to see what the gadgets do to your image. For this reason, never use Save As when saving for the web.

Figure 15.6
What does all this stuff mean?

Now, in the File menu just below Save As, you can find the option Save For Web. The Save For Web dialog box has some huge advantages over the Save As option, the biggest being that when you adjust all those doohickeys, you can see instantly how the settings will affect the image. This way, you can make an intelligent choice between image quality and file size! Hoo hah!

Saving for the Web

If you're following along with the downloaded image, go to File, Save As to open the Save For Web dialog box.

When the dialog box opens, you see the image displayed in two windows. The left-hand image is the original; the right hand image is referred to as the Optimized window and will display how your settings will alter the image, as shown in Figure 15.7.

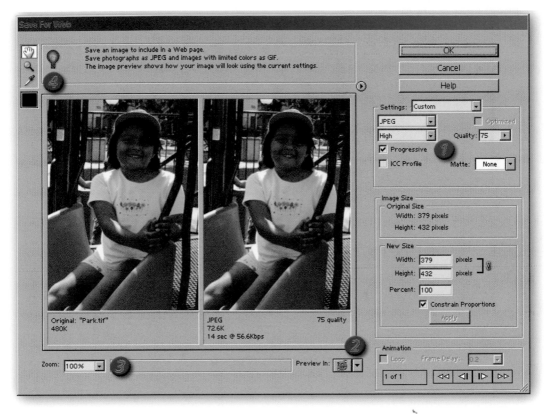

Figure 15.7
The primary advantage of the Save For Web dialog box is that you can see the effects of your settings on the image before you commit to them.

When your cursor enters the image area, it changes into the Hand tool, so you can maneuver around the image. Use the Hand tool to move to Rachel's face. Now look in the Settings area (indicated by the number 1 in Figure 15.7). If you click in the file format box, you can change to another format, such as GIF. The Progressive box is checked in this figure; if you are planning on sending an image through email, you might want to check this box, but if you are placing the image on a web page, be aware that not all browsers support progressive JPEGs.

The box you want to focus on in this area is the one marked Quality. If you click the area, a slider appears. Move the slider down to about 75 percent. Elements will do some calculations and, if you look in the Optimized window just under the image, you can see the new total file size to be around 72k, which is a perfectly fine file size to email someone. If you were placing this image on a web site, you might try lowering the file size further, such as 20k, by moving the Quality slider, watching the file-size number change, and checking the image for compression artifacts. If you want to see compression artifacts easily, look for the red areas of the image (this is true of any area of solid color, but red shows artifacts most obviously), move the Quality slider to 100 percent, and then move the slider in 10-percent increments (but, put it back to 75 percent after you finish). You're actually done with this exercise and can click OK, but before you do, let's take a quick tour of the Save For Web dialog box.

The default modem speed that's shown in the Optimized window is 28kbps. Grandma has a 56kbps modem, so the modem speed was adjusted by clicking in the right-facing arrow just above and to the left of the word Settings, which is just to the left of the top of the Optimized window.

Below the Settings area is an area for resampling your images. I recommend that you stay with the Image Size dialog box for doing that work.

Below that is a control panel for doing web animations on layered images.

In area 2, shown in Figure 15.7, you see Preview In and the Internet Explorer icon. Click the icon to display a preview of the image in a new web-browser window to see how it will look on the web. Internet Explorer is displayed by default. If you have Netscape installed and want to use it, click the downward-facing arrow next to the Internet Explorer icon.

In area 3, you can choose to zoom in or out to see how the image looks at different zoom factors. This can be useful for checking the overall image, but to best see compression artifacts, use 100 percent zoom.

In area 4 of Figure 15.7 are the available tools. By default, the Hand tool is active, but you can choose the Zoom tool (the Magnifying Glass icon) to zoom in or out.

After you finish taking the 5¢ Save For Web dialog box tour, you can click to save the file to your hard drive. Because you did so much editing (particularly image downsampling), I recommend that you save the file with a different name so that the old file isn't written over (you might need the big version for printing). In this case, I saved the file to my hard drive as Rachel, ready to attach to an email.

Attaching Your Images to Email

Attaching images using the three big email programs (Internet Explorer Outlook, Netscape Composer, or AOL) to send email is straightforward. You can attach images to either new emails or to a reply email. You can simply look for the paperclip icon or the word Attachments, as shown in Figure 15.8. Clicking these buttons enables you to search your hard drive to locate the masterpiece you just made in Elements. You might attach multiple images, but you don't want the files to be too large, or the entire email bounces like flubber.

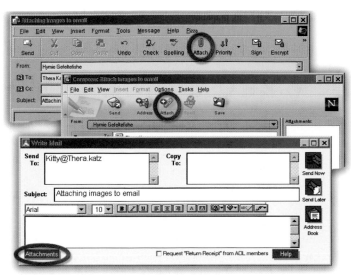

Figure 15.8
You should have no trouble locating the attachment buttons in the three big email programs.

TIP

As an aside, if more than one file is attached using AOL, a zip file (or a `*.sit` file if a Mac) is created and sent to the recipient. If your friend is also on AOL and uses the same platform as you, the AOL software automatically opens the `.zip` or `.sit` files for you when you download them off the AOL server. If you are on Windows and your Mac friend sends you several images, you need to download StuffIt Expander for Windows from `www.aladdinsys.com`. It has a free version that lets you expand `.sit` files. If you need a zip program, I suggest downloading a copy of WinZip from `www.winzip.com`. After the StuffIt or WinZip programs are installed on your system, you can double-click the `.sit` or `.zip` file to launch the program. You should be able to see the individual filenames. Click the files and drag them to your desktop temporarily or drag them into a folder on your hard drive for safekeeping. If you get unsolicited files from a complete stranger, you might want to scan for viruses at the very least or not open the files at all.

I would be remiss if I didn't mention a feature in Elements called Attach to Email (which is located in the File menu). Why didn't I just instruct you to use the Attach to Email feature with the original image? If you were to choose that option with the unedited `Park.jpg` image, a dialog box would have opened saying that the file is too large— "Would you like to Auto-convert?" If you choose Yes, the *file size* is lowered through image compression so that the image can be sent and attached into your default email program, but the file remains that super close-up mess that I talked about at the beginning of this chapter. You still need to reduce the *image size* by cropping and/or downsampling to make it manageable, and if you want, you might use Attach to Email.

Automated Web Photo Gallery Creation

Now, let's explore some other features within Elements geared toward the web: the next one being the Web Photo Gallery. This is a great tool, whether you are an artist or just someone looking to put pictures up on a family web page for friends from all over to come and see.

Before you open the Web Photo Gallery dialog box, you want to first place all the images you want to use for the gallery into one folder on your hard drive. This serves as your source folder. You don't need to worry about size if your images are large. Elements resizes copies of the files automatically to make them relatively uniform for the gallery. If you need to sort your files visually for your gallery, you might use the File Browser in Elements. If you use the How To palette, choose Common Issues from the drop-down menu, and click the Create New Web Gallery link for semiautomatic Web Photo Gallery help.

Also, you want to make a new folder in which to store the completed Web Photo Gallery files at this time. Sadly, Adobe doesn't enable you to create a new folder for your destination inside the Web Photo Gallery dialog box.

After you make your preparations, you can choose File, Create Web Photo Gallery. The first adjustment that you'll want to make is to choose a style from the drop-down menu. I chose the Vertical Frame style, as shown in Figure 15.9. A thumbnail image appears on the right to give you a rough idea of how the finished gallery will look.

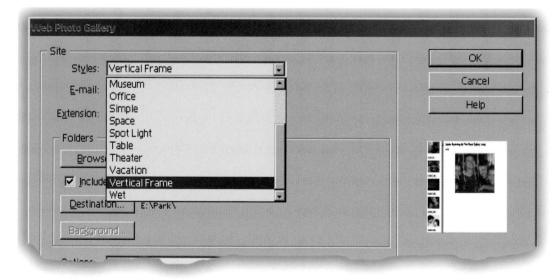

Figure 15.9
Elements provides a number of page layouts to choose from, such as the Vertical Frame style.

Next, make sure to enter the locations of your source and destination folders on your hard drive, as shown in Figure 15.10. You might also use the information that I've added to the other fields as a guideline.

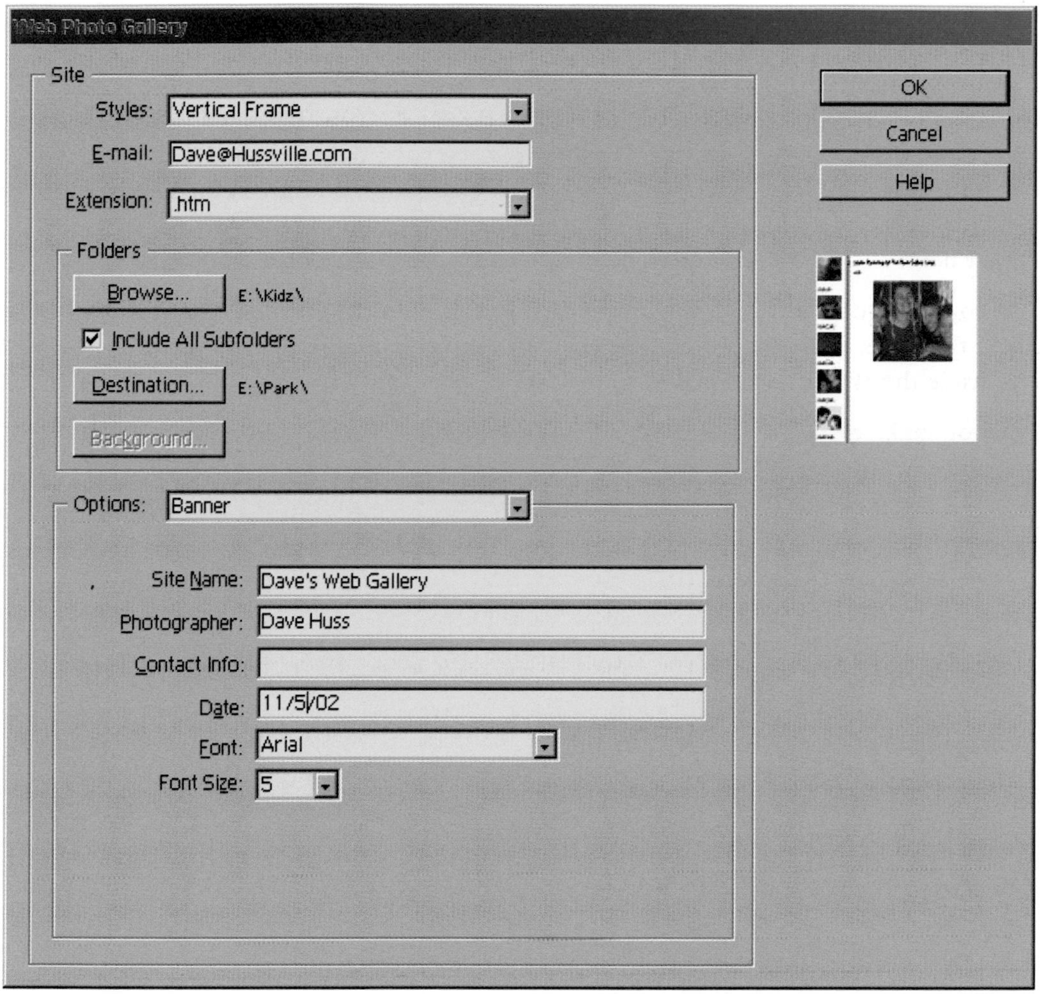

Figure 15.10
Use the information in this figure as a guide for filling out the information fields for your web gallery.

There is an Options drop-down menu at about the middle of the Web Photo Gallery dialog box. You can customize the settings for a number of features, but I recommend that you leave them at their defaults initially. If you are an artist that wants to protect the rights of your images, one Option you might want to use is Security. Choose Security from the drop-down list and enter your specific information using the information shown in Figure 15.11 as an example. When the large images appear in the gallery, large text will be written over them.

Figure 15.11
Protect your images with the Security feature.

After you fill out all the fields to your liking, click OK. Elements begins to work its magic. After a few moments (depending on how many files you placed in your gallery and how fast your computer is), a browser window opens with your new photo gallery, as shown in Figure 15.12. If you click a thumbnail image in the browser, you're taken to a larger gallery image. Pretty cool, eh? Simply close the browser when you're finished looking at the gallery.

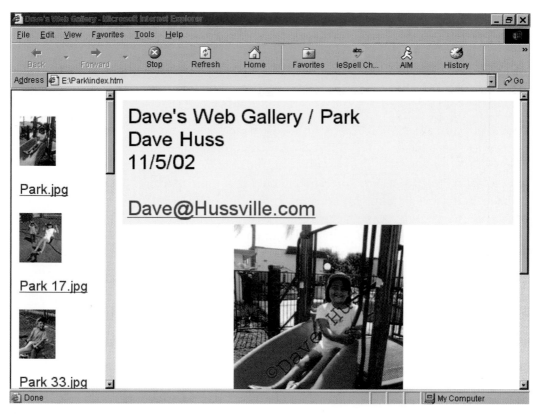

Figure 15.12
Now, you've got a custom-made web gallery of all your favorite images. Life couldn't be better.

Generating a PDF Slideshow

Oh boy, are you in for a treat. This is such a cool feature! Do you know what a Portable Document File (PDF) file is? If you have Adobe Acrobat or Acrobat Reader, you know that PDF files can be sent through email, posted on web sites, or stuck on CD-ROMs. A PDF file can be shared with anyone who owns the Acrobat Reader program, so if you create a slideshow for someone in particular, you might want to ensure the recipient has Acrobat Reader installed on his or her system. Adobe provides free downloads of Acrobat Reader from its web site (www.adobe.com).

What is a slideshow anyway? It's where one image is displayed on your monitor full screen for a few seconds, then dissolves, cuts, or fades into another image, moving through the group of selected images.

Before you jump in and begin creating your own little slideshow, you need to do a bit of preparation, just as you did with the Web Photo Gallery. You want to make a source folder, just as you did for the photo gallery, but you will want to put edited files in this folder. By edited, I mean that you want to reduce the file size of each image, just as you did at the very beginning of this chapter. (See, there was a reason you spent so much time covering that material. You'll use it extensively when doing web work.)

Let me give you an example. I took 11 unedited images and made a slideshow from them, and the result was a 13MB file. To show that to anyone, I'd have to burn the file onto a CD-R, then head to the post office and snail mail the images to them. I don't want to sound too down on a 13MB file. I could post it on a web site somewhere and let people suffer through painful downloads. I took those same files, however, and by using the techniques outlined earlier, I reduced the files to between 20–60KB each. The resulting PDF file was just 746KB! This file is OK to email people. You might still want to ask permission first…remember your web etiquette!

My rule of thumb for resampling the images for the slideshow was slightly different than the guidelines I gave you for the web. For images that had a greater vertical dimension, I only entered a value of 600 pixels in the Height box of the Pixel Dimension area of the Image Size dialog box. For images with a greater horizontal dimension, I only entered a value of 800 pixels in the Width box. The Resample Image and Constrain Proportions boxes were both checked, so I only needed to enter these single values to get the results I wanted for slideshow presentation.

Another quick tip about preparing these images for your slideshow—if you want them to be displayed in a particular order, you need to rename them numerically. For example, `Lovely01.jpg`, `Lovely02.jpg`, `Lovely03.jpg` assures these images will display in the order chosen from one to three. Also, you might choose to rename the files alphabetically if you find that easier.

Preparing the files for your slideshow is most of the work. After that is complete, you're almost done! You might open the Slideshow dialog box from the menu by navigating to File, Automation tools, PDF Slideshow. In the Source section, click the Browse button and navigate to where the source files you prepared on your hard drive are stored, as shown in Figure 15.13.

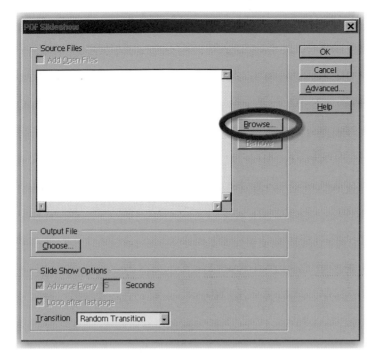

Figure 15.13
Click the Browse button to access your source files.

Click the first file in the folder, hold the Shift key, and click the last file. This selects all the files, as shown in Figure 15.14. Click OK after you select all the files.

Figure 15.14
Choose every file once by holding the Shift key.

Next, you need to identify where you want the finished PDF file to be written. In the Output section, click the Choose button (see Figure 15.15) and name the file My Slideshow.PDF (or something equally profound).

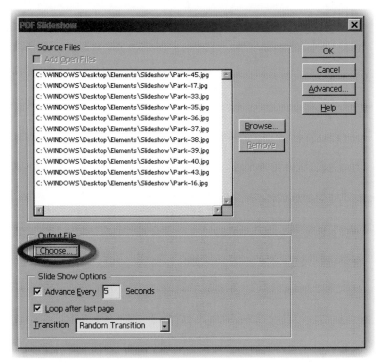

Figure 15.15
Press the Choose button to decide where your slideshow will be stored.

Now you need to pick the method of change as one image changes to the next. From the Transition menu, I suggest Random Transition, as shown in Figure 15.16. Also, I recommend checking the Loop After Last Page box; it makes the slideshow run until the recipient presses the Escape key. I repeat: The slideshow fills the entire screen when it runs, so it's very important to let people know they need to press Esc on their keyboard to exit the slideshow.

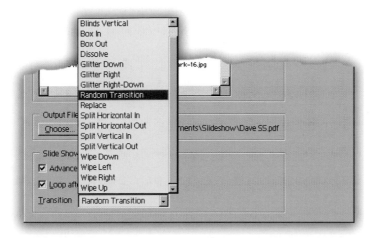

Figure 15.16
Choosing Random Transition keeps the changes between images interesting.

Finally, I recommend that you tweak the slideshow settings by clicking the Advanced button and checking JPG Encoding and moving the slider to about 3, as shown in Figure 15.17. This helps guarantee a small slideshow file! Click OK.

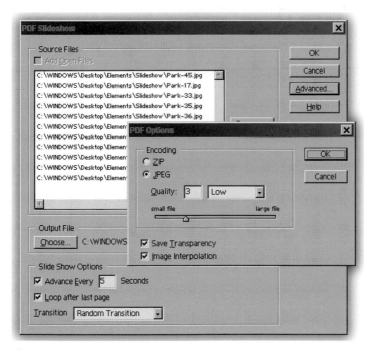

Figure 15.17
These settings help lower your PDF slideshow file size.

Now that everything has been set, click OK in the Slideshow dialog box. A small box pops up announcing the slideshow was successful. Click OK.

So where's the slideshow? Minimize Elements and go to the place on your hard drive where you told Elements to write the PDF file. Assuming that you have Acrobat Reader installed, double-click to open the file. Figure 15.18 cannot do justice to how cool the Slideshow feature is, but don't take my word for it. Try it for yourself!

Figure 15.18
This is one of the transitions that you'll see in the Slideshow. Note that there is a second image forming in the random squares.

Summary

In this chapter, we reiterated that images might be larger than they appear on your monitor. We also learned that for the web, smaller files are better, and there are a number of ways to achieve the goal of small-sized web images. We learned a simple rule of thumb for reducing the size of images of auction items. Also, we learned that before you use the PDF Slideshow and Web Photo Gallery features, you want to prepare folders filled with images first. That wraps things up for this chapter on publishing your photos to the web. In Chapter 16, we find out how to get the best prints using Elements.

16 Making Great Photos on Your Printer

In the previous chapter, we learned how to publish our photos on the Internet. But not everyone uses the Internet and, to further complicate things, you can't put your favorite snapshots or a copy of your web page in your wallet or purse to show friends or coworkers. Printing from Elements, as with any other program, is easy. Just select the Print command and your photo prints. But, regardless of how good you make your photographs look on the computer, if you cannot get good-quality prints from your printer, it can be frustrating. If you ever printed something using Adobe Photoshop, you were faced with a bewildering selection of features, options, and what-have-yous to pick from. You'll be relieved to learn that Elements has really streamlined the printing process.

In this chapter, we learn about how to make all kinds of cool picture packages with the click of a button. Also, we learn much about how to make great photos on almost any inkjet printer. Finally we explore some of the options available to you for making hard copies of your masterpieces.

Fast Track Printing

Basic printing from Elements is easy: Just select Print from the File menu and, when the dialog box opens (see Figure 16.1), make sure the name of the printer in the Name box is the printer that you want to use. If the printer isn't the one you want to use, click the down arrow next to the printer name and select the correct printer.

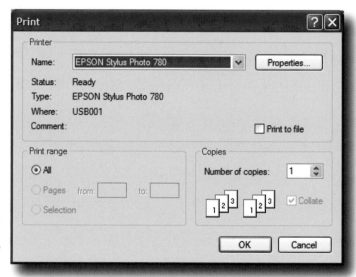

Figure 16.1
Check and make sure that the printer name that appears in the Name box is the one you want to print to before you click the OK button.

Next, click the Properties button and the Printer Properties dialog box appears (two samples are shown in Figures 16.2 and 16.3). Each dialog box is unique to its manufacturer, but they all have certain items in common. The following items must be checked before you start printing your first job of the day:

- **Type of paper**—With inkjet printers, this setting is critical. Many users are disappointed with the photographs they print because the printer is set up to print to plain paper when photo paper is installed.

- **Paper size**—Generally, it should be set to letter size in the United States.

- **Orientation**—Is the photo in landscape or portrait orientation? Does the setting of the printer match the orientation of what you are printing?

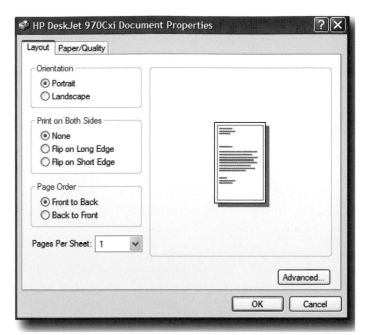

Figure 16.2
The dialog box that appears for the printer properties is designed and provided by the printer manufacturer and, therefore, is unique.

Figure 16.3
The Properties dialog box for an Epson Photo Stylus printer contains more choices for you to make when compared to the dialog box shown in Figure 16.2.

Previewing Your Print Job

If you're a novice to printing photos, use the Print Preview feature to make sure that what you are about to print will be the size that you are expecting. For example, in Figure 16.4, the photograph fills the screen. Only when the photo is previewed in the Print Preview dialog box does its true printed size become apparent (see Figure 16.5).

Figure 16.4
This photograph is so large, it fills the entire Photoshop Elements workspace.

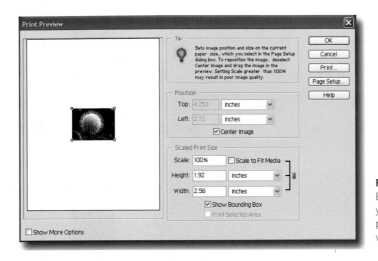

Figure 16.5
By using the Print Preview feature, you sometimes discover that the printed size is a little different from what's onscreen.

Speeding Up Your Print Jobs

Printing a photo can take a lot of time. This section discusses some ways in which you can speed up the job while maintaining excellent results.

Flatten Your Picture

If you are about to print a photograph that contains layers, you can print out a photo quicker if you flatten the image before you print it. First, you need to save the photo as a PSD file to preserve the layers, but then save a copy and flatten the photo by using the Flatten Image command (found in the Layer menu).

Resolution—More Is Slower

Every printer manufacturer that sells printers that will be used for graphic or printing photos heavily advertises the resolution of its printers. I am using an Epson Stylus Photo 780 to proof my pages for this book. It advertises that it can print at a resolution of 2,880dpi. That is an incredible resolution, so it stands to reason that a photo printed at that resolution would be razor sharp with fantastic detail, right? Actually, that's not true. The first stumbling block to this printing miracle is your eyes. That is more than most anyone's eyes can resolve. Ignoring that minor problem, when you print at the highest resolution that the printer can spit out, it consumes large amounts of ink and takes up to four times as long to print.

Getting the Best Quality Prints from Your Printer

The three most important things that affect the quality of the photographs that you print are the resolution setting, the paper quality, and the ink quality.

Optimum Resolution Settings

So, what resolution setting should you use to get the best possible photographic prints? For a majority of your printings, the default automatic photo setting should work great. If you go into one of the advanced settings pages (see Figure 16.6), you might be surprised to discover that the printer normally prints quality photographs at a resolution of 720dpi. The reason has to do with a funny thing about the human eye that we previously mentioned. If a photograph has a wide palette of colors, it's almost impossible to tell the difference between a photo printed at 720dpi and one printed at 2,880dpi.

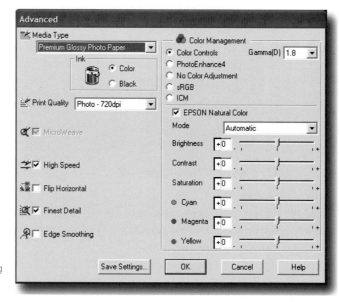

Figure 16.6
For all the advertising for monsterly high resolutions, most photo printers print beautifully at their default setting of 720dpi.

So, when should you use the higher resolutions? If the photograph you are printing is 5x7 or larger, you might benefit from printing at 1,440dpi. But don't take my word for it—run a little test and print your favorite photograph at the top three resolutions of your printer. See how long it takes to print each one and write on the back of each photo what resolution it was printed at. After you do that, put the photos in a file folder or one of those big manila envelopes and the next time you are tempted to print at a higher resolution, pull out those prints to remind yourself of the difference (or lack thereof).

Your Photo Is Only as Good as the Paper

Like it or not, the best photo printer in the world produces pretty crummy photos when it prints them on copier paper. Another general fact of life: Your printer will do better on its own brand of specialty paper than it will with the generic stuff you bought at the local super center. This has nothing to do with the superiority of the printer manufacturer's paper. It has to do with the settings of the printer software being fine-tuned to get the best-looking result using its own paper. Look at the list of papers (media) that are listed for my HP 970 Cxi printer (see Figure 16.7). Two types of paper are listed: HP papers and others. So, when I have important samples of my photographs I need to produce on my HP printer, I use their premium photo stock and get great results.

Figure 16.7
For the best possible photos from
your printer, you should always use
the specialty paper provided by the
printer's manufacturer.

Now, if you are printing cute sticker buttons for your
kids' birthday paper, making invites for a bash, or punch-
ing out the dreaded annual holiday newsletter, get the
best deal on paper you can and go for it.

Ink Quality, Refills, and Other Fun Stuff

Because the cost of ink refills is getting to be almost as
expensive as the printers, it becomes tempting to get
generic ink cartridges or refill kits. I cannot address the
non-photo ink refills because I haven't done any tests,
but I have done some serious testing of the photo-printer
inks, and they don't compare to the real thing. The
colors are not the same; they are never as vivid as the
original—period.

Printing Multiple Copies of a Picture

One of the coolest features in Photoshop Elements is the
capability to print many different-size copies of a single
image with a single click of a button. I'm talking about the
Picture Package feature located in the File Menu under
Print Layouts.

TIP

Anytime you notice that the colors of
your inkjet printer aren't quite right,
you need to run the test pattern and
see if any of the printer's ink nozzles
are blocked. If just one of the print-
head nozzles are not working, a few of
the colors in your photo can radically
change. Clean the nozzles. This is especially true if you haven't printed on
the printer in over a week. The print-
head nozzles tend to dry up a bit.

The Picture Package feature doesn't print directly to the printer. Instead, it takes the image(s) and the layout you selected and creates an Elements document that you can print or save and print at a later time.

When you select this feature, a huge dialog box appears (see Figure 16.8) that almost covers the entire screen (and I have a 21-inch screen).

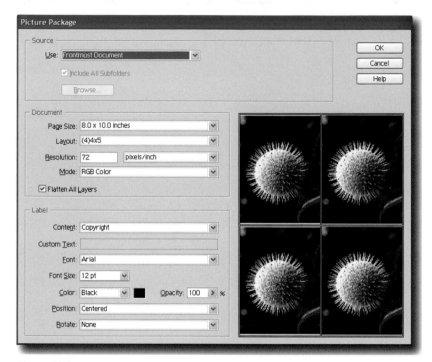

Figure 16.8
Finally, you can make the same photo sets that are offered for school pictures.

The operation of this dialog box is mostly self-explanatory, but a few items deserve some consideration.

The Source Document

You have three choices for the source documents. If you have a photograph open, the default choice is the image that's open. If more than one image is open, the one you select becomes the default.

If you want to create multiple copies of more than a single picture, click an image in the layout and you can then choose a new source image. If you have added several different photos to your picture layout, be aware that if you change the layout selection, all the photos in the new layout revert back to the original single photo.

Document Choices

In this section of the Picture Package dialog box, you can choose one of the many available combinations for the page size you have selected (see Figure 16.9).

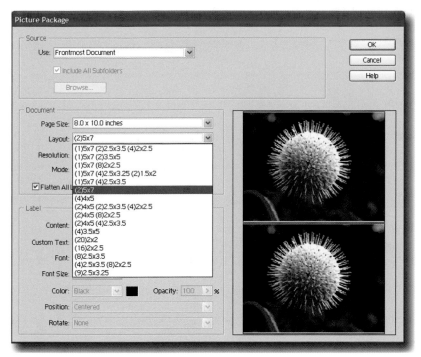

Figure 16.9
Depending on the document page size you select, there can be a vast array of available combinations from which to choose.

One item might cause confusion: the Resolution setting. Note that it's in pixels per inch (ppi), which is not how we are used to seeing the setting. My recommendation is to leave this setting at 72. If you want to increase it, print a test photo at 72 and then try printing a second one at a higher resolution, and see if you can see any difference.

Photo Labels

The Labels section also might cause a little confusion if this is your first time using this section. You might notice in the drop-down list that you have a large number of available choices from which to select (see Figure 16.10). The Custom Text (as you might imagine) enables you to add some text to each photo. The others, such as Copyright, Caption, and so on, if they are selected, are printed from information that was added to the file using the File Info command (located in the File menu). Therefore, if you haven't added anything to the photo, even if you select one of these choices, nothing will print.

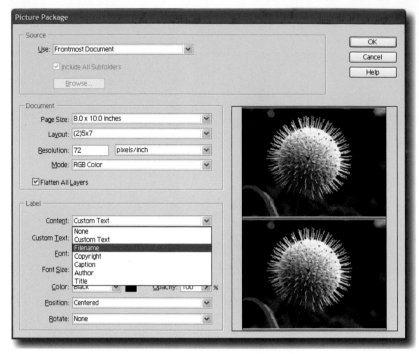

Figure 16.10
Most of the labels on this list require that the information be added to the
photograph using the File Info feature.

Summary

For the record, I buy all of my own printers, ink, and media. I felt I should add that
because, in rereading this chapter, it looks like I might be an agent for one of the printer companies. The truth is, I think they are painfully expensive as well, but when you
need really good-quality photos, there's no better alternative. I spend a lot of time printing color photographs, and what I have said reflects what I have learned about extracting the best possible image from printers that range in price from $99 to $3,000 (which
is what my Stylus Photo 780 cost).

Index

A

Acrobat Reader, downloading, 287
action events, digital cameras, 77
adding
    light to dark photos, 106-110, 112
    objects to photos, 238-242
    styles to shapes, 151-153
    text to images, 134-139, 141-143
adjusting
    color, 257-258
    versus enhancing images, 32
Adjustment layers, 233
    creating, 251-253
    versus copies, 249-251
AE (automatic exposure) settings, 184
Aligned mode, Clone Stamp tool, 266-267
alpha channel, 216
AOL, attaching images to email, 283
Artistic filter library, 170-171
Attach to Email feature, 52
attaching images to email, 282-283
Auto Color Correction, 96-98
Auto Contrast, 122

Auto Convert button, 52
Auto Levels, 107
automatching panoramas, incorrect automatching, 193-195
automated web photo gallery creation, 283-286
automatic exposure (AE) settings, 184
automatic tools, correcting color casts, 97-99
avoiding blowouts, 116

B

backgrounds
    blurring, 73-76, 127
    changing, 213-215
    modifying, 127
    removing items from, 70-72
    replacing, 78-80
barrel distortion, 84
    removing, 87
batch processing, 6
blowouts, 115-116
    avoiding, 116
blurring backgrounds, 73-76, 127
borders, creating, 140
Brightness and Contrast controls, 122-123
brightness, 123-126. *See also* tonal adjustments
Brush Selection tool, 8

Burn tool, 113-115
buttons
    Auto Convert, 52
    Perspective, 189
    Print Size, 13

C

cameras, 21. *See also* digital
    cameras
        connecting to comput-
        ers, 21-22
Canvas Size command,
    61-62, 130
canvases, resizing, 61-62
changing backgrounds,
    213-215
channels, alpha
    channel, 216
checking tonal quality, 245
Clone Stamp tool
    aligned versus non-
        aligned, 266-267
    restoring photos,
        254-256
Clone tool, 79-80, 129
cloning, aligned versus
    non-aligned, 266-267
color
    accuracy versus
        appearance, 92-93
    adjusting, 257-258
    Auto Color
        Correction, 96
    faded color, restoring,
        268-271
    selective color removal,
        180-182
Color Cast command,
    103-104

color casts, 93-96
    correcting, 96
        with automatic
        tools, 97-99
        Color Cast command,
        103-104
        selective color
        correction, 99-101
Colorize features,
    Hue/Saturation
    command, 174
combining filters for
    painterly effects, 176
commands
    Canvas Size, 61-62, 130
    Color Cast, 103-104
    Import, 23-24
    Levels, 123-126
    Liquify, 236
    Paste, 204
composition
    guidelines for, 89-90
    improving, 68
        blurring back-
        grounds, 73-76
        cropping, 68-69
        removing items from
        background, 70-72
computers, connecting to
    cameras, 21-22
contrast, loss of details,
    123. *See also* tonal
    adjustments
controlling
    Magnetic Lasso tool,
    215-216

overlap in
    panoramas, 185
copies versus Adjustment
    layers, 249-251
copyright laws,
    scanning, 28
correcting
    color casts, 96
        with automatic
        tools, 97-99
        Color Cast command,
        103-104
        selective color
        correction, 99-101
    distortion in images,
        84-88
Crop tool, 35, 68, 276
cropping images, 35-38,
    68-69, 135-137
    creatively, 81-82
    for retouching, 231
    versus picture size, 38
    suggestions for, 39-40
Custom Shape tool,
    145-147
Cylindrical Mapping, 196

D

Deep Paint, 178
deleting. *See* removing
details, contrast, 123
digicams. *See* digital
    cameras
digital cameras, 18, 21. *See
    also* cameras
    action events, 77

software, 22-23
dimensions, pixels, 54
distortion
    barrel distortion, 84
        removing, 87
    correcting, 84-88
dividing images for
    restoration, 121
document choices, print-
    ing multiple copies of
    images, 301
Dodge tool, 112-115, 206
dots per inch (dpi), 57
downloading
    Acrobat Reader, 287
    Photoshoop Elements, 9
    recipes, 16
downsampling images, 278
dpi (dots per inch), 57
Dust and Scratches filter,
    259-261
    applying, 264-265

E

editing text, 143-144
effects, previewing, 47
Ellipse tool, 145
Elliptical Marquee tool,
    203-208
email
    attaching images to,
        282-283
    sizing images for, 52-53
endpoints, 247
enhancing versus adjusting
    images, 32
Eraser tool, 110
errors. *See* mistakes, 14

evaluating
    painterly effects,
        167-169
    photos, 245-247
        for retouching, 230

F

fastening point, 215
feathering selections,
    Marquee tools, 209-210
File Browser, 25-26
    rotating images, 26-27,
        33-34
file formats, 64
    graphic standard
        formats, 65
    Internet formats, 64-65
    native formats, 66
File Info feature, managing
    images, 29-30
file management tools, 6
files, managing, 66
Fill Flash, 108, 115
film scanners, 20-21
filters
    Artistic filter library,
        170-171
    combining for painterly
        effects, 176
    covering up poor
        photos, 172-176
    Dust and Scratches,
        applying, 264-265
    Dust and Scratches
        filter, 259-261
    Poster Edge, 170-171
    Rough Pastels, 174

Smart Blur, 234
Spatter, 142
Unsharp Mask, 128
Watercolor, 165-169
flash photography, 229-230
flatbed scanners, 20
flattening images, speeding
    up print jobs, 297
folders, managing
    images, 29
formats, saving in different
    formats, 62
frames, creating
    borders, 140
framing images, 130-132,
    142, 177-178

G

generating PDF slideshows,
    287-292
GIF versus JPEG, 65
graphic standard formats,
    64-65
guidelines
    for composition, 89-90
    for taking panorama
        photos, 185-186

H

Hand tool, 212
help, 15
    recipes, 16
Hemera, 21
highlighting hair, photo
    retouching, 233
highlights, 113-115

home pages, images, 279-280

horizons, 76
    leveling, 77-78

Horizontal Type tool, 138

HP ScanJet scanners, 27

Hue/Saturation, 236

Hue/Saturation command, Colorize features, 174

I

image correction, QuickFix. *See* QuickFix

images. See also photos; pictures
    adjusting versus enhancing, 32
    attaching to email, 282-283
    backgrounds
        blurring, 73-76
        replacing, 78-80
    borders, 140
    correcting distortion, 84-88
    cropping, 35-38, 68-69, 135-137
        creatively, 81-82
        suggestions for, 39-40
        versus picture size, 38
    dividing for restoration, 121
    downsampling, 278
    flattening to speed up print jobs, 297
    framing, 130-132, 142, 177-178

home pages, 279-280

importing, 23-24

managing, 29
    with File Browser, 25-26
    with File Info, 29-30
    with folders, 29
    with naming conventions, 29

oversharpening, 49

pixels, 53

printing, 32
    cropping images, 35-38
    image correction, 41
    multiple copies, 299-301
    rotating images, 32-34
    sharpening, 45-50

reducing for Internet auctions, 278-279

removing
    items from, 129
    items from background, 70-72

resampling, 60-61, 288

resizing, 57
    resampling, 60-61
    Resize Image dialog box, 58-59
    resolution, 59

resolution, speeding up print jobs, 297

restoring, blurring backgrounds, 127

rotating, 32-34
    with File Browser, 33-34

saving, 62-63
    options for, 63
    for web, 280-282

sharpening, 45, 47-50, 128
    Unsharp Mask, 46

sizing
    for email, 52-53
    for the web, 274-275

text
    adding, 134-139, 141-143
    editing, 143-144
    web, 276-278
    saving for, 280-282

Import command, 23-24

importing images, 23-24

improving composition, 68
    blurring backgrounds, 73-76
    cropping, 68-69
    removing items from background, 70-72

ink, quality of printed images, 299

installing Photoshop Elements 2.0, 10

Internet auctions, reducing images, 278-279

Internet formats, 64-65

isolating selections, 262

items, removing from images, 129

J

JPEG versus GIF, 65
JPG, 279

K

keystoning, 84

L

Lasso tools, 210, 213-215
    Magnetic Lasso
        tool, 211
    Polygonal Lassso
        tool, 211
layers
    Adjustment layers, 251
    creating, 136
Layers palette, 135
level horizons, 76
level of horizons, 77-78
Levels Adjustment
    layers, 250
Levels command, 123-126
libraries, Artistic filter
    library, 170-171
lighting
    adding to dark photos,
        106-110, 112
    highlights, 113-115
    in panoramas, 191-192
    problems with, 106
    shadows, 113-115
Line tool, 145
Liquify command, 236
loading selections, 217

M

Magic Wand tool, 218-220
    tips for using, 220
Magnetic Lasso tool,
    73, 211
    controlling, 215-216
managing
    files, 66
    images, 29
        naming
            conventions, 29
        with File Browser,
            25-26
        with File Info, 29-30
        with folders, 29
Marquee tools, 203-208
    feathering selections,
        209-210
    Options bar, 208-209
    tips for using, 208
matting photos, 130-132
mistakes, undoing, 14
    Undo History
        palette, 15
modifying
    backgrounds, 127
moire pattern, 28
Move tool, 78
moving
    objects, photo
        retouching, 235
    selections, 212

N

naming images, 29
native formats, 64, 66
new features
    Brush Selection tool, 8
    file management
        tools, 6
    online
        documentation, 7
    Picture Package, 8-9
    QuickFix, 8, 41
        demonstration of,
            42-44
        recipes for using, 42
    recipes, 7
Non-Aligned mode, Clone
    Stamp tool, 266-267

O

objects
    adding to photos,
        238-242
    removing from photos,
        255-256
online documentation, 7
options, revealing tool
    options, 11
Options bar, 11-12
    Marquee tools, 208-209
    Zoom tool, 13-14
outlining, text, 157-161
overcast skies, replacing,
    221-223
overlap, controlling in
    panoramas, 185
oversharpening images, 49

P

paint jobs, restoring, 126
painterly effects, 165-166
   Artstic filter library,
     170-171
   evaluating, 167-169
   filters, combining, 176
   options for, 178-180
   Poster Edge filter,
     170-171
   Watercolor filter,
     167-169
palettes
   Layers, 135
   Swatches, 159
panels, panoramas,
  multiple panels
  overlaid, 199
panning, 77
panoramas
   controlling overlap, 185
   creating
     challenging panora-
       mas, 193-197
     from three photos,
       189-193
     from two photos,
       186-188
   Cylindrical
    Mapping, 196
   examples, 198, 200
   incorrect automatching,
     193-195
   lighting, 191-192
   multiple panels over-
     laid, 199
   Perspective button, 189

Photomerge, 184
   size of, 199
   taking pictures for, 184
     guidelines, 185-186
paper, quality of printed
  images, 298-299
Paste command, 204
patterns, moire pattern, 28
PDF slideshows, generat-
  ing, 287-292
Perspective button, 189
photo galleries, automated
  web photo gallery
  creation, 283-286
photo labels, printing
  multiple copies of
  images, 301
Photomerge, 184
photos. *See also* images;
  pictures
   adding light to dark
     photos, 106-110, 112
   blowouts, 115-116
   covering up poor
     photos with filters,
     172-176
   creating panoramas
     challenging panora-
       mas, 193-197
     from three photos,
       189-193
     from two photos,
       186-188
   evaluating, 245, 247
   matting, 130-132
   overcast skies, replacing,
     221-223

red eye, 116
   removing, 116-118
restoring
   adjusting color,
     257-258
   Clone Stamp tool,
     254-255
   determining the
     problem, 244-245
   Dust and Scratches
     filter, 259-261
   establishing a plan of
     attack, 247
   faded colors, 268-271
   isolating
     selections, 262
   removing objects,
     255-256
   Selection brush,
     263-264
   understanding what
     can and cannot be
     repaired, 248-249
retouching, 236-237
   adding objects,
     238-242
   cropping, 231
   evaluating, 230
   highlighting hair, 233
   moving objects, 235
   removing red
     eye, 232
   removing
     reflections, 234
   resizing objects,
     235-236
   smoothing out
     pixels, 234

whitening eyes and
teeth, 232
scanning damaged
photos, 259
tips for better
pictures, 226
composition, 228
deciding on subject,
226-227
flash photography,
229-230
simplifying
photos, 228
Photoshop Elements 2.0
downloading, 9
installing, 10
introduction to, 6
Picture Package, 8-9,
299-301
pictures. *See also* images;
photos
rotating with File
Browser, 26-27
taking for
panoramas, 184
guidelines, 185-186
pixels, 53-55
examples of, 55-56
resolution, 56-57
smoothing out, 234
pixels per inch (ppi), 57
plug-ins
Deep Paint, 178
Virtual Painter, 178
Polygon tool, 145
Polygonal Lasso tool,
211, 239

Poster Edge filter, 170-171
ppi (pixels per inch), 57
previewing
effects, 47
print jobs, 296-297
print jobs
previewing, 296-297
speeding up
flattening
pictures, 297
resolution, 297
Print Preview feature,
296-297
Print Size button, 13
printing
images, 32
cropping, 35-38
image correction, 41
rotating, 32-34
sharpening, 45-50
multiple copies of
images, 299-301
quality prints
ink, 299
paper, 298-299
resolution
settings, 298
from Photoshop
Elements, 294-295
problems
determing problems
with photos for
restoration, 244-245
with lighting, 106

Q

quality of printed images
ink, 299

paper, 298-299
resolution settings, 298
QuickFix, 8, 41
demonstration of, 42-44
recipes for using, 42

R

Random Transition, 290
recipes, 7, 16
downloading, 16
Rectangle tool, 145
Rectangular Marquee
tool, 70
red eye, 116
photos, retouching, 232
removing, 116-118
Red Eye Brush tool,
116-118
Redo, 14
reducing images for
Internet auctions,
278-279
reflections, removing, 234
removing
barrel distortion, 87
color, selective color
removal, 180-182
items
from backgrounds,
70-72
from images, 129,
255-256
red eye, 116-118
reflections, photo
retouching, 234
replacing
backgrounds, 78-80
overcast skies, 221-223

resampling images,
60-61, 288
Resize Image dialog box,
58-59
resizing. *See also* reducing
canvases, 61-62
images, 57
for email, 52-53
resampling, 60-61
Resize Image dialog
box, 58-59
resolution, 59
objects, photo
retouching, 235-236
resolution, 56-57
of images, speeding up
print jobs, 297
resizing images, 59
settings for quality
printed images, 298
restoring
images
blurring back-
grounds, 127
dividing for
restoration, 121
paint jobs, 126
photos
adjusting color,
257-258
Clone Stamp tool,
254-255
determining the
problems, 244-245

Dust and Scratches
filter, 259-261
establishing a plan of
attack, 247
faded colors, 268-271
isolating
selections, 262
removing objects,
255-256
Selection brush,
263-264
understanding what
can and cannot be
repaired, 248-249
retouching photos, 236-237
adding objects, 238-242
cropping, 231
evaluating, 230
highlighting hair, 233
moving objects, 235
removing red eye, 232
removing
reflections, 234
resizing objects, 235-236
smoothing out
pixels, 234
whitening eyes and
teeth, 232
revealing tool options, 11
rotating
images, 32-34
with File Browser,
33-34
pictures with File
Browser, 26-27

Rough Pastels filter, 174
Rounded Rectangle
tool, 145

S

saturation, 236
saving
images, 62-63
options for, 63
for web, 280-282
selections, 217
scaling
canvases, 61-62
images, 57
for email, 52-53
resampling, 60-61
Resize Image dialog
box, 58-59
resolution, 59
objects, photo
retouching, 235-236
scanners, 19
film scanners, 20-21
flatbed scanners, 20
HP ScanJet scanners, 27
scanning, 27-28
copyright laws, 28
damaged photos, 259
printed material, 28
scans, straightening out,
82-83
Selection brush, 263-264
Selection Brush tool, 110
selection tools, 202
selections, 202-203

alpha channel, 216
feathering with
    Marquee tools, 209-210
isolating, 262
Lasso tools. *See*
Lasso tools
loading, 217
Magic Wand tool,
    218-220
Marquee tools, 203-208
    feathering selections,
    209-210
moving, 212
rough cut
    selections, 211
saving, 217
shaping, 212
zooming in, 212
selective color correction,
    correcting color casts,
    99-101
selective color removal,
    180-182
semitransparent text,
    154-155, 157
shadows, lighting, 113-115
Shape Selection tool,
    145-147
shapes
    adding styles to, 151-153
    creating, 145-147
shaping selections, 212
sharpening, images,
    45-50, 128
    Unsharp Mask, 46
Shortcuts bar, 12

size
    of panoramas, 199
    of pictures versus
        cropping, 38
sizing images
    for email, 52-53
    for the web, 274-275
slideshows, generating PDF
    slideshows, 287-292
Smart Blur filter, 234
smoothing out pixels,
    photo retouching, 234
software, digital camera
    software, 22-23
source documents, print-
    ing multiple copies of
    images, 300
Spatter filter, 142
speeding up print jobs
    flattening pictures, 297
    resolution, 297
spot metering, 120
Straighten and Crop
    feature, 83
straightening scans, 82-83
stroke, 157
styles, adding to shapes,
    151-153
Swatches palette, 159

T

Tagged Image Format File
    (TIFF), 65
text
    adding to images,
        134-139, 141-143
    editing, 143-144
    outlining, 157-161

semitransparent text,
    154-155, 157
transforming,
    154-155, 157
unwarping, 148-150
warping, 148-150
Text tool, 139
    editing text, 143
textures, matting
    images, 130
TIFF (Tagged Image
    Format File), 65
tonal adjustments, 121,
    245-247
    Brightness and Contrast
        controls, 122-123
    Levels command,
        123-126
tonal quality, checking, 245
Toolbox, 11-12
tools
    automatic tools, correct-
        ing color casts, 97-99
    Brush Selection tool, 8
    Burn, 113-115
    Clone, 79-80, 129
    Clone Stamp, restoring
        photos, 254-256
    Crop, 35, 68, 276
    Custom Shape, 145-147
    Dodge, 112-115, 206
    Ellipse, 145
    Elliptical Marquee,
        203-208
    Eraser, 110
    file management
        tools, 6
    Hand, 212

Horizontal Type, 138
Lasso, 213-215
Lasso tools, 210-211
Line, 145
Magic Wand, 218-220
    tips for using, 220
Magnetic Lasso, 73, 211
    controlling, 215-216
Marquee, 203-208
    feathering selections,
        209-210
    Options bar, 208-209
    tips for using, 208
Move, 78
Polygon, 145
Polygonal Lasso, 211
Polygonal Lasso
    tool, 239
Rectangle, 145
Rectangular
    Marquee, 70
Red Eye Brush, 116-118
Rounded Rectangle, 145
Selection Brush, 110
selection tools, 202
Shape Selection,
    145-147
Text, 139
    editing text, 143
Unsharp Mask, 46
Zoom, 13
    Options bar, 13-14
transforming text, 154-155,
    157
transitions, 290

U

Undo, 14
Undo History palette, 15
undoing mistakes, 14
    Undo, 14
    Undo History
        palette, 15
Unsharp Mask, 46
Unsharp Mask filter, 128
unwarping text, 148-150

V

vanishing point, 85
Virtual Painter, 178-180

W

Warped Text, 148-150
warping text, 148-150
Watercolor filter, 165-169
web
    automated photo
        gallery creation, 283-
        286
    images, 276-278
        for home pages,
            279-280
        saving, 280-282
        sizing for, 274-275
    Internet auctions,
        reducing images for,
        278-279
Welcome Screen, 10
white space, creating, 136
whitening eyes and teeth,
    photo retouching, 232
WIA (Windows Imaging
    Acquisition) interface, 23

window panes, Magic
    Wand tool, 218-220
Windows Imaging
    Acquisition (WIA)
    interface, 23

X-Y-Z

Zoom tool, 13
    Options bar, 13-14
zooming, 13
    previewing effects, 47
    in selections, 212

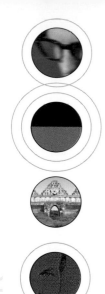

VOICES THAT MATTER

HOW TO CONTACT US

VISIT OUR WEB SITE

WWW.NEWRIDERS.COM

On our Web site you'll find information about our other books, authors, tables of contents, indexes, and book errata. You will also find information about book registration and how to purchase our books.

EMAIL US

Contact us at this address: **nrfeedback@newriders.com**

- If you have comments or questions about this book
- To report errors that you have found in this book
- If you have a book proposal to submit or are interested in writing for New Riders
- If you would like to have an author kit sent to you
- If you are an expert in a computer topic or technology and are interested in being a technical editor who reviews manuscripts for technical accuracy

- To find a distributor in your area, please contact our international department at this address. **nrmedia@newriders.com**

- For instructors from educational institutions who want to preview New Riders books for classroom use. Email should include your name, title, school, department, address, phone number, office days/hours, text in use, and enrollment, along with your request for desk/examination copies and/or additional information.
- For members of the media who are interested in reviewing copies of New Riders books. Send your name, mailing address, and email address, along with the name of the publication or Web site you work for.

BULK PURCHASES/CORPORATE SALES

The publisher offers discounts on this book when ordered in quantity for bulk purchases and special sales. For sales within the U.S., please contact: Corporate and Government Sales (800) 382-3419 or **corpsales@pearsontechgroup.com**. Outside of the U.S., please contact: International Sales (317) 581-3793 or **international@pearsontechgroup.com**.

WRITE TO US

New Riders Publishing
201 W. 103rd St.
Indianapolis, IN 46290-1097

CALL US

Toll-free (800) 571-5840 + 9 + 7477
If outside U.S. (317) 581-3500. Ask for New Riders.

FAX US

(317) 581-4663

New
Riders

Publishing
the Voices
that Matter

OUR AUTHORS

PRESS ROOM

| web development | design | photoshop | new media | 3-D | server technologies |

EDUCATORS

ABOUT US

CONTACT US

You already know that New Riders brings you the **Voices That Matter**.

But what does that mean? It means that New Riders brings you the

Voices that challenge your assumptions, take your talents to the next

level, or simply help you better understand the complex technical world

we're all navigating.

Visit **www.newriders.com** to find:

▸ **10% discount** and **free shipping** on all book purchases

▸ Never before published chapters

▸ Sample chapters and excerpts

▸ Author bios and interviews

▸ Contests and enter-to-wins

▸ Up-to-date industry event information

▸ Book reviews

▸ Special offers from our friends and partners

▸ Info on how to join our User Group program

▸ Ways to have your Voice heard

New
Riders

WWW.NEWRIDERS.COM

informIT

www.informit.com

YOUR GUIDE TO IT REFERENCE

New Riders has partnered with **InformIT.com** to bring technical information to your desktop. Drawing from New Riders authors and reviewers to provide additional information on topics of interest to you, **InformIT.com** provides free, in-depth information you won't find anywhere else.

Articles

Keep your edge with thousands of free articles, in-depth features, interviews, and IT reference recommendations— all written by experts you know and trust.

Online Books

Answers in an instant from **InformIT Online Books'** 600+ fully searchable online books.

POWERED BY

Catalog

Review online sample chapters, author biographies, and customer rankings and choose exactly the right book from a selection of over 5,000 titles.

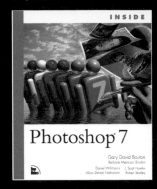

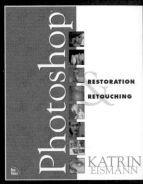
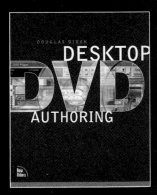